# 风格

## 写作的清晰与优雅

Style

lessons in clarity and grace

Joseph M. Williams
Joseph Bizup

[美] 约瑟夫·M. 威廉姆斯  约瑟夫·毕萨普 著
张飞龙 译

著作权合同登记号 图字：01-2014-4170

**图书在版编目(CIP)数据**

风格：写作的清晰与优雅／(美)约瑟夫·M.威廉姆斯（Joseph M.Williams），(美)约瑟夫·毕萨普（Joseph Bizup）著；张飞龙译.—北京：北京大学出版社，2020.3
 ISBN 978-7-301-29265-5

Ⅰ.①风… Ⅱ.①约…②约…③张… Ⅲ.①英语－写作－研究 Ⅳ.① H315

中国版本图书馆 CIP 数据核字 (2018) 第 036443 号

Authorized translation from the English language edition, entitled STYLE:LESSONS IN CLARITY AND GRACE,11th Edition by WILLIAMS,JOSEPH M.; BIZUP,JOSEPH, published by Pearson Education,Inc,Copyright©2014

All rights reserved. No part of this book may be reproduced or transmitted in any form or by any means, electronic or mechanical, including photocopying, recording or by any information storage retrieval system, without permission from Pearson Education, Inc.

CHINESE SIMPLIFIED language edition published by PEKING UNIVERSITY PRESS. Copyright©2020 ALL RIGHTS RESERVED.

本书中文简体翻译版由 Pearson Education, Inc. 授权给北京大学出版社发行。
本书封面贴有 Pearson Education（培生教育出版集团）激光防伪标签。无标签者不得销售。

| | |
|---|---|
| **书　　名** | 风格：写作的清晰与优雅 |
| | FENGGE：XIEZUO DE QINGXI YU YOUYA |
| **著作责任者** | [美]约瑟夫·M.威廉姆斯（Joseph M. Williams） |
| | [美]约瑟夫·毕萨普（Joseph Bizup）著 张飞龙 译 |
| **责任编辑** | 于海冰 |
| **标准书号** | ISBN 978-7-301-29265-5 |
| **出版发行** | 北京大学出版社 |
| **地　　址** | 北京市海淀区成府路205号 100871 |
| **网　　址** | http://www.pup.cn 新浪微博：@北京大学出版社 @培文图书 |
| **电子信箱** | pkupw@qq.com |
| **电　　话** | 邮购部010-62752015　发行部010-62750672　编辑部010-62750112 |
| **印刷者** | 天津联城印刷有限公司 |
| **经销者** | 新华书店 |
| | 880 毫米×1230 毫米　32 开本　13.25 印张　300 千字 |
| | 2020年3月第1版　2020年3月第1次印刷 |
| **定　　价** | 68.00元 |

未经许可，不得以任何方式复制或抄袭本书之部分或全部内容。
**版权所有，侵权必究**
举报电话：010-62752024　电子信箱：fd@pup.pku.edu.cn
图书如有印装质量问题，请与出版部联系，电话：010-62756370

致我的母亲和父亲

……英语的语体风格是:平易但不粗鄙;优美但不浮华。

——塞缪尔·约翰逊

## 英语写作的十把密钥：

1. 区分语法规则和习惯用法。（第 33—50 页）

2. 用故事中的人物做句子主语。（第 92—101 页）

3. 用动词描述主要动作。（第 68—79 页）

4. 句子开头要体现熟悉的信息。（第 126—130 页）

5. 快速找到动词：

    * 避免使用冗长的引导语。（第 248—250 页）

    * 避免使用较长的抽象主语。（第 250—252 页）

    * 避免在主语和谓语之间加入插入语。（第 252—253 页）

6. 将新的、复杂的信息放在句子末端。（第 146—151 页）

7. 句子开头就要展现主语和话题，并使之连贯起来。（第 133—137 页）

8. "简洁"的要求：

    * 删除无意义的、重复的和暗示性的成分。（第 218—222 页）

    * 用一两个词代替冗长的短语。（第 222—223 页）

    * 将否定式转换成肯定式。（第 224—225 页）

9. 重新整理散乱的句子：

    * 关系从句后最多只能再附加一个从句。（第 258—260 页）

    * 用重复性、总结性或自由修饰语替代不必要的从句。（第 261—266 页）

    * 动词之后宜用并列结构代替从句，这样能够使句子条理清晰。（第 266—268 页）

10. 希望别人的作品如何写，自己就怎么写。（第 317—318 页）

# 目录

中文版序 .................... viii
前　言 ...................... 001
致　谢 ...................... 007

**第一部分　风格是种选择** .................... 015
　　第一课　风格的内涵 .................... 017
　　第二课　准确性 ........................ 031

**第二部分　清晰** ............................ 059
　　第三课　动　作 ........................ 061
　　第四课　人　物 ........................ 091
　　第五课　衔接与连贯 .................... 123
　　第六课　强　调 ........................ 145

**第三部分　形式的简洁** ...................... 169
　　第七课　动　机 ........................ 171
　　第八课　整体连贯 ...................... 195

**第四部分 优美** ......................................... 215

　　第九课　简 洁 ........................... 217

　　第十课　条理性 ........................... 245

　　第十一课　典 雅 ........................ 285

**第五部分 伦理** ......................................... 313

　　第十二课　伦 理 ........................ 315

　　附录一　标 点 ........................... 345

　　附录二　资源的使用 ............... 381

　　参考答案 ..................................... 395

　　术语表 ......................................... 405

# 中文版序

写作是一种社会行为。作者虽不为社会而生,作品却为社会而写。但作品能否被社会所接受,或被接受的程度如何,则主要取决于写作的风格。

风格是文之灵魂,既涉及形式,也涉及内容。文之优劣,虽以内容为重,而内容能否首先被看重、被理解和被欣赏,还需有平易的表达、优美的文字和清晰的思想。

风格是个性。个性鲜明者能迅速而充分地展现内涵,仿佛穿衣戴帽,款式颜色多能体现人之性格,包括外在风度和内在品格。

风格是选择。选择不是即席决定,而由惯习养成。惯习不是规训,不是教育,而由日常知识生活使然。读书习文,朝暮情思,凡有思想,行诸文字,久而久之,终成惯习。

此书讨论风格,似为创写而作,但文中所含"密钥",凡十余种,也适于学术文类,因为清晰和优雅是一切文之命脉。古今中外,所谓文者,无非诗文与散文。诗文之"诗",在古为律,在今为美,而美则在于朴实而不浮夸,清晰而不晦涩,准确而无谬误。散文之"散",并非说其无诗。散文有诗,自有妙境,亦以朴实、清晰、准确为美。且散之妙用，散之风味，散之诗意，尝为诗所不及。如庄周之散，磅礴恢弘；陶潜之散，风味隽永；逸少之散，平和自然。确为文之观止矣。

此书讨论英文写作。虽一国之语，一语之用，然天下作文之道，写作之法，大同小异，因此也适于中文。况今之世界，只持母语或外语而偏执一方者，终不成器。若放眼全球，立志于美美与共，大同之业，非二者之综合提高不可。具体而言，即中外文素质与写作能力之综合，其终极目的，在于语际视野与批判思维之通识能力的培养，其相互借鉴之妙，乃克服时之文弊，相互促进，中外多语共勉之道。

今人作文，或论题空泛，或言不由衷，或语焉不详。而修辞文法则生搬硬套，小词不用，大词堆砌；语法繁冗，内容晦涩，读来味同嚼蜡。在学术界则尤甚。言不晦而难以惑众，语不涩则不显论之高深。惟复杂长句方达深意；惟生涩字眼才显笔头功夫。更有甚者，如此晦涩之文风尚有大批追随者在，甚或亦成利禄功名之本，终于酿成时下文弊之风，致使主题困惑、文法不通、逻辑混乱、词不达意等匪夷所思之文章四处泛滥。

常言道，文不在写，而在于改。所谓改，指的是先把在阅读中或实践中出现的闪光思想形诸书面，或片段或小文，然后仔细咀嚼，慢慢细品，因只有自己参透，别人才能理解，此即清晰之意。如此反复，多而达到意思精确，文法简洁，风格悦目，可读性强。读之又读，改之又改，按书中所指，文风必有大进。

此书所赠与读者之宝贵经验，于克服上述弊端，培养改写习惯，掌握美文之诸法，均有助益。凡五部十二课，讲解详细，内容全面，技巧精到，大至篇章行文，小至标点符号，均有指点。尚有名人之妙语，有论者之佳评，也有详尽之例证。凡此，皆出自著者多年教创写之经验，读后必收益良多。且译笔顺畅，中英对照，相得益彰。

是为序。

陈永国

2020年1月21日于清华大学荷清苑

# 前 言

> 大多数人意识不到写作其实是一门技术。
> 你不得不像一个学徒似的,经过学习才能掌握。
> ——凯瑟琳·安·波特
> (Katherine Anne Porter)

## 第十一版

在第十版的前言中,格雷格·科洛姆(Greg Colomb)开篇直言,"按理来说,前言应该由乔·威廉姆斯(Joe Williams)来写,校正工作也应由他完成,但是我还是很荣幸地能够替他来完成。"同理我也可以说,这版的前言应该由格雷格来写,而且校正工作也应由他完成,我也很荣幸能够替他(格雷格)做这些事情。但是我们二人与此书的关系并不相同,所以我的校正之法必然与他的不同。近三十年来,格雷格和乔交情深厚,学术上相互合作,自然格雷格有资格为乔捉刀代笔。我了解乔,但我不能因此而对他横加指责。相反,乔所教授的课程对我写作此书大有裨益,尤其是在作家和读者的关系方面让我获益良多。

乔认为,作家对读者的使命是尽可能地写出清晰的文章。反过来,读者也会对那些全心全意为读者着想的作家心存感激。乔说:"为什么我们通常能够对别人的作品讲得头头是道,对自己的错误却视而不见呢？这是因为我们总希望读者能够从我们的作品中读到我们想要表达的东西。"乔认识到，作家可能最清楚自己想要表达的内容，但是读者最清楚作家在多大程度上表达出了本意。因此，乔叮嘱作家要相信读者的判断，因为读者不能直接了解作家的想法，只能从"书本上的词句"中读出来。几十年来，乔持续修订本书，把对读者的责任履行得淋漓尽致。我不仅心怀尊敬，而且以重新审视的态度检视他所写的内容，从而履行了我对他的责任。

**新特点**

最明显的一点是，我对本书的章节顺序进行了重新编排。在修订上一版的过程中，乔越来越强调本书的整体性。在第七版，他增加了一个关于调动读者的积极性、界定问题和组织章节的结语。在第八版，他在前一版基础上又拓展了一个结语，从而把统率句子的清晰性原则和统率段、节、章之间的连贯性原则清晰地对接起来。在第九版中，他把这两个后记提升到了章节的层面，即第十章的"动机连贯性"和第十一章的"整体连贯性"。为了与他的思路保持一致，我把这两章放到了书的中间部分，即第七章和第八章。这样，本书按照副标题的逻辑，从"清晰"开始，再到"优雅"，改变了以往从"句子"到"篇章"的问题探讨模式。

我修改了课后的练习。有的进行了重新整理，有的进行了删除，另外还增添了一些。当前版本中从第三章到第十二章课后的练习都是重新修改过的，归放在"自我检测"这一栏目之下。这些练习都是让读者从自己所写的文章着手，首先单独修改，然后再邀请读者参与意见。

从始至终，我整合了格雷格2012年修订本书第四版《风格：清晰和优雅的基础》(Style: The Basic of Clarity and Grace, 2012) 时所做的工作。

作为对读者建议的回应，我简化了一些解释，更新了一些例子，删除了一些冗余的内容，并从各章节的正文中撤掉了一些图表。现在这些图表都放在每一章末尾的"总结"部分。我还在一些我认为不准确的地方做了调整。

为了"简洁"起见，我还修改了一些格言，删除了几个无关紧要话题的相关讨论。为了保持第九章（原第七章）的简洁，我削减了涉及初学者的"多产的冗余"这一讨论。为了保持第十一章（原第九章）的优雅，我删除了"隐喻"一节。

最后，我调整了行间距，这项工作的量非常巨大。在第十版的修正过程中，在评价调整行间距时说，乔"不会原谅哪怕一丁点的瑕疵……故意留在后面。"我也试着让自己的工作达到这个标准。

**相同之处**

尽管此书有些变化，但书还是乔的书，仍同以往，一直在回应下列这些问题：

句子中，是什么让读者评判它的好坏？
我们如何对自己的文章进行诊断从而来预知读者的判断？
我们如何来修改一个句子从而让读者更好地理解？

关于这些问题的重要性,乔的解释是:

> 有关写作的标准建议一般都对这些问题忽略不计。这些建议,诸如"制订一个计划""不要使用被动语态"和"想想你的读者",只是一些陈词滥调。当我们在各种观点中反复思量并把它们落实在纸上时,大部分人却把这些建议抛诸脑后了。在写这一段话的时候,我也并没有考虑到你们(读者);而是在努力想法子把观点直接表达出来。我的确知道我还会回到这些句子上,看一遍,再看一遍(但是我没想到会反复斟酌长达二十五年之久)。只有在修改的时候,我才会想到你们(读者),才会想到与草稿一致的写作计划。此外,我知道还存在着一些赖以应用的原则,就像我对这些原则秉持不弃。本书就是在阐释这些。

格雷格从这段文章当中看出了《风格》经久不衰的精髓:这些**原则能够帮助作家准确地预知读者的反应,从而据此做出修改**。我也对乔的决定感到震惊,因为他把这当作作家的轶事呈现给读者,而不是作为一个摘要式的声明。

像格雷格那样,我也保留了乔的个人观点,这不是风格的问题,而是因为这一观点对整本书的信息传递来说至关重要。乔当然清楚每一种风格都是一种选择,即使是最简单易懂的那个也不例外。把格雷格所谓的"无处不在的 I's(第一人称)"添加到文章当中时,乔还添加了局限性讨论以及普通作家的事例。如果把《风格》的长盛不衰归功于乔的建议,那么本书所激发的热情可以归功于作者和读者共同努力的结果。

前言中，以下的内容几乎都是乔写的。首先是格雷格，然后是我，对之进行了些微的修改，目的是处理乔所用的第一人称，调整我们过度卷入其文章的问题。

## 不是药方，而是原则

这里的原则看上去像是规定性的（必须遵守），但本意却并非如此。它们是用来帮助你预知读者如何判断你的文章，并且帮助你决定是否修改或者如何修改文章。当你尝试着遵循这些原则的时候，你可能会写得比较慢，这是不可避免的。每当我们写作时，无论何时思考所写的内容，我们都会把反思当作一种自觉行为，从而丧失了写作的感觉，有时甚至到了使写作陷入瘫痪的地步。这个阶段经常发生。不过不要紧。如果你时刻记得，这些原则对于修改的作用大过对于起草的作用，那么这些原则就不会打乱你的修改进程。如果这是**起草文章**的第一原则，那么你大可不必理会那些针对这个原则而提出的其他建议。

## 一些前期工作

为了学习如何有效地修改文章，你需要了解一些基本知识：

你需要掌握一些语法术语知识：主语（SUBJECT）、动词（VERB）、名词（NOUN）、主动语态（ACTIVE）、被动语态（PASSIVE）、从句（CLAUSE）、介词（PREPOSITION）以及并列（COORDINATION）。所有的语法词汇第一次出现时都是大写的，并且正文部分或是书末的术语表中有相关定义。

你需要知道两个老词儿的新意义：主题（TOPIC）和强调（STRESS）。

你还需要学习一些新词，比如：名词化（NOMINALIZATION）、元话语（METADISCOURSE）、重复性修饰语（RESUMOTIVE MODIFIER）、总结性修饰语（SUMMATIVE MODIFIER）以及自由性修饰语（FREE MODIFIER）。学习新术语的过程很难受，唯一可以避免的办法就是从不学习任何新的术语。

最后，如果你是自学，那么一定要慢一些。这不是那种一两口气就能读完的休闲小文。一次看几章，然后做课后练习。修改一下别人的作品，再修改几周之前你自己写的文章，最后修改一下当天所写的内容。

对本书中的学术性和教学内容感兴趣的人，还可以选用《指导手册》(*Instructor's Manual*)。

约瑟夫·比萨普（Joseph Bizup）

马萨诸塞州，波士顿

# 致 谢

很多人都为这一版做出了贡献,在此我必须要感谢他们。感谢提供给我这个项目的培生教育出版集团的凯瑟琳·格林女士(Katharine Glynn),十分感谢她在编辑方面给予我的帮助。我也十分感谢培生教育出版集团的梅根·迪玛伊奥先生(Meghan DeMaio),他一直在为本书的出版做协调工作。还要感谢普利美迪亚全球出版社的奇特拉·加内桑女士(Chitra Ganesan),感谢她为这本书所做的准备工作。

感谢我的同仁,尤其是波士顿大学 CAS 写作课程中的同仁,感谢我们就乔·威廉姆斯(Joe Williams)的理念所进行的交流。我也十分感谢海瑟·巴雷特(Heather Barrett)、艾米·班尼特-赞迪昂(Amy Bennett-Zendzian)、凯特·尼尔森(Kate Neilsen)以及凯西·赖利(Casey Riley),他们的建议和回应对于我的修改和校正大有裨益。

感谢以下评论者对于第十版的评论,他们分别是德堡大学的大卫·阿尔瓦雷斯(David Alvarez)、德州农工大学的詹姆斯·贝克(James Baker)、杨百翰大学的艾米丽·贝朗格(Emily

Belanger）、旧金山大学的雷切尔·克劳福德（Rachel Crawford）、特拉华大学的克里斯汀·柯柯安瑞（Christine Cucciarre）、华盛顿大学的凯瑟林·麦金尼斯（Kathleen McGinnis）、圣泽维尔大学的艾米·费迪南·斯托雷（Amy Ferdinandt Stolley）、利普斯科姆大学的玛特·赫恩（Matt Hearn）、杨百翰大学的贝丝·何丹格林（Beth Hedengren）、路易斯安那州立大学的芭芭拉·A.海佛荣（Barbara A. Heifferon）、密里根学院的海瑟·M.胡佛（Heather M. Hoover）、阿拉巴马大学伯明翰分校的安德鲁·W.基特（Andrew W. Keitt）、内布拉斯加大学的克雷格·M.劳森（Craig M. Lawson）、马里兰大学的琳达·C.马克里（Linda C. Macri）、马里兰大学帕克分校的丹尼尔·潘蒂克（Daniel Pendick）、斯坦福大学的康斯坦斯·莱朗斯（Constance Rylance）、新学院的约瑟夫·塞尔瓦托（Joseph Salvatore）、波士顿大学的克里斯多夫·沃尔什（Christopher Walsh）以及康奈尔大学的雷切尔·韦伊（Rachel Weil）。

十分感激2008年和乔·威廉姆斯在一起度过的时光，那时候他参观了我所指导的写作项目。我也万分感激格雷格·科洛姆，他不仅让我开阔了眼界、拓展了技能，而且还有我们之间的友情。

最后，感谢安玛莉（Annmarie）、格蕾丝（Grace）和夏洛特（Charlotte），感谢我们能彼此相爱，分享欢乐。

## （来自第十版）

感谢金妮·布兰福德（Ginny Blanford）以及培生朗文出版社的每一位成员，是他们给了我继续这项由乔·威廉姆斯开创的工作机会。我的致谢和乔的有很多相同之处，所以我还是让乔自己来一一感谢这些人吧。感谢乔恩·德埃里克（Jon D'Errico），在我一直忙于这个手稿时，他替我做了大量工作。我欠家人一个道歉，因为我有两本书稿在同一天到期。在没有我的陪伴下，桑德拉（Sandra）、罗宾（Robin）、凯伦（Karen）和劳伦（Lauren）已经习惯了自得其乐，但是他们知道他们常驻我心。

## （来自第九版）

在过去的25年中，太多的人给予了我支持和建议，以至于我不能对此表示一一感谢了。但我和194名英国学生及一名教师再一次开始了这项工作，学生们忍受着印刷模糊的纸页（这告诉人们这本书已经问世很多年了），老师也总是和他们一样困惑。

我从本科生、研究生、专业学生以及在芝加哥大学参加过小红学舍写作项目（又名高级学术及专业写作）的博士后那里学到了很多。同样感谢那些讲解过这些原则并给了积极反馈的研究生们。

十分感谢那些在语言心理学、话语语言学以及功能句法学方面有开创之功的人们。熟悉这些方面的人则熟知查尔斯·费尔默（Charles Filmore）、贾恩·费尔巴斯（Jan Firbas）、尼尔斯·恩奎斯特（Nils Enkvist）、迈克尔·韩礼德（Michael Halliday）、诺姆·乔姆斯基（Noam Chomsky）、托马斯·贝佛（Thomas Bever）、维克·英韦（Vic Yngve）等人的影响。艾莉诺·罗施（Eleanore Rosch）的作品很好地解释了为什么动词应该是动作而人物是主语。她的《原型语义学》是本书所探讨风格类型的理论基础。

就早期的版本来说，我十分感谢特丽莎·安米莱迪（Theresa Ammirati）、伊冯·阿特金森（Yvonne Atkinson）、玛格丽特·贝特斯克勒（Margaret Batschelet）、南希·贝仁思（Nancy Barendse）、兰迪·柏林（Randy Berlin）、谢丽尔·布鲁克（Cheryl Brooke）、肯·布鲁菲（Ken Bruffee）、克里斯多夫·巴克（Christopher Buck）、道格拉斯·巴特夫（Douglas Butturff）、唐纳德·拜克（Donald Byker）、布鲁斯·坎贝尔（Bruce Campbell）、伊莱恩·茶伊卡（Elaine Chaika）、埃文·克里斯摩尔（Avon Crismore）、康斯坦斯·盖富沃特（Constance Gefvert）、达伦·坎布里奇（Darren Cambridge）、马克·加拿大（Mark Canada）、保罗·孔蒂诺（Paul Contino）、吉姆·加勒特（Jim Garrett）、吉尔·格莱德斯坦（Jill Gladstein）、凯伦·高科斯克（Karen Gocsik）、理查德·格兰德（Richard Grande）、珍妮·戛纳（Jeanne Gunner）、马克辛·海尔斯顿（Maxine Hairston）、乔治·霍夫曼（George Hoffman）、丽贝卡·摩尔·霍华德（Rebecca Moore Howard）、约翰·海曼（John Hyman）、桑德拉·贾米森（Sandra Jamieson）、理查德·詹斯（Richard Jenseth）、伊丽莎白·布尔克·约翰逊（Elizabeth Bourque

Johnson)、朱莉·卡丽什(Julie Kalish)、赛斯·卡茨(Seth Katz)、伯纳黛特·隆戈(Bernadette Longo)、特德·劳(Ted Lowe)、布里杰·鲁尼(BrijLunine)、理查德·麦克莱恩(Richard McLain)、乔尔·马古利斯(Joel Margulis)、苏珊·米勒(Susan Miller)、琳达·米歇尔(Linda Mitchell)、埃伦·穆迪(Ellen Moody)、艾德·莫里茨(Ed Moritz)、帕特里夏·莫里(Patricia Murray)、尼尔·那柯达特(Neil Nakadate)、贾尼斯·尼蕾比(Janice Neuleib)、安·帕克维奇(Ann Palkovich)、马修·帕菲特(Matthew Parfitt)、唐娜·伯恩斯·菲利普(Donna Burns Philips)、迈克·波纳尔(Mike Pownall)、皮特·普利斯特(Peter Priest)、约翰·瑞斯凯韦可(John Ruszkiewicz)、玛格丽特·夏克立(Margaret Shaklee)、南希·萨默斯(Nancy Sommers)、劳拉·巴特利特·斯奈德(Laura Bartlett Snyder)、约翰·泰勒(John Taylor)、玛莉·泰勒(Mary Taylor)、比尔·范德柯普(Bill Vande Kopple)、斯蒂芬·威特(Stephen Witte)、约瑟夫·瓦浦耳(Joseph Wappel)、艾莉森·瓦瑞纳(Alison Warriner)、温蒂·韦曼(Wendy Wayman)、帕特里夏·韦布(Patricia Webb)以及凯文·威尔逊(Kevin Wilson)。

非常感谢斯坦·亨宁(Stan Henning)在威斯康星大学麦迪逊分校教授的班级给予的反馈。同时也感谢琳达·齐夫(Linda Ziff)所发现的错误用法。特别感谢能够和凯斯·罗德斯(Keith Rhodes)就第十二课的内容交流意见。

感谢詹姆斯·范登·博世(James Vanden Bosch)在术语表中运用法国作家蒙田的引语,感谢弗吉尼亚·图福特(Virginia

Tufte)在其著作《风格中的句法》(*The Syntax of Style*)中引用 W. H. 加斯(W. H. Gass)的话,我以此来作为第十二课的格言。感谢韦氏公司(G. & C. Merriam Company)的弗雷德里克·C. 米什(Frederick C. Mish)安置了第二课中三个最好的引文例证;感谢查尔斯·巴扎曼(Charles Bazerman),他贡献了第九课中克里克和沃森 DNA 论文的第一段。

在过去的几年当中,我有幸和一个好同事、好朋友一起工作,他缜密的思维帮助我更好地思考了许多专业的和个人的事情,他就是唐·弗里曼(Don Freeman)。唐的文本让我避免了许多滑稽可笑的错误。感谢他在第十课中引用了威廉·布莱克(William Blake)的格言。

再次感谢那些为我做出贡献的人:奥利佛(Oliver)、米歇尔(Michele)和艾莉诺(Eleanor)、克里斯(Chris)和英格丽德(Ingrid)、戴夫(Dave)、帕蒂(Patty)、欧文(Owen)和马蒂尔德(Matilde)、梅根(Megan)、菲尔(Phil)、莉莉(Lily)和卡尔文(Calvin),以及乔(Joe)、克里斯汀(Christine)、尼古拉斯(Nicholas)和凯瑟琳(Katherine)。自始至终,琼(Joan)付出的耐心和关爱远远多于我应得的。

# 纪 念

约瑟夫·M. 威廉姆斯（Joseph M. Williams），1933—2008

最好的工匠（il miglior fabbro）

[格雷格·科洛姆题词]

2008年2月22日，世界失去了一名伟大的学者、教师，我失去了一位亲密的朋友。近三十年来，乔·威廉姆斯同我一道教学、研究、写作、喝酒、旅行，我们争争吵吵、分分合合。上一版的前言中，他把那些足以能够导致我们分道扬镳的争论说成"我们肆无忌惮的争吵"，然而我们却比之前更加亲近了，写得更为细致。我知道他的缺点，但他是我所知道的最优秀的人。

"最好的工匠"（il miglior fabbro）是我为乔所作的墓志铭，以让他能与名流做伴。这句话出自意大利诗人但丁，用以纪念12世纪抒情诗人阿尔诺·丹尼尔（Arnaut Daniel），他被普鲁塔克（Plutarch）赞为诗歌"大师"（"Grand Master"）。20世纪，T. S. 艾略特（T. S. Eliot）用这句话恰当地评价了美国著名意象派代表诗人埃兹拉·庞德（Ezra Pound）。当然我们都知道，这些诗人之所以被称为大师，除了他们创作清晰、优雅之外，还有作品的深度和难度。无论如何，在技术层面他们是最出色的，没有人可以比肩，正如在作品修改方面没有人比乔还出色一样。乔还有一绝，所有的论文、报告、备忘录以及其他文件一经他的品提润色，立马增色千倍。正因为他，它们才更好地被读者理解。

# 纪 念

**格雷格·科洛姆，1951—2011**

我们最大的幸福并不是由因缘际会而得到的生活条件，而往往是我们合理追求良知、健康、职业以及自由的结果。

(Our greatest happiness does not depend on the condition of life in which chance has placed us, but is always the result of a good conscience, good health, occupation, and freedom in all just pursuits.)

这是格雷格的女儿为父亲挑选的墓志铭，是托马斯·杰斐逊（Thomas Jefferson）的名言。格雷格的一生确实体现了杰斐逊所呼唤的理想。但是与其说杰斐逊的名言是格雷格女儿的猜测，不如说确有此意，因为在《弗吉尼亚州州志》(Notes on the State of Virginia) 的原文中，这些话并不是空头支票，而是杰斐逊针对教育的具体提议，是格雷格毕生追寻的信念。格雷格曾是最出色的教师，他曾指导过无数学生（包括律师、会计、记者，甚至教授）学会思考、学会写作。他还教导我们这些熟人要好好生活。他在学识和学术水平上从不打折扣，无论是在专业还是私人事情上，极其慷慨。他拥有超级自信，并且有足够的信心由衷地称赞他人。他爱笑，是我所认识的最会讲故事的人。格雷格教过很多课程，最重要的是他以身作则。

# 第一部分 风格是种选择

> 如果有话要说,就一定要说得尽可能清楚,这是风格唯一的秘密。
>
> ——马修·阿诺德（Matthew Arnold）

[ 第一课 ]

# 风格的内涵

本质上说,文章的风格类似于良好的行为举止。它源于对不同作品风格坚持不懈的领悟,源于对他人而不是自己风格的分析,或源于用心地思考。

——亚瑟·奎勒-库奇
（Arthur Quiller-Couch）

不真诚是影响语言清晰的最大障碍。

——乔治·奥威尔
（George Orwell）

就重要性而言,风格远比真诚重要得多。

——奥斯卡·王尔德
（Oscar Wilde）

## 简洁的内涵

本书坚持以下两个理念：一是语言简洁是有益处的；二是人人都可以写得清晰简练。第一条是显而易见的，尤其是对于读过大量类似下面风格文章的人来说尤其如此：

An understanding of the causal factors involved in excessive drinking by students could lead to their more effective treatment.

但是就第二条来说，对于那些想要表述清楚而又无法达到下面语句所表达的效果的人而言，似乎太过乐观：

We could more effectively treat students who drink excessively if we understand why they do so.

当然，写作不成功的原因有很多，几个不简练的语句尚构不成十分严重的后果。如果我们不能把复合观点连贯地组织起来，读者就会感到迷惑不解（我在第八课还要探讨这个问题）。除非激励他们，否则他们就不愿意继续读下去了（我在第七课讲到了这个问题）。然而，一旦我们系统地阐发自己的观点，组织支撑观点的论据，在翔实的例子上展开论述，然后激励读者认真地阅读，我们还必须做到表述清楚。这对于大多数作者来说是一项艰巨的任务，也会令许多人望而却步。

这个问题已经使历代作家头疼不已，不仅读者，甚至有时候他们自己也对其所写不明所以。政府条文使用的语言，我们称之为官话；法律文件使用的语言，我们称之为法律语言；学术文章中那些以小见大的论证过程中使用的语言，我们称之为学术语言。写得过分随意或过分谨慎，是整个社会所不能容忍的语言的两种极端形式，而且也是一个长期以来的历史问题。

## 关于"写作晦涩"的简短回顾

直到16世纪中期，作家们才意识到，英语也能够表达得足够明了，可以在一些重要的语境中取代法语和拉丁语。然而最初，他们殚精竭虑创作的文本中，写作风格过于艰涩难懂：

> If use and custom, having the help of so long time and continuance wherein to [re]fine our tongue, of so great learning and experience which furnish matter for the [re]fining of so good wits and judgments which can tell how to refine, have griped at nothing in all that time, with all that cunning, by all those wits which they won't let go but hold for most certain in the right of our writing, that then our tongue has no certainty to trust to, but write all at random.

——理查德·穆尔卡斯特，《英语基础词汇》（1582年）

17世纪，英语成为科学领域的语言。我们或许期望科学家清

楚简单地表述科学事实,但是这种复杂的写作风格已经蔚然成风了。正如一个人所抱怨的:

> 就所有对人类的研究而言,我们从中得到的无非是这邪恶的庞大词汇、隐喻技巧,以及为世界制造着巨量聒噪之音的饶舌之语。
> ——托马斯·斯布拉特,《英国皇家学会史》(1667年)

> ( Of all the studies of men, nothing may sooner be obtained than this vicious abundance of phrase, this trick of metaphors, this volubility of tongue which makes so great a noise in the world.
> —Thomas Sprat, *History of the Royal Society*, 1667 )

早在第一批欧洲移民到北美大陆定居时,作家们或许就为这个新兴的民主国家奠定了一种全新的、自由的写作风格。事实上,托马斯·潘恩于1776年出版了《常识》,他用平实的语言激发了北美大陆人民的革命热情:

> 接下来,我呈现的只是简单的事实、简单的论据以及常识。

> ( In the following pages I offer nothing more than simple facts, plain arguments, and common sense. )

令人遗憾的是,他的著作并没有引发本民族的关于写作风格转变的革命。

半世纪后,詹姆斯·费尼莫·库柏曾如此抱怨当时的写作状况:

> 浮夸的表达日益得势,这应得到纠正。一个最能支持人之学养的证据,便是其平实的言语:即摆脱了庸俗和夸张的朴素……在摆脱庸俗之后,平实应该成为其坚定的目标,……然而,在任何情况下,那些以浮夸的语言、夸张的感情或迂腐的话语为目标的人,都枉活于世。
>
> ——詹姆斯·费尼莫·库柏,《美国民主党人》(1838 年)

> ( The love of turgid expressions is gaining ground, and ought to be corrected. One of the most certain evidences of a man of high breeding, is his simplicity of speech: a simplicity that is equally removed from vulgarity and exaggeration... Simplicity should be the firm aim, after one is removed from vulgarity... In no case, however, can one who aims at turgid language, exaggerated sentiments, or pedantic utterances, lay claim to be either a man or a woman of the world.
>
> —James Fenimore Cooper, *The American Democrat*, 1838 )

不幸的是,库柏在抨击的同时也采用了这种风格。如果遵循他的建议,应该写成这样:

> 我们应该贬斥浮夸的语言。饱学之士言语平实,既不会庸俗,也不会夸张。故作夸张之态,或者言语浮夸、迂腐之

人都枉活于世。

（We should discourage those who promote turgid language. A well-bred person speaks simply, in a way that is neither vulgar nor exaggerated. No one can claim to be a man or woman of the world who deliberately exaggerates sentiments or speaks in ways that are turgid or pedantic.）

大约五十年后，马克·吐温的文章被认为是美国散文的经典。他这样评价库柏的风格：

曾经有些人大胆地说库柏会写作，但是他们都已去世，朗斯波里却是赞赏库柏中硕果仅存的学者。他说，《杀鹿人》是一部纯粹的艺术品……（但是）库柏使用的是现存英语语言里最糟糕的那部分，并且《杀鹿人》里的语言也是库柏所有作品中最糟糕的。

（There have been daring people in the world who claimed that Cooper could write English, but they are all dead now—all dead but Lounsbury [an academic who praised Cooper's style] ... [He] says that *Deerslayer* is a "pure work of art." ... [But] Cooper wrote about the poorest English that exists in our language, and... the English of *Deerslayer* is the very worst tha[t] even Cooper ever wrote.）

尽管我们对马克·吐温直白的表达钦佩不已，但很少有人能模仿它。

在当代关于英语写作风格的最著名的文章《政治与英语语言》("Politics and the English Language")中，乔治·奥威尔分析了政治、官僚、学术和其他领域中的浮夸语言：

[矫揉造作风格的]关键在于，它一般不用简单动词。它往往采用名词或者形容词附着在一般动词上面，组成一个词组，比如 prove（证明）、serve（服务、担当）、form（形成）、play（承担、担当）、render（回报、产生），而不用诸如 break（打破）、stop（停止）、spoil（纵容）、mend（修理）、kill（杀害）等简单动词。此外，只要能用被动语态，主动语态就得退避三舍，名词结构也比动名词更受青睐（比如，常用 by examination of，而不用 by examining）。

[The keynote (of a pretentious style) is the elimination of simple verbs. Instead of being a single word, such as *break, stop, spoil, mend, kill,* a verb becomes a phrase, made up of a noun or adjective tacked on to some general-purposes verb such as *prove, serve, form, play, render.* In addition, the passive voice is wherever possible used in preference to the active, and noun constructions are used instead of gerunds (by examination of instead of by examining).]

但是正如库柏一样，奥威尔也在抨击的同时使用了这种风格。他本可以写得更简洁：

> 矫情的作家总避免使用简单动词。他们不用单个动词，诸如 break、stop、kill，相反，却把动词变为名词或者形容词，然后附着在通用动词上，例如 prove、serve、form、play、render。只要可能，他们就用被动语态代替主动语态，用名词结构代替动名词（比如，名词结构 by examination 比 by examining 用得更多）。

> [ Pretentious writers avoid simple verbs. Instead of using one word, such as *break, stop, kill,* they turn the verb into a noun or adjective, then tack onto it a general-purpose verb such as *prove, serve, form, play, render.* Wherever possible, they use the passive voice instead of the active and noun constructions instead of gerunds ( *by examination* instead of *by examining* ). ]

如果最著名的评论家都不能抵制浮夸的风格，那么当政治家和学者们推崇这种风格时，我们不应该感到惊讶。
关于社会科学语言的评论，

> 社会科学领域，使用浮夸的语言和多音节词的文章泛滥成灾……我认为，这种晦涩的表达几乎与思想的复杂性无关。它似乎完全揭示了学术文章的作者对于自己地位的某些困惑。

——赖特·米尔斯，《社会学的想象力》

关于医学语言的评论：

> 在医学界，表达必须晦涩难懂，似乎是一种根深蒂固的传统……（医学著作）总是千方百计地迷惑读者……医生总是认为，论文的语言表述越清晰，其思想就越显得简单，从而评不上副教授。
>
> ——迈克尔·克莱顿，《新英格兰医学杂志》

关于法律语言的评论：

> 律师和法官开始担心在法学文章和演讲中，在课堂和法庭上被误解的频率。他们发现有时甚至不能理解彼此。
>
> ——汤姆·戈德斯坦，《纽约时报》

关于科学语言的评论：

> 有时候作者（对猿猴交流的方式）解释得越多，人们却理解得越少。猿类似乎肯定能够使用语言进行交流。不管科学家的观点如何，这依然值得我们怀疑。
>
> ——道格拉斯·查德威克，《纽约时报》

大部分人首先会在课本中遇到类似的晦涩文字：

> Recognition of the fact that systems [ of grammar ] differ from one language to another can serve as the basis for serious consideration of the problems confronting translators of the great works of world literature originally written in a language other

than English.

简单地说,上文的意思是:

> When we recognize that languages have different grammars, we can consider the problems of those who translate great works of literature into English.

多少年来,学生们在晦涩难懂的著作中艰难地阅读,很多人认为自己不够聪明,因而无法领悟作者的深刻思想。一部分人这样想是对的,然而更多的人本应该将此归咎于作者不能(或不愿)清晰地表达意思。不幸的是,很多学生并没有这么做;更不幸的是,另一些人不仅习惯读这类风格的著作,而且还用其写作,反过来再折磨他们的读者。从而,缺乏可读性的写作传统延续了 450 年。

## 表述晦涩的个人原因

表述不清是一个社会问题,但常常也有个人原因。迈克尔·克莱顿提到其中之一:一些作家在文章中使用了大量复杂的句子,希望以此传达深刻的思想。特别是,当我们自己都不知道要说些什么的时候,我们尤其会用抽象的词堆砌成冗长复杂的句子。

另外一些作家的文章并不优美,这绝非刻意而为,而是因为,他们坚持认为好的作品一定不能犯下只有语法家才能解释的错误。他们不是把纸张当作探索观点的阵地,而是将之视为潜在错误的雷区。他们在词与词之间徘徊，较多的心思停留在能否不犯错误的层面上，却很少关注读者的理解状况。我在第二课还要探讨这个问题。

还有一些作家的著作之所以表述不清晰，是因为他们思路不够开阔，尤其是在一种陌生的学术或专业背景下学习思考和写作的时候。我们对熟悉观点的写作远比对新观点更加得心应手。在这一点上，并没有良方，只能靠经验积累。

但是，多数人表述不清的最大原因，是他们不知道何时读者会感到晦涩难懂，更别说原因了。作者比读者更了解文章的内容，因为他们在文章中所呈现的正是希望读者能够发现的。因此，作者不会为了满足读者的需要而修改作品。相反地，当达到了自己的要求时，就会将其发表。

当然，所有这些都是一个巨大的讽刺：当我们就一个自己都会感到困惑的主题写作时，我们可能也会使别人感到不解。但当我们对复杂风格感到迷惑不解时，我们很容易假定这种复杂性暗示着深刻的思想，因此我们极力效仿，结果就形成了这种匪夷所思的作品。本书将回答如何避免这两个极端的问题。

## 写作和阅读

这是一本从阅读习惯角度阐发如何写作的著作。我们一旦明白了如何判断一个句子是晦涩抽象的、还是清晰的，就会知道如何既能辨别他人作品的复杂程度是否超出了其应有的深度，又能这样辨别自己的作品。问题在于，我们不能像别人判断我们的作品那样判断自己的作品,因为我们想到的与他们读到的是不同的。一旦你知道了读者读完文章的感觉就可以避免这一难题。

你可以自觉地尝试下述原则,这将对你的阅读有所裨益:当遇到难懂的文章时,从文中找出一些信息,从而判断困难来自材料必要的复杂性,还是写作中不必要的复杂性。如果是后者,这些原则能帮助你从思想上把抽象和简洁的内容转化成易于理解的信息(当知道自己本可以表述得更清楚时会暗自欢喜)。

## 写作和改写

警告:如果在起草阶段考虑这些原则,就可能永远完不成起草。大部分有经验的作家会尽可能快地写下一些东西,然后把第一稿修改得比较清楚,然后他们会更好地理解自己的想法。当作者能够较好地理解自己的想法时,就能表达得更清楚,表达得越清楚他们理解得也会越好……如此反复,直到耗尽精力、兴趣或时间,作品就完成了。

对于少数的幸运者来说,他们在几周、几个月或者几年后完成了作品。然而,对于多数人来说,只能坚持到第二天早上。人们不得不完善并不完美的著作,但只是在有限的时间内我们会尽力做到最好(完美可能是一种理想化的状态,但文章就没意义了)。

所以,起草时不要把规则生搬硬套到每个句子中,而是用这些原则来识别可能使读者困惑的语句,然后进行修改。

尽管清晰性十分重要,但一些场合有更多的要求:

现在那号角又再度召唤我们——不是号召我们掮起武器，虽然武器是我们所需要的；不是号召我们去作战，虽然我们准备应战；那是号召我们年复一年地肩负起持久和胜败未分的斗争，"在希望中欢乐，在患难中忍耐"；这是一场对抗人类公敌——暴政、贫困、疾病以及战争本身——的斗争。

——约翰·F.肯尼迪,《就职演讲》(1961年1月20日)

（Now the trumpet summons us again—not as a call to bear arms, though arms we need; not as a call to battle, though embattled we are; but a call to bear the burden of a long twilight struggle, year in and year out, "rejoicing in hope, patient in tribulation," a struggle against the common enemies of man: tyranny, poverty, disease and war itself.

—John F. Kennedy, Inaugural Address, January 20, 1961）

被召去写总统演讲稿的人毕竟为数不多，但即使在不太正式的情形下，一些人也总以写出优美的句子为乐趣，即使没人会在意。如果你不仅享受写作的乐趣，而且还喜欢润色你的文章，第四部分将有相关的建议。

写作也是一种社会行为，可能会也可能不会满足读者的兴趣。在第十二课中，我提到了一些有关风格的准则。附录一是有关标点的风格。附录二解释了如何使用和引用引文及原材料。

多年前，H.L.门肯曾这样写道：

除极少数外，所有关于风格的英文书籍都是由不会写作的人来完成的。的确，这个写作学科在女教师、乡间大学教授和其他假知识分子中产生了一种特别的、发狂的魔力……当然，其核心目标在于，把写作简化为一套简单的规则——它们能随时随地征服内心的忧郁。

（With precious few exceptions, all the books on style in English are by writers quite unable to write. The subject, indeed, seems to exercise a special and dreadful fascination over school ma'ams, bucolic college professors, and other such pseudoliterates... Their central aim, of course, is to reduce the whole thing to a series of simple rules—the overmastering passion of their melancholy order, at all times and everywhere.）

门肯是正确的——没人仅凭规则就能学好写作，尤其是那些不善于观察、少有感触或缺乏思考能力的人。但我也知道，许多人能够清楚地观察、深切地感受、认真地思考，但他们却不能写出一些能够清楚地表现思想、感触及想象力的语句。我还发现，写得越清晰，观察到的、感触到的、考虑到的就越清楚。规则不能帮人做到这些，但是一些原则却能。

是这样的。

[ 第二课 ]

# 准确性

> 上帝不在乎蹩脚的语法,但对此也不会有特殊的好感。
> ——伊拉斯谟
> (Erasmus)

> 对于语言的习惯用法,任何语法规则都没有足够的权威加以控制。为了解决语言和风格中存在的争议,人们不得不将口语和写作中已经形成的习惯作为最后的参考标准。
> ——休·布莱尔
> (Hugh Blair)

> 有时,英语使用惯例不仅仅体现了作者的偏好、判断力,以及教育状况——偶尔有点像过马路一样,纯属运气。
> ——E. B. 怀特
> (E. B. White)

## 准确性的内涵

对一个认真的作家来说,选择最重要。例如,如果想让读者看明白,你会选择下列哪一个句子?

1. Lack of media support was the cause of our election loss.
2. We lost the election because the media did not support us.

大部分人会选择第二个句子。

然而不同于简洁,准确性似乎与选择无关,而只要遵守习惯用法就够了。选择的缺乏的确使事情显得简单化了:"准确性"只要求作者拥有良好的记忆力,而不是合理的判断力。例如,如果人们一直记得 irregardless 是错的,那就无可选择了。一些教师和编者认为人们应记住一堆这样的"规则":

> 句首绝不要使用 and 或 but。
> 绝不使用双重否定。
> 绝不能将不定式分离。

然而,实际情况却更加复杂。如果我们忽略下列合理的规则,我们就会被贴上"文盲"的标签:**动词必须与主语保持一致**;代词必须与**所指**保持一致，还有许多其他的规则。但是很多经常重复使用的规则并没有人们想象的那么重要，有些规则甚至不合理。如果拘泥于这些规则，就不能既快速又清晰地写作。这就是我为什么要把准确性放到简洁性之前来讲解的原因。

## 语法规则及其权威性的基础

关于语法规则的社会功能，人们的意见并不统一。对于一些人来说，语法规则只不过是**体制内的人**用来控制**体制外的人**的工具，通过这些规则给**体制外的人**的语言打上标记，借此来压制他们的社会和政治理想。对于另外一些人来说，**标准英语**的规则已经被历代受过教育的演说者和作家们完善，以至于最优秀的英文作家必须遵循这些规则。

这两种观点都有一定道理。几个世纪以来，思想的统治者就曾经利用语法"错误"来将那些不愿意，或不能够顺从受过教育的中产阶级习惯的人踢出门外。但是一些评论家却错误地认为规则只是为了这个目的而制定的。其实任何一种语言的标准形式都含有地理和经济实力的因素。如果一种语言包含着不同的区域方言，其中被最有实力的人使用的方言通常会变得最为权威，因而成为该国"准确"写作的基础。

因此，如果是爱丁堡而不是伦敦成为了英国的经济、政治以及文化的中心，人们所说或所写的语言风格就会更像苏格兰诗人博比·彭斯（左），而非莎士比亚（右）：

| A ye wha are sae guid yourself | (All you who are so good yourselves |
| Sae pious and sae holy, | So pious and so holy, |
| Ye've nought to do but mark and tell | You've nothing to do but talk about |
| Your neebours' fauts and folly! | Your neighbors' faults and folly!) |

另一方面，保守的观点也有道理，他们认为标准英语的众多规则形成于有效的表达。例如，人们不再使用一千年前所要求的动词结尾。人们省略了现在时态的屈折变化，除了这种情况（我们不需要用它）：

|  | 第一人称 | 第二人称 | 第三人称 |
|---|---|---|---|
| 单数 | I know + φ | You know + φ | She know + **S** |
| 复数 | We know + φ | You know + φ | They know + φ |

但是，一旦他们认为**标准英语**已经沿袭了受过教育的演讲家和作家的文化逻辑而得以完善，并且就其本质而言，它必定在社会层面和道德层面优于所谓的劣等阶层的语言，那么他们就犯了错误。

诚然，**标准英语**的众多规则反映了该语言朝着更有逻辑性的方向演进。如果我们用"逻辑性"意指语言具有规律性因而具有可预测性，那么标准英语在很多方面上**不如**非标准英语更具逻辑性。例如，句子"I'm here, aren't I?"中，标准英语缩写式是 aren't，但是还有比句子"I am here, are I not?"的完整形式更不合乎语法的吗？逻辑上讲，我们应该把"am + not"缩写成"amn't"，这其实是非标准的"ain't"的原型之一（另外一个原型是 are + not）。因此，标准英语中的"aren't I"并不比非标准英语中的"ain't I"更有逻辑性。我能举出一大堆**标准英语**中不合语法的例子，但正是这些语法中的违规现象反映了某种逻辑思维，它使得英语语法更具一致性。

当然，对那些以**标准英语/非标准英语**来区分人群的人来说，正是标准英语的**不一致性**才使得语法规则显得更加有用：要想掌握标准的英语口语和书面语，我们要么必须出生在标准英语环境里，要么必须投入大量时间来学习它（同时还要学习标准英语者的价值观）。

> **要点** 这些决心以语言区别人群的人会利用任何一个语言上的差异。但是语言看似比邮政编码更直接地反映着思想的品质，因此，容易瞧不起别人的人认为语法错误暗示着精神或道德的缺陷。但这一观点不仅仅是事实层面的错误，在我们这样的国度里，它具有社会性的破坏力。尽管"ain't"在逻辑上是正确的，但是社会的规约力量十分强大，因而这种用法并不可取；至少假如因严肃的写作目的，或者我们希望自己的作品被当作严肃作品，我们就要避免它。

## 三类规则

历代文法家的观点，直接鼓励了这种腐朽的关于"准确性"的社会看法的滋生，他们在执着地编码"好"英语的过程中，混淆了下面三个规则：

## 1. 合理性规则

合理性规则定义了英语的语法构成，**冠词**放在**名词**前："the book"，而不是 "book the"。生于英语国家的人写作时完全不用考虑这些规则，只有在疲惫或思想不集中时才会违反这些规则。

## 2. 社会性规则

社会性规则将**标准英语**与非标准英语区分开来："He doesn't have any money" 和 "He don't have no money"。受过教育的作家自然地遵守这一规则，就像遵守合理性规则一样，并且只有在他们注意到别人违反这些规则时，他们才会想到这些规则。那些有意识去遵循这些规则的人，都不是出生在标准英语环境中的人，他们想努力跻身于受教育的行列。

## 3. 虚构的规则

最后，一些文法家虚构了很多他们认为我们**应该**遵循的规则。语法警察喜欢将这些规则付诸实施，但很多受过教育的作家被这些规则所困扰。大部分规则可追溯到 18 世纪后半叶：

> 不能将不定式分开，例如，"to **quietly** leave"。
> 不能把介词放在句子的结尾。

少数规则源于 20 世纪：

> 不要用 "hopefully" 表达 "I hope" 的意思，例如，

**Hopefully**, it won't rain.

不要用 which 代替 that，例如，a car **which** I sold。

250年来，文法学家们指责那些犯了类似语法错误的优秀作家；而250年来，那些优秀的作家们对这些规则视而不见。这对于文法学家来说是一件幸事，因为如果作家们遵循了所有的原则，那么文法学家们就不得不创造新的规则或寻找另一种新的工作。事实上，任何一条新创的规则都未曾让优秀的作家在写作中有意识地加以运用。

这一课主要讲第三类的语法规则，因为这些规则令使用**标准英语**写作的人备感困惑。

## 对语法规则的观照

如果想被读者认为你写得"准确"，那么使用这些虚构的规则并不是一件容易的事情。你可以选择最坏的策略，即时刻遵守所有的规则，因为有些人偶尔会因某些事吹毛求疵，例如句子开头使用了"and"，结尾使用"up"。

但是如果时刻试图遵循所有的规则，你会被这些规则所束缚，从而感到困惑不已，早晚会把这些合理的或者不合理的规则强加给别人。毕竟，如果人们仅仅是遵守这些语法规则，而不做其他用途，那研究它还有什么用呢？

与盲目遵守相对的是选择性遵守。但是你就不得不判断需要遵守哪些规则，忽略哪些规则。如果你忽略了一条所谓的规则，就不得不应付那些出于对"好"语法的热衷而认为把不定式分开来用就是道德腐败和社会败退标志的人们。

如果你不想被指责"缺乏标准",但又不想被从中学书本上得来的任何规则所限制,那你就不得不比规则的主宰者更了解这些新规则。这一课剩下的部分会帮你做到这一点。

## 两类虚构性规则

大多数的虚构性规则可以分为两类:**民俗规则和典雅规则**

### 约定俗成规则

这些规则包括那些最细心的读者和作家都会忽略的规则。你可能还没把这些规则强加给自己,但你将来可能会这样做。下面的引文包含着"违规现象",这些引文来源于学识渊博的作家,或者那些在惯用法上值得信赖的保守派(有些人两者都是)。尽管一些文法家仍持有异议,打对号的句子表明的是可接受的**标准英语**。

**1. 句子开头不能用"and"或者"but"**,下文两次忽略了这一"规则":

> √ **But**, it will be asked, is tact not an individual gift, therefore highly variable in its choice? **And** if that is so, what guidance can a manual offer, other than that of its author's

prejudices—mere impressionism?

——威尔逊·福莱,
《现代英语美式用法入门》,雅克·巴赞等人编辑完成

一些缺乏经验的作家在很多句子中把"and"放在句首,但这是风格上的错误而不是语法错误。

一些不自信的作家还认为不应把 because 放在句首。据说不能这样写:

√ **Because** we have access to so much historical fact, today we know a good deal about changes within the humanities which were not apparent to those of any age much before our own and which the individual scholar must constantly reflect on.

——瓦尔特·翁, S. J.,
《美国现代语言协会会刊》,美国现代语言协会出版物

我所知道的手册中没有一本提到过"because"的约定俗成规则,但它却越来越盛行。它源于为避免下列**片段化句子**的目的:

The plan was rejected. **Because** it was incomplete.

> **快速提示** 语法中没有涉及 because 的规则,它确实反映了风格上一个不起眼的事实。在第五课中我们会看到一个关于风格的规则,它告诉我们如何安排句子成分,使得读者头脑中首先呈现的是熟知的信息而不是生疏的信息

（请略读 126—132 页的小结）。在英文风格中，用 because 开头的从句通常引入新信息。因此，这类从句通常在句末：

√ Some writers write graceless prose because they are seized by the idea that writing is good only when it's free of errors that only a grammarian can explain.

如果颠倒顺序的话，句子就显得有些蹩脚：

Because some writers are seized by the idea that writing is good only when it's free of errors that only a grammarian can explain, they write graceless prose.

如果你想把从句放在句首表达因果关系的已知信息，从句应以"since"开头。因为"since"表明读者已经知道了从句信息：

√ Since our language seems to reflect our quality of mind, it is easy for those inclined to look down on others to think that grammatical "errors" indicate mental or moral deficiency.

这一规则也有例外，但总体是合理的。

**2. 在限定性从句中使用关系代词"that"，而不是"which"。** 据说不能这样写：

√ Next is a typical situation **which** a practical writer corrects "for style" virtually by reflex action.

——雅克·巴赞,《简单与直接》

对于前面这些句子,巴赞(最杰出的文化史学家与风格评论家之一)坚持认为:

> 除非是写作风格的需要,否则定语从句(例如,限定性从句)一般由 that 引导。

(以上引用的句子没有风格原因。)

这一"规则"相对来说比较新,最早出现于 1906 年亨利·福勒和弗朗西斯·福勒写的《标准英语》(牛津大学出版社)中。他们认为引导限定性从句时,如果随机使用 that 和 which,句子就会显得很混乱,所以他们认为自此以后,应该只用 which 来引导非限定性从句。

你可以回想一下,非限定性从句修饰一个名词——先行词,不用参考从句信息就可以清楚地识别这个先行词。例如:

√ ABCO inc. ended its first bankruptcy, **which** it had filed in 1997.

公司只能有一个首次破产,所以人们可以不参照后面的从句就能清楚地识别破产这个先行词。因此,我们称这类从句为非限定性从句,因为从句没有进一步限制或规定名词所指。在这一语境下,我们在修饰从句前放一个逗号,用 which 来引导该从句。这一规则基于历史和当代的惯用法。

但是,富勒兄弟曾说,在限定性从句中我们只能使用 that 不能使用 which。例如:

> √ ABCO inc. sold a product **that** [ *not* **which** ] made millions.

因为 ABCO 公司可能生产很多产品,从句 that made millions "限定"能赚上百万的产品。所以他们说应该用 that 引导。

弗朗西斯 1981 年去世之后,亨利继承家族传统,继续编纂《现代英语用法词典》(牛津大学出版社,1926 年),其中他忧心忡忡地说:

> 现在一些人遵守这一规则;但是假使大部分或最好的作家们不使用这一规则,那它就没有用处。(635 页)

(关于另外一个所谓不正确的 which,参见 39 页瓦尔特·翁的文章。)

我承认我遵从了福勒的说法,不是因为限制性的 which 是错的,而是因为 that 听上去更入耳。在一个句子内或有两个 that 同时存在,我确实会选择使用 which 代替其中一个 that,因为不喜欢两个 that 靠在一起时发出来的声音:

> √ We all have **that** one rule **that** we will not give up.
>
> √ We all have **that** one rule **which** we will not give up.

**3.** "fewer" 修饰可数名词,"less" 修饰不可数名词。据此规则,下面这句话是不对的：

> √ I can remember no **less** than five occasions when the correspondence columns of *The Times* rocked with volleys of letters...
>
> ——诺埃尔·吉尔洛·安南、洛尔·安南，《今天英国大学里的生活观念》载于《美国学术团体协会电子报》

物质名词前不使用 fewer（fewer dirt），然而受过教育的作家通常用 less 修饰可数名词复数（less resources）。

4. "since" 和 "while" 只表示时间，不表示 because 和 although 的意思。大部分细心的作家用 since 表示和 because 接近的意思，但正如上文提到的，since 给人一种感觉，即下文提到的事情是已知的：

> √ **Since** asbestos is dangerous, it should be removed carefully.

大部分细心的作家也不只局限于用 while 表示时间（We'll wait while you eat），而且用它来表达与这句相近的意思 "I assume you know what I state in this clause, but what I assert in the next will qualify it"：

> √ **While** we agree on a date, we disagree about the place.

> **要点** 如果那些被认为有能力的作家经常违反已有的规则而且大部分细心的读者从来没注意到,那么这些规则就形同虚设了。在这类情况下,不是需要作家们改变规则的用法,而是需要文法家们改变规则。

**典雅的规则**

**典雅规则**是对合理性规则的补充。如果你一直遵循着合理性规则,那么大部分读者不会注意到,但一旦你违背了它,他们就会意识到。另外,如果你违背了典雅规则中的一条,很少读者会注意到,但是如果你遵循了它,就会引起他们的注意,因为这样会使写作的正式文体显得更像有意为之。

**1. 不能分离不定式。**因为下面这个句子(我在下面所有的句子中都做了强调),有语言纯正癖的人经常指责犯了类似极端保守的语言学家德怀特·麦克唐纳所犯的错误:

> √ One wonders why Dr. Gove and his editors did not think of labeling knowed as substandard right where it occurs, and one suspects that they wanted **to slightly conceal** the fact...
> ——德怀特·麦克唐纳,《不协调的音符》载于《纽约人》

他们会要求:

> they wanted **to conceal slightly** the fact...

不定式频繁地被分离，一旦你没有分离，不管你有意还是无意，细心的读者都会觉得你在刻意地保持正确。

**2. 用 whom 做动词宾语或介词宾语。** 有语言纯正癖的人也会经常指责犯了类似威廉·津泽所犯的 "who" 的用法错误：

> √ Soon after you confront this matter of preserving your identity, another question will occur to you: "**Who** am I writing for?"
>
> ——威廉·津泽，《论典雅写作》

他们坚持认为：

> another question will occur to you: "For **whom** am I writing?"

真正的规则是：用"who"做从句中动词的主语，只用"whom"做从句中动词的宾语。

---

**快速提示** 当关系从句修饰名词时，如果省去关系代词后仍要保持句子的意义，应使用 whom：

√ The committee chose someone **whom** they trusted.
√ The committee chose someone [　] they trusted.

如不能省去"who"或者"whom"，就应选择"who"：

√ The committee chose someone **who** earned their trust.

> √ The committee chose someone [ ] earned their trust.
>
> 以下两种情况例外：（1）从句是动词宾语时，不能省略"whom"。在这类情况下你必须参照从句语法：
>
> √ The committee decided **whom** they should choose.
>
> √ The committee decided **who** was to be chosen.
>
> （2）使用"whom"作为介词的宾语。
>
> The committee chose someone **in whom** they had confidence.

**3. 不能把介词放在句尾**。有语言纯正癖的人经常指责犯了类似《标准英语》（第二版）的编辑所犯的错误：

> √ The peculiarities of legal English are often used as a stick to beat the official **with.**

——《简明词汇汇编》

他们坚持认为下面的句子更典雅：

> ... a stick **with which** to beat the official.

第一句是正确的，第二句则显得更加正式。（再次参见 39 页的文章）把介词和 whom 放在左侧，看上去更正式。试比较下列两个句子：

[ 046 ]　风格：写作的清晰与优雅

√ The man I met **with** was the man I had written **to**.

√ The man **with whom** I met was the man **to whom** I had written.

但是，介词可以勉强地置于句末（见150—152页）。在下面这个句子中，乔治·奥威尔可能把"from"放在句末，使英语语法显得更灵活。但是我怀疑它只能用于这种情况（标出"不正确的"which）：

[ The defense of the English language ] has nothing to do with...

the setting up of a "standard English" **which** must never be departed **from**.

——乔治·奥威尔，《政治与英语语言》

下面这句的表达看上去没那么蹩脚，而且重点更加突出：

We do not defend English just to create a "standard English" whose rules we must always obey.

**4.** "none"和"any"用作单数。最初，"none"和"any"是单数的，但是现在大多数的作家把他们用作复数。因此，如果把它们作为单数时，一些读者就会注意到。下面第二句比第一句更正式一些：

√ **None** of the reasons **are** sufficient to end the project.

√ **None** of the reasons **is** sufficient to end the project.

如果文章被严格审查，你可能会选择遵循所有的高雅规则。尽管它们常常被大部分细心的作家们忽略，也就是说，它们根本就不是规则，而是能够创造出一种使语气更加正式的语体选择。如果不得已选择了这种表达方法并且时刻遵循，很少有读者会信任你，他们只会注意到你的文本有多正式。

**怪癖规则**

不知道是什么原因，一些规则总是被滥用。也没有任何理由，它们既不影响文章的清晰性，也不影响简明性。

**1.** 不能把"like"当作"as"或"as if"来用。依理，下列表达是不准确的：

√ These operations failed **like** the earlier ones did.

而是：

√ These operations failed **as** the earlier ones did.

18 世纪时，当作家们把 as 从连词短语 like as 中去掉，只剩下 like 作为连词时，like 就变成了从属连词。这种处理方法被称作省音。这是一种常见的语言变化。据说《福勒词典》（语言保守主义者最喜欢的词典）第二版的编辑从"illiteracies"词条中把"like"当作"as"去掉了，把 like 添加到"Sturdy Indefensibles"

的条目之下了。

**2.** 不能用"**hopefully**"表示"**I hope**"的意思。依理，下列表达是不准确的：

√ Hopefully, it will not rain.

而是：

√ I hope that it will not rain.

这一"规则"可追溯到20世纪中叶。该规则既没有逻辑基础，也没有语法基础。hopefully 与那些没有受到质疑的词汇用法差不多，譬如 candidly、frankly、sadly 和 happily：

√ Candidly, we may fail.（That is, **I am candid when I say we may fail.**）

√ Seriously, we must go.（That is, **I am serious when I say we must go.**）

**3.** 不能用"**finalize**"表示"**finish**"或"**complete**"的意思。finalize 不仅仅表示"finish"，它表示"清理最后的细节"，这是其他词汇无法表达出来的意思。此外，要是我们认为"finalize"很糟糕是因为词尾"-ize"看着不顺眼，那么，我们也可以拒绝使用"nationalize""synthesize"和"rationalize"，以及其他众多类似的词汇。

**4.** 不能把 **impact** 当作动词使用，例如，The survey impacted our strategy, 这句话里"impact"的用法不准确；"impact"只能

用于名词，例如，"The survey had an impact on our strategy."其实"impact"用作动词已经有 400 年了，但是他们却对历史的证据视而不见。

**5. 不能用"very、more quite"等词修饰表示绝对意义的词，例如"perfect""unique""final"或者"complete"。**要是按照这一规则的话，下面我们所熟悉的句子就不会存在了：

√ We the People of the United States, in order to form a **more perfect** union...

（尽管如此，这仍是一个值得遵循的规则。）

**6. 不能用"irregardless"指代"regardless"或者"irrespective"。**不管这一规则多么武断，我们都要遵循它。如果使用 irregardless，一些人就会觉得你无可救药。

### 值得关注的词

一些词在意义上经常与其他词混淆，例如"flaunt"和"flout"，细心的读者更可能会注意到这些。如果使用得准确，那些关注语言差异的人至少会认为你清楚"flaunt"的意思是"故意地表现"，而"flout"的意思是"轻视某个规则或标准"。因此，如果没有注意到"flaunt"和"flout"之间的差别的话，一不小心就掉到沟里了。下面是一些其他的词：

**aggravate** 指"使恶化"，不指"annoy"（令人讨厌）。可以指使伤势恶化，而不能用于"使人恶化"。

**anticipate** 指"预先准备",和"expect"的语义不尽相同。当你在提问前准备好问题的答案时,可以说"anticipate a question"(预测一个问题)。如果问题快出现了,而你还没有准备好答案,就只能用"expect"。

**anxious** 指"uneasy"(焦虑的),而不是"eager"(急切)。如果离开时的心情很愉快,就要说"You're eager to leave";如果离开时的心情很紧张,就说"You're anxious about leaving"。

**blackmail** 指"to extort by threatening to reveal damaging information"(想通过揭露重磅信息进行威胁,以达到敲诈的目的)。它不单指"coerce"(胁迫)。如果一个国家只是威胁要使用核武器,就不能用"blackmail"这个词。

**cohort** 指"a group who attends on someone"(同党)。它不单指"a single accompanying person"(一个伙伴)。威廉王子和凯特·米德尔顿结婚,她成为他的"consort"(伴侣、配偶);他的 hangers-on(拥护者)是他的 cohort。

**comprise** 指"各个部分组成一个整体"。它不同于"constitute"(构成)。The alphabet is not comprised by its letters.(注:需要把"by"换成"of"。)it comprises them.(它包含了字母。)Letters **constitute** the alphabet, which is thus constituted by them.(字母构成了字母表。)

**continuous** 指"without interruption"(连续的、没有间断的)。它不同于"continual"(持续是指活动在一定的时间中进行,伴随有间断)。If you **continuously** interrupt someone,

第二课 准确性

that person will never say a word because your interruption will never stop.（如果你连续不断地打断别人，所以这个人插不上话）。If you **continually** interrupt, you let the other person finish a sentence from time to time.（如果你不停地打断他，他就可以时不时地插上一句话。）

**disinterested** 指 "neutral"（中立的、无偏见的）。它不同于 "uninterested"（不感兴趣的）。A judge should be disinterested in the outcome of a case, but not uninterested in it. 对一件事情的判断应该保持中立而不是漠不关心。（某些情况下，disinterested 的原意是"漠不关心的"。）

**enormity** 指 "hugely bad"（罪不可恕的），不同于 "enormous"（过分的）。例如：In private, a belch might be enormous, but at a state funeral, it would also be an enormity.（在私人场合，打嗝可能只是过分的，但是在国葬上就是不可饶恕的。）

**fortuitous** 指 "by chance"（意外的），不指 "fortunate"（幸运的）。例如，You are fortunate when you fortuitously pick the right number in the lottery.（如果你意外中奖了，就是幸运的。）

**fulsome** 指 "sickeningly excessive"（过度的），不单指 "much"（多，或者程度高）。例如：We all enjoy praise, except when it becomes fulsome.（我们都喜欢被称赞，除非称赞过度。）

**notorious** 指 "known for bad behavior"（臭名昭著的），不同于 "famous"（出名的）。例如，Frank Sinatra was a famous singer but a notorious bully.（法兰克·辛娜特拉是一个著名的歌手，但也是一个臭名昭著的流氓。）

现在，只有少数读者关注这些区别，他们的意见却举足轻重。将词汇放在检测写作准确与否的过程中学习，我们只需几分钟就能掌握它们的用法，尤其当你也认为这些差别值得保留的时候。

另一方面，人们只期望受过教育的作家能够准确地区分"imply"和"infer"，"principal"和"principle"，"accept"和"except"，"capital"和"capitol"，"affect"和"effect"，"proceed"和"precede"，"discrete"和"discreet"。当一个拉丁语或希腊语的复数名词被当作单数的时候，绝大多数细心的读者也是能够注意到的。因此我们需要把下列词汇的单复数弄清楚：

| 单数 | datum | criterion | medium | stratum | phenomenon |
| 复数 | data | criteria | media | strata | phenomena |

> **要点** 不能仅凭逻辑性或一般规则来预测语言是否符合语法，是否用法准确。人们不得不逐条地学习这些规则，并且接受这样的事实：一些规则（可能是大多数规则）非常武断和怪僻。

## 问题：代词与性别偏见

**代词及其所指**

我们期望有文化的作家在写作中动词与主语保持一致：

> √ Our **reasons** ARE based on solid evidence.

我们也期望代词和先行词保持一致。下面的句子不准确：

> Early **efforts** to oppose the hydrogen bomb failed because **it** ignored political issues. **No one** wanted to expose **themselves** to anti-Communist hysteria.

应该是：

> √ Early **efforts** to oppose the hydrogen bomb failed because **they** ignored political issues. **No one** wanted to expose **himself** to anti-Communist hysteria.

然而当代词与所指保持一致时，会出现两个问题：

第一个问题：如果指代一个在语法上是单数而意义上却是复数的名词时，我们选用单数代词还是复数代词？如果我们指代单数名词，例如"group、committee、staff、administration"等等，我们选用单数动词还是复数动词？当集合名词作为单数整体使用时，一些作家往往使用单数动词和代词：

> √ The **committee** HAS met but has not yet made **its** decision.

当作单独成员使用时，他们用复数动词和代词：

> √ The **faculty** HAVE the memo, but not all of **them** have

read it.

当今,复数在这两方面使用时并没有规律(但是在英国英语中复数的使用是有规则可循的)。

第二个问题:要指代如"someone、everyone、no one"等类似的代词,以及指代诸如"teacher、doctor、student"等没有性别指向的单数普通名词,我们选用哪个代词,it 还是 they?通常情况下,使用 they:

**Everyone** knows **they** must answer for **their** actions.

When **a person** is on drugs, it is hard to help **them**.

正式文体要求选用单数代词:

√ **Everyone** realizes that **he** must answer for **his actions.**

但是这一规则提出了语言偏见问题。

## 性别和语言偏见

常识告诉我们,不能无缘无故地冒犯读者。如果我们在类属代词中不选 he,因为它带有性别偏见色彩,也不选 they,因为读者认为它不合语法,那么我们就别无选择了。一些作家就选用了蹩脚的标识法,即"he or she";其他的作家则选用了更糟糕的"he/she",甚至"s/he":

If **a writer** ignores the ethnicity of **his or her** readers, **s/he** may respond in ways **the writer** would not expect to words that to **him or her** are innocent of bias.

一些作家用复数替代单数：

> √ When **writers** ignore **their** readers' ethnicity, **they** may respond in ways **they** might not expect to words that are to **them** innocent of bias.

但是在上面句子中"they、their、them"指代不清楚，因为它们既能指代作者又能指代读者。对于一些认真的人来说，包含单数名词和代词的句子似乎稍微清晰一些：

> When a **writer** ignores **his** reader's ethnicity, **his reader** may respond in ways that **he** might not expect to words that are to **him** innocent of bias.

我们还可以尝试使用第一人称"we"：

> √ If **we** ignore the ethnicity of **our** readers, they may respond in ways **we** would not expect to words that to **us** are innocent of bias.

但是"we"也存在歧义。我们也能够尝试使用非人称的抽象词，但这也会有它自己的问题：

> Failure to consider ethnicity may lead to unexpected responses to words considered innocent of bias.

最终，如果需要的话，我们可以交替选用"he"和"she"。

但这也不是一个完美的解决方法，因为一些读者发现，在风格上"she"和"he/she"一样都具有性别偏见的意味。例如，《纽约时报》的一个评论家质疑作家的品质时，控诉道：

> ... right history's wrongs to women by referring to random examples as "she", as in "Ask a particle physicist what happens when a quark is knocked out of a proton, and she will tell you...," which strikes this reader as oddly patronizing to women.

但我们想知道的恰好是，女性量子物理学家又有怎样的反映。

未来几年内，我们还不容易处理单数的类属代词问题。对一些读者而言，任何解决方法都很拙劣。我怀疑我们最终会接受把复数 they 当作正确的单数使用：

√ **No one** should turn in **their** writing unedited.

一些人声称，类似的妥协将会导致不求甚解的意义模糊。无论未来会怎样，我们可以选择，这并不是坏事，因为我们的选择决定了我们的风格。

## 总结

我们必须写得准确。但是如果在定义准确性的时候，我们忽略了事实和约定俗成规则之间的差别，我们就会有忽视真正重要问题的风险，即选择写得杂乱和冗长，还是选择清晰和简练。仅仅做到正确使用"which"和"that"，以及不用"finalize"和

"hopefully"，仍然是不够的。过度纠缠于类似细节的人常常无视下列更为严重的意义含混：

> Too precise a specification of information processing requirements incurs the risk of overestimation resulting in unused capacity or inefficient use of costly resources or of underestimation leading to ineffectiveness or other inefficiencies.

上段的意思是：

> √ When you specify too precisely the resources you need to process information, you may overestimate. If you do, you risk having more capacity than you need or using costly resources inefficiently.

这两段话在语法上都是正确的，谁会更愿意读第一段呢？

我怀疑那些时刻遵循所有规则的人这样做，确实不是因为他们想去保护语言的整体性或者文化的品质，而是为了确定他们自己的风格。一些人语言平实；另一些人喜欢用高雅的词汇，只要它不是用于与别人区隔的借口，而是另有更重要的目的，即接下来要讨论的简洁和高雅，我们就不该对它嗤之以鼻。

# 第二部分 清晰

一切能够思考的东西，都能被思考得清楚，一切能够讲清楚的东西，亦能被阐释得清晰。
——路德维希·维特根斯坦
（Ludwig Wittgenstein）

清晰、直接的写作远比文体华丽的写作更费力气。
——弗雷德里希·尼采
（Friedrich Nietzsche）

[ 第三课 ]

# 动 作

让行动符合台词，台词也符合行动。

——威廉·莎士比亚，《哈姆雷特》, 3.2

（William Shakespeare, *Hamlet*, 3.2）

我不可能相信那些信手拈来的句子。

——威廉·加斯

（William Gass）

## 判断的内涵

我们有足够多的词汇去称赞自己喜欢的作品,诸如写作**清晰**、**明快**、**简洁**;同时我们也有足够多的词汇去批评所不喜欢的作品,如表述**不清晰**、**繁琐**、**抽象**、**晦涩和杂乱**。那么,我们可以运用这些词汇来评价下面这两个句子:

1a. The cause of our schools' failure at teaching basic skills is not understanding the influence of cultural background on learning.

1b. Our schools have failed to teach basic skills because they do not understand how cultural background influences the way a child learns.

大多数人认为句子(1a)表述得太复杂,而(1b)更清楚也更明快;但是这些评价并不指代句子中的任何具体的东西,它们只是用来描述这些句子给我们的**感受**。当我们说(1a)表述**不清**时,我们是指句子理解起来很费劲;而当我们绞尽脑汁去读它时,我们会认为句子**晦涩难懂**。

问题是作者要去理解读者读这两个句子时的感受,然后,作者才能对自己作品有更好的了解,从而发现读者认为需做修改的地方。要达到这种程度,你就必须知道精彩的故事之所以精彩的奥秘所在。(要从这一课和后面的三课获益,你需要能够辨别动词、简单主语和总主语。参见术语表。)

## 人物和人物的动作

下面的故事存在问题:

2a. Once upon a time, as a walk through the woods was taking place on the part of Little Red Riding Hood, the Wolf's jump out from behind a tree occurred, causing her fright.

我们更喜欢读下面这样的句子:

√ 2b. Once upon a time, Little Red Riding Hood was walking through the woods, when the Wolf jumped out from behind a tree and frightened her.

大多数读者会认为(2b)比(2a)讲述得更清楚,因为(2b)遵循了下面这两条原则:

> 句子的主要人物是动词的主语。
> 这些动词表达特定动作。

**清晰原则之一:让主要人物做主语**

看下面句子中(2a)的主语。划线部分是简单主语,不是句子的核心；斜体部分是主要人物。

> 2a. Once upon a time, as a walk through the woods was taking place on the part of *Little Red Riding Hood*, *the Wolf's* jump out from behind a tree occurred, causing *her* fright.

这些主语并不指称人物；它们指称的是抽象名词"walk"和"jump"：

| 主语 | 动词 |
| --- | --- |
| a walk through the woods | was taking place |
| the Wolf's jump out from behind a tree | occurred |

occurred 的总主语中确实包涵着人物：the **Wolf's** jump。但是"the Wolf"不是主语，它只从属于简单主语 jump。

同抽象主语形成对比的是，下面句子里的主语（斜体部分）也是简单主语（划线部分）：

> 2b. Once upon a time, *Little Red Riding Hood* was walking through the woods, when *the Wolf* jumped out from behind a tree and frightened *her*.

现在，主语和主要人物都是同一个词：

| 主语 / 主要人物 | 动词 |
| --- | --- |
| *Little Red Riding Hood* | was walking |
| *the Wolf* | jumped |

## 清晰原则之二：用动词表达主要动作

现在看一下（2a）中动作和动词的不一致之处：动作没有用动词来表达，而是采用了抽象名词（黑体字是动作；大写的词是动词）：

2a. Once upon a time, as a **walk** through the woods WAS TAKING place on the part of Little Red Riding Hood, the Wolf's **jump** out from behind a tree OCCURED, causing her **fright**.

注意动词的模糊程度："was taking""occurred"在（2b）中，句子显得更清晰，因为它是用动词表达特定动作的：

√ 2b. Once upon a time, Little Red Riding Hood WAS WALKING through the woods, when the Wolf JUMPED out from behind a tree and FRIGHTENED her.

> **要点** 在（2a）中，句子似乎显得冗长、啰唆，两个主要人物（Little Red Riding Hood 和 the Wolf）不做主语，并且人物的动作（walk、jump 和 fright）都没有做动词。而在（2b）中，句子更加的直接，其中两个人物是主语，他们的主要动作是动词。这是我们偏爱（2b）的原因。

# 神话故事、学术或专业写作

在大学期间或者工作中,神话故事似乎离我们的写作很遥远。其实,它们并不遥远,因为大多数的句子依然和动作的执行者相关。比较下面两句:

> 3a. The Federalists' argument in regard to the destabilization of government by popular democracy was based on their belief in the tendency of factions to further their self-interest at the expense of the common good.

> √ 3b. The Federalists argued that popular democracy destabilized government, because they believed that factions tended to further their self-interest at the expense of the common good.

我们可以用分析"Little Red Riding Hood"的方法来分析这些句子。

有两个原因使句子(3a)感觉晦涩难懂。第一个原因是,句子的人物不做主语。它的简单主语(划线部分)是"argument",但是人物(斜体部分)是"Federalists""popular democracy""government"和"factions":

> 3a. The *Federalists'* <u>argument</u> in regard to the destabilization of *government* by *popular democracy* was based on *their* belief in the tendency of *factions* to further *their* self-interest at the

expense of the common good.

第二个原因是，大部分的动作（黑体字）不是用动词（大写字体）表达的，而是用的抽象名词：

> 3a. The Federalists' **argument** in regard to the **destabilization** of government by popular democracy WAS BASED on their **belief** in the **tendency** of factions to FURTHER their self-interest at the expense of the common good.

注意（3a）的总主语有多长、多复杂，并且由主要动词"based"表达的意思有多少：

| 总主语 | 动词 |
|---|---|
| The Federalists' argument in regard to the destabilization of government by popular democracy | was based |

读者们认为（3b）表述得更清晰基于两个原因：人物（斜体字）做主语，动作（黑体）是用动词（大写字）表达的：

> 3b. The *Federalists* ARGUED that *popular democracy* DESTABILIZED government, because *they* BELIEVED that *factions* TENDED TO FURTHER *their* self-interest at the expense of the common good.

同时注意：所有的总主语非常简短、明确且具体：

| 总主语 / 人物 | 动词 / 动作 |
| --- | --- |
| the Federalists | argued |
| popular democracy | destabilized |
| they | believed |
| factions | tended to further |

本课余下的部分探讨动作和动词；下一课探讨人物和主语。

## 动词和动作

我们的原则是：**如果主要动作用动词表示，句子就会显得清晰。**

观察句子（4a）和（4b）中动作是如何表达的。在（4a）中，动作（黑体字）没有用动词（大写字）表达；它们用的是名词：

> 4a. Our **lack** of data PREVENTED **evaluation** of UN **actions** in **targeting** funds to areas most in **need** of **assistance**.

另一方面，在（4b）中，动作几乎全是用动词表示的：

> √ 4b. Because we LACKED data, we could not EVALUATE whether the UN HAD TARGETED funds to areas that most NEEDED assistance.

如果使用大量的抽象名词，尤其是用从动词和形容词派生出来的词，还有以"-tion""-ment""-ence"等结尾的名词，**特别是用类似的抽象名词作为动词的主语时**，读者会认为该文章晦涩难懂。

从动词或形容词派生出来的名词有专业称谓：**名词化**。该词表明了其意义：当我们把"nominalize"名词化时，我们就创造了 nominalize 的名词 nominalization。下面有些例子：

动词 → 名词化　　　　　　形容词 → 名词化

discover　→　discovery　　　careless　→　carelessness
resist　→　resistance　　　different　→　difference
react　→　reaction　　　proficient　→　proficiency

我们也可以在动词后加 ing，使动词名词化（使其变为**动名词**）：

She flies → her flying　　　We sang → our singing

有些被名词化了的词和其动词同形：

Hope → hope　　result → result　　repair → repair

We REQUEST that you REVIEW the data.
Our **request** IS that you DO a **review** of the data.
（有些动作隐含在形容词里："It is applicable → It applies."还有些其他词："indicative""dubious""argumentative""deserving"。）

　　在抽象、冗长、艰涩、浮夸的写作风格中，最突出的特点是使用了大量的名词化词，尤其是那些可以做动词主语的词。

> **要点** 在小学阶段，我们就知道主语是人物（或执行者），动词表示动作。这通常是正确的：
>
> ```
>   subject        verb         object
>   We          discussed    the problem.
>   doer         action
> ```
>
> 但是这个意义几乎相同的句子，却不正确：
>
> ```
>   subject      verb
>   The problem   was   the topic   of our discussion.
>                                    doer    action
> ```
>
> 我们可以调换人物和动作的位置，不必让主语和动词指称任何特殊的成分。但是如果在大部分句子里，用人物做主语，用动词表示动作，读者会认为文章清晰、明快、易读。

## 练习 3.1

----⁂----

如果不确定自己是否能辨别动词、形容词和名词化词，你可以做下面的练习。把动词和形容词转换为名词化词，把名词化词转换为形容词和动词。切记一些动词和名词化词是同形的：

Poverty predictably CAUSES social problems.

Poverty is a predictable CAUSE of social problems.

| | | | | |
|---|---|---|---|---|
| analysis | believe | attempt | conclusion | evaluate |
| suggest | approach | comparison | define | discuss |
| expression | failure | intelligent | thorough | appearance |
| decrease | improve | increase | accuracy | careful |
| emphasize | explanation | description | clear | examine |

## 练习 3.2

在这些成对的句子中，辨识出主语、人物、动词和动作。前一句是表述不清晰的；后一句有所改善。你注意到了句子中的人物和主语、动作和动词是如何保持一致的吗？

1a. There is opposition among many voters to nuclear power plants based on a belief in their threat to human health.

1b. Many voters oppose nuclear power plants because they believe that such plants threaten human health.

2a. There has been growth in the market for electronic books because of the frequent preference among customers for their convenience and portability.

2b. The market for electronic books has grown because customers frequently prefer their convenience and portability.

3a. There is a belief among some researchers that consumers' choices in fast food restaurants would be healthier if there were postings of nutrition information in their menus.

3b. Some researchers believe that consumers would choose healthier foods if fast food companies posted nutrition information in their menus.

4a. The design of the new roller coaster was more of a struggle for the engineers than had been their expectation.

4b. The engineers struggled more than they expected when designing the new roller coaster.

5a. Because the student's preparation for the exam was thorough, none of the questions on it were a surprise.

5b. Because the student prepared thoroughly for the exam, she was not surprised by any of the questions on it.

## 练习 3.3

用练习 3.1 中的动词和形容词造三个句子。然后用相对应的名词化词（保证相同的意思）改写这三句。例如，用"suggest""discuss"和"careful"造句：

I SUGGEST that we DISCUSS the issue CAREFULLY.

然后，用这三个词的名词化形式将这句话改写为：

My **suggestion** is that our **discussion** of the issue be done with **care**.

只有在看到一个清晰的句子被写得晦涩后，你才能理解为什么原句表述得更清楚。

## 诊断与修改：人物和动作

用动词表达动作、人物做主语的原则，能解释读者评判文章好坏的原因。但更重要的是，也能用这些原则去辨别和修改那些对作者清晰却使读者困惑的句子。修改文章有下面三个步骤：诊断、分析、改写。

**1. 诊断**

a. 忽略稍短的（四或五个词）引导短语，并在每句的前七个和八个词下面划线。

<u>The outsourcing of high-tech work to Asia</u> by corporations means the loss of jobs for many American workers.

b. 然后寻找两个答案：

划线部分是否包含做简单主语的抽象名词（黑体字）。

The **outsourcing** of high-tech work to Asia by corporations means the loss of jobs for many American workers.

划线部分（前七、八个词）是否在动词之前。

The outsourcing of high-tech work to Asia by corporations （10个词）**means** the loss of jobs for many American workers.

**2. 分析**

a. 首先决定谁是主要人物，尤其是有血有肉的人物（下一课会涉及得更多）。

The outsourcing of high-tech work to Asia by **corporations** means the loss of jobs for **many American workers**.

b. 然后寻找这些人物执行的动作，尤其是那些从动词派生出来的抽象名词。

The **outsourcing** of high-tech work to Asia by corporations means the **loss** of jobs for many American workers.

## 3. 修改

a. 如果用名词化的词表达动作的话，将名词化的词改为动词。

outsourcing → outsource　　　　loss → lose

b. 人物做动词的主语。

corporations outsource　　　　American workers lose

c. 用从属连词如"because""if""when""although""why""how""whether"或"that"改写句子。

√ Many middle-class American workers are losing their jobs, **because** corporations are outsourcing their high-tech work to Asia.

## 常见句型

你可以快速地辨别和修改五个名词化词的常见句型。

**1.** 名词化词是虚动词的主语，如"be""seems""has"等：

The **intention** of the committee IS to audit the records.

a. 将名词化词转化为动词：

intention → intend

b. 找出可以做动词主语的人物：

The intention of *the committee* is to audit the records.

c. 使人物做新动词的主语：

√ The committee INTENDS to audit the records.

**2.** 名词化词紧跟虚动词：

The *agency* CONDUCTED an **investigation** into the matter.

a. 将名词化词转换为动词：

investigation → investigate

b. 用新动词替换虚动词：

conducted → investigated

√ The agency INVESTIGATED the matter.

**3.** 名词化词做虚动词的主语，且后面跟着另一个名词化的词：

Our **loss** in sales WAS a result of their **expansion** of outlets.

a. 将名词化词改为动词：

loss → lose      expansion → expand

b. 辨别这些可以做动词主语的人物：

*Our* **loss** in sales was a result of *their* **expansion** of outlets.

c. 使这些人物做动词的主语：

we lose      they expand

d. 用逻辑连词连接从句：

要表达简单的小句：because, since, when

要表达条件句：if, provided that, so long as

要表达和预期矛盾的句子：though, although, unless

| Our **loss** in sales | → | We LOST sales |
| was the result of | → | **because** |
| their **expansion** of outlets | → | they EXPANDED outlets |

### 4. 一个名词化词跟着"there is"或"there are"句型：

There IS no **need** for our further **study** of this problem.

a. 将名词化词转化为动词：

need → need　　　study → study

b. 辨识应该做动词主语的人物：

There is no **need** for *our* further **study** of this problem.

c. 让人物做动词的主语：

no need → we need not　　　our study → we study

√ We NEED not STUDY this problem further.

**5. 由介词连接的一组两个或三个名词化词：**

We did a **review** of the **evolution** of the brain.

a. 将第一个名词化词转化为动词：

review → review

b. 保留第二个名词化词，或者将它转化为以"how"或"why"引导的从句中的动词：

evolution of the brain → how the brain evolved

√ First, we REVIEWED the **evolution** of the *brain*.

√ First, we REVIEWED how the brain EVOLVED.

> **快速提示** 如果修改一个复合句，会产生由人物和动作组成的多个从句。斟酌如何将从句恰当地组合在一起，然后试着从下列句型中挑出合适的句型：X because Y; Since X, Y; If X, then Y; Although X, Y; X and / but / so Y.

## 满意的结果

如果一贯用动词表示主要动作，读者就会在许多方面受益：

1. 句子内容会显得更加具体，因为句子里包含更具体的主语和动词。对比下面两句：

> There WAS an affirmative **decision** for **expansion**.
> √ The Director DECIDED to EXPAND the program.

2. 句子会显得更加简洁。如果使用名词化词，作者不得不添加"a"和"the"之类的冠词，以及诸如"of""by""in"之类的介词。如果使用动词和连词，就不需要它们了：

> A **revision** of the program WILL RESULT in **increase** in our **efficiency** in the **servicing** of clients.
> √ If we REVISE the program, we CAN SERVE clients more EFFICIENTLY.

3. 句子的逻辑性会更清晰。如果用名词化动词，那么动作和模糊介词就需要连接起来，如"of""by"和"on the part of"。

但是，如果使用动词，就只需将句子和简洁的从属连词连接起来，如"because""although"和"if"：

Our more effective presentation of our study resulted in our success, despite an earlier start by others.

√ **Although** others started earlier, we succeeded **because** we presented our study more effectively.

4. 故事叙述得更连贯。名词化词会打乱动作的顺序（下列句子标注的数字是事件发生的真实顺序）。

Decisions[4] in regard to administration[5] of medication despite inability[2] of an irrational patient appearing[1] in a Trauma Center to provide legal consent[3] rest with the attending physician alone.

如果你将这些动作修改为动词，并且调整它们的顺序，你就会得到一个更加连贯的叙述：

√ When a patient appears[1] in a Trauma Center and behaves[2] so irrationally that he cannot legally consent[3] to treatment, only the attending physician can decide[4] whether to medicate[5] him.

## 已解决的常见问题

多数人可能有过这样的经历：他们认为自己的作品写得不错，但是读者却不这样想。他们怀疑是否只是这位读者的阅读有问题，但是他们还是咬紧牙关努力去修改，尽管他们认为对于任何一个能阅读杜斯博士（Dr. Deuss）作品的人来说，他们的著作表述得还算清楚。如果这件事发生在我身上（以后我会不时地提到），到最后我几乎总是意识到我的读者是正确的，因为他们比我更清楚作品中需要修改的地方。

为什么我们通常可以正确评判他人的作品，却对自己的作品产生错觉？因为我们总是希望读者按照我们的方式阅读作品。这也解释了两个读者对同一篇文章的清晰度有不同的看法的原因：很熟悉文章内容的读者可能会认为文章十分清晰。当然，他们都没错，但是旁观者或多或少地真正了解文章的清晰度。

这就是我们需要用一种近乎机械的方式去审查作品的原因，从而避免高估它。最快速的方式就是在每句话的前七个或八个词下面划线。如果在这些句子中，没有发现做主语的"人物"和表示特殊动作的动词，就需要进行修改。

> **快速提示** 如果修改的篇幅较长，首先查看那些难写的段落，因为你不能完全理解自己的观点。如果我们不确定自己想要表达什么，或者不知道怎么表达，我们更容易写得糟糕。

## 练习3.4

———— ❧ ————

下面每组句子中，有一个是表述清晰的，它让人物做主语，用动词表达动作；另一个则表述得不清楚，它没有让人物做主语，而且用名词化的词表达动作。首先，辨别出它们；然后圈出名词化的词，用括号括出动词，并且在主语下面画线。然后在想要表达动作的"人物"前面加上字母C。

1a. Some people argue that atmospheric carbon dioxide does not elevate global temperature.

1b. There has been speculation by educators about the role of the family in improving educational achievement.

2a. The store's price increases led to frustration among its customers.

2b. When we write concisely, readers understand easily.

3a. Researchers have identified the AIDS virus but have failed to develop a vaccine to immunize those at risk.

3b. Attempts by economists at defining full employment have been met with failure.

4a. Complaints by editorial writers about voter apathy rarely offer suggestions about dispelling it.

4b. Although critics claim that children who watch a lot of television tend to become less able readers, no one has demonstrated that to be true.

5a. The loss of market share to Japan by domestic automakers resulted in the disappearance of hundreds of thousands of jobs.

5b. When educators embrace new-media technology, our schools will teach complex subjects more effectively.

6a. We need to know which parts of our national forests are being logged most extensively so that we can save virgin stands at greatest risk.

6b. There is a need for an analysis of library use to provide a reliable base for the projection of needed resources.

7a. Many professional athletes fail to realize that they are unprepared for life after stardom because their teams protect them from the problems that the rest of us face every day.

7b. Colleges now have an understanding that yearly tuition increases are impossible because of strong parental resistance to the soaring cost of higher education.

## 练习 3.5

———❦———

现在，修改练习 3.4 中使用名词化词的句子，把动作改用动词表示。把每组中用动词的那句作为模本。例如，如果口头句子用"when"开头，那么你修改的那句也用"when"开头。

| | |
|---|---|
| Sentence to revise: | 2a. The store's price **increases** led to **frustration** among its customers. |
| Model: | 2b. When we WRITE concisely, readers UNDERSTAND more easily. |
| Your revision: | 2a. When the store INCREASED prices,... |

## 练习 3.6

———❦———

修改下面的句子，将名词化词改为动词，让人物做主语。在 1—5 句中，斜体字是"人物"，名词用黑体表示。

1. *Lincoln*'s **hope** was for the **preservation** of the Union without war, but the

*South's* **attack** on Fort Sumter made war an **inevitability**.

2. **Attempts** were made on the part of the *president's aides* to assert *his* **immunity** from a *congressional* subpoena.

3. There were **predictions** by *business executives* that the *economy* would experience a quick **revival**.

4. *Your* **analysis** of *my* report omits any data in **support** of *your* **criticism** of *my* **findings**.

5. The *health care industry's* **inability** to exert cost **controls** could lead to the *public's* **decision** that *congressional* **action** is needed.

下面 6—10 中，人物已用斜体字表示出来，请找出表达动作的词，并加以修改。

6. A *papal* appeal was made to the world's rich *nations* for assistance to those facing the threat of *African* starvation.

7. Attempts at explaining increases in *voter* participation in this year's elections were made by *several candidates*.

8. The agreement by the *class* on the reading list was based on the assumption that there would be tests on only certain selections.

9. There was no independent *business-sector* study of the cause of the sudden increase in the trade surplus.

10. An understanding as to the need for controls over drinking on campus was recognized by *fraternities*.

## 练习 3.7

用句尾的提示词,修改下面的句子。例如:

Congress's **reduction** of the deficit resulted in the **decline** of interest rates. [ because ]

√ Interest rates DECLINED because Congress REDUCED the deficit.

1. The use of models in teaching prose style does not result in improvements of clarity and directness in student writing. [ Although we use... ]

2. Precision in plotting the location of building foundations enhances the possibility of its accurate reconstruction. [ When we precisely plot... ]

3. Any departures by the members from the established procedures may cause termination of membership by the Board. [ If members... ]

4. A student's lack of socialization into a field may lead to writing problems because of his insufficient understanding about arguments by professionals in that field. [ When..., ..., because... ]

5. The successful implementation of a new curriculum depends on the cooperation of faculty with students in setting achievable goals within a reasonable time. [ To implement..., ... ]

## 限制条件:正确使用名词化的词

我曾经很严厉地要求把名词化的词转化为动词,所以你可能会认为绝对不能采用它们。但是，实际上，如果没有它们，也写不出好文章。下面的方法教你如何保留或者修改它们。请遵守下列原则：

**1. 指代前句的简短主语的名词要保留：**

√ **These arguments** all depend on a single unproven claim.

√ **This decision** can lead to positive outcomes.

这些名词化的词把前后两个句子连贯地组合在一起，这个问题我会在第五课更详细地探讨。

**2. 代替蹩脚的"The fact that"的简短名词要保留：**

The fact that she ADMITTED guilt impressed me.

√ Her **admission** of guilt impressed me.

但是，下面的句子更恰当：

√ *She* IMPRESSED me when *she* ADMITTED her guilt.

**3. 做动词宾语的名词化的词要保留：**

I accepted *what she* REQUESTED [ that is, *She requested something* ].

√ I accepted her **request**.

这类名词比抽象词汇让人感觉更具体。但是，相对于上面的

"request"，下面这句里的"request"能更准确地表达动作。

Her **request** for **assistance** CAME after the deadline.

√ She REQUESTED **assistance** after the deadline.

**4.** 指代读者所熟悉的概念的名词化词时，它充当的是实质的人物（下一课会重点探讨）要保留：

√ Few problems have so divided us as **abortion** on **demand**.

√ The Equal Rights **Amendment** was an issue in past **elections**.

√ **Taxation** without **representation** did not spark the American **Revolution**.

这些名词化的词指称熟悉的概念：abortion on demand, amendment, election, taxation, representation, revolution。你必须擦亮双眼，把表达普通观点的词和要修改为动词的名词区分开来：

There is a **demand** for a **repeal** of the **inheritance** tax.

√ We DEMAND that Congress REPEAL the **inheritance** tax.

## 清晰不等于直白

读者希望读到清晰的作品，但它并不等于小儿科的作品。一些人认为所有的句子都应该简短，不应该超过十五或二十个字。但是许多完善的观点太复杂，无法如此简洁地表达出来。在第十课和第十二课我们探讨了一些方法，将过于简短、过于直白的句子修改为既具有可读性又能够表达复杂观点的句子。

## 自我检测

### 练习3.8

仔细检查文章中的一页,在总主语下画线,用括号括住动词。现在考虑你所讲述的故事。圈出主要人物、框出人物的动作,特别要找出隐含在名词中的动作。你注意到了什么?你怎样让读者感受到文章的清晰?如果有必要的话,修改相应的人物做主语,用动词表示特定的动作。

### 练习3.9

相对于读者来说,作者们更容易认为自己的作品表述清晰。从作品中选出一页,和一位读者分享它。两人在1—10的数值范围内评估它的清晰度,10表示完全的清晰,1表示难以理解。用这些步骤去诊断和分析75—77页的句子,然后解释评估中出现的任何差异。必要的话,修改你的文章。

## 总结

表述清晰有两个基本原则:一个是让主要人物做动词的主语;另一个是用动词表达人物主要的动作。

我们能用表格来表示这两个原则。在思维上,读者必须把两个层面的句子结构连接到一起。其中一个是语法层面,它是一系列相对固定的主语和动词(下面的空表里可以填写任何伴随动词的词):

| 固定格式<br>(Fixed) | 主语<br>(Subject) | 动词<br>(Verb) | _____ |

另一个则是叙事层面上的,它以人物和人物的动作为基础,没有固定的顺序。读者更喜欢将两个层面搭配在一起,让人物做主语,动词表达动作。我们可以把这些原则和图表结合在一起:

| 固定格式<br>(Fixed) | 主语<br>(Subject) | 动词<br>(Verb) | _____ |
| 变体<br>(Variable) | 人物<br>(Character) | 动作<br>(Action) | _____ |

记住:人物不只**充**当主语,而且也会出现在下面两种情况里:

The *president's* veto of the bill infuriated Congress.

The veto of the bill by *the president* infuriated Congress.

然而,读者愿意看到用人物**充**当主语的句子,例如:

When *the president* (subject) VETOED VERB the bill, *he* (subject) INFURIATED (verb) Congress.

如果没有实现预期的效果,读者阅读起来就会更费劲。所以,修改时要遵循下面这些原则：

1. 用动词表示动作：

The **intention** of the committee is improvement of morale.

√ The committee **INTENDS** to improve morale.

2. 使动词的主语和动作人物一致：

A decision by *the dean* in regard to the funding of the program by *the department* is necessary for adequate *staff* preparation.

√ The *staff* CAN PREPARE adequately, only after *the dean* DECIDES whether *the department* WILL FUND the program.

3. 在下面的情况中，不要修改名词化的词：

a. 它们指代前一句：

√ **These arguments** all depend on a single unproven claim.

b. 它们替代这个蹩脚的"The fact that"句型：

**The fact that she strenuously objected** impressed me.

√ **Her strenuous objections** impressed me.

c. 它们指代动词的宾语：

I do not know **what she** INTENEDS.

√ I do not know **her intentions**.

d. 它们指代读者熟悉的概念,即实际的人物:

- √ Few problems have so divided us as **abortion** on **demand**.
- √ The Equal Rights **Amendment** was an issue in past **elections**.

[ 第四课 ]

# 人物

在同一种语言之内，任何句子如果可以用另外更简洁的句子替换，且不造成意义流失或有失庄重，那它就不是好句子。

——萨缪尔·泰勒·柯勒律治
（Samuel Taylor Coleridge）

丢失了人物，就损失了一切。

——匿名
（Anonymous）

## 人物重要性的内涵

如果句子中主要动作是用动词来表达的,那么读者就会觉得句子清晰直接。比较(1a)和(1b):

1a. The CIA feared the president would recommend to Congress that it reduce its budget.

1b. The CIA had fears that the president would send a recommendation to Congress that it make a reduction in its budget.

大多数读者认为(1a)比(1b)清晰,但也强不了多少。现在比较(1b)和(1c):

1b. The CIA had fears that the president would send a recommendation to Congress that it make a reduction in its budget.

1c. The fear of the CIA was that a recommendation from the president to Congress would be for a reduction in its budget.

大多数读者认为(1c)明显不如(1a)和(1b)清晰。

原因在于:在(1a)和(1b)中,主要的人物(斜体部分)都是简短具体的动词主语(下划线部分):

1a. <u>The CIA</u> FEARED *the president* WOULD RECOMMEND to *Congress* that it REDUCE its budget.

1b. <u>The CIA</u> HAD fears that *the president* WOULD SEND a recommendation to *Congress* that *it* MAKE a reduction in its budget.

但是在（1c）中，两个主语（下划线部分）并不是具体的人物，而是抽象名词（粗体加黑部分）：

1c. The *fear* of the <u>CIA</u> WAS that a **recommendation** from the *president* to *Congress* WOULD BE for a **reduction** in its budget.

（1a）和（1b）中不同的动词产生了不同的效果，而（1c）中使用抽象名词做主语产生的区别更明显。更糟糕的是，主语完全被省略掉，例如：

1d. <u>There</u> WAS **fear** that <u>there</u> WOULD BE a **recommendation** for a budget **reduction**.

到底是谁感到害怕？是谁提出建议？语境或许能帮助读者准确猜出来，但如果语境有歧义，那么就有猜错的风险了。

> **要点** 读者希望用动词来表示动作，但是他们更希望用人物做主语。当我们没有很好的理由说明为什么不用人物做主语，或者更糟的是把主语完全省略时，我们就为读者制造了麻烦。用动词来表示动作很重要，但是做

第四课 人物 [093]

> 到表达清晰的首要原则,是用故事中的主要人物做大多数动词的主语。

## 诊断并修改句中的人物

要让人物做主语,就要知道下面三点:

1. 何时人物不做主语?
2. 如果主语不是人物,那么怎样找到做主语的人物?
3. 一旦找到了(或没找到),接下来应该怎么办?

例如,下面这个句子总让人有点雾里看花终隔一层的感觉,且没有人情味儿:

> Governmental intervention in fast-changing technologies has led to the distortion of market evolution and interference in new product development.

我们可以诊断一下这个句子:

**1. 把前七八个单词加上下划线:**

> <u>Governmental intervention in fast-changing technologies has led</u> to the distortion of market evolution and interference in new product development.

在前几个词中,读者希望看到的**不仅仅是**人物做动词的总主语,就像 government 在 governmental 中暗含着一样,人物还要做动词的简单主语。在上述例子中,情况并非如此。

**2. 找出主要人物。**

主要人物可能是**物主代词**加名词化的词,可能是做了介词宾语(尤其是"by"和"of"的宾语),或者只是隐含的词。在此句中,一个主要人物就在形容词"governmental"中隐含着;另外一个主要人物"market"则做了介词的宾语:of market evolution。

**3. 快速浏览文章,找出与人物相关的动作,尤其是名词化的词语中隐含的动作。试着回答:是谁?他正在干什么?**

| governmental **intervention** | → | √ | government **intervenes** |
| **distortion** | → | √ | [ government ] **distorts** |
| market **evolution** | → | √ | markets **evolve** |
| **interference** | → | √ | [ government ] **interferes** |
| **development** | → | √ | [ market ] **develops** |

要想对句子进行修改,将这些新主语和动词重新组成一个句子,并使用诸如 if, although, because, when, how, why 等连接词。

√ **When** a government INTERVENES in fast-changing technologies, it DISTORTS how markets EVOLVE and INTERFERES with their ability to DEVELOP new products.

请注意,不仅动作可以暗含在形容词中(reliable → rely),人物也可以:

Medieval *theological* debates often addressed issues considered trivial by modern *philosophical* thought.

如果在形容词中发现了人物，也以同样的方式进行修改：

√ Medieval *theologians* often debated issues that modern *philosophers* consider trivial.

> **快速提示**
>
> 诊断一篇结构复杂的文章首要看主语。如果发现主语并不是用几个简短具体的词来表达的，那就先找主语。他们可能隐藏在介词宾语、物主代词，或者形容词之中。一旦找到了主语就要找出与之相关的动作。
>
> **在修改文章的过程中：**
>
> 让人物做动词（指称动作的词）的主语，然后将不同的人物与各自动作组成完整的句子。
>
> **在阅读的过程中：**
>
> 在将注意力集中在人物上的同时，试着一句一句地重述故事，一次一个动作。如果行不通，就将各个人物与各自的动作分别列出，以自己的方式重组句子。

## 重构缺席的人物

对读者来说，没有人物的句子最难读懂：

A decision was made in favor of doing a study of the

disagreements.

这个句子可理解为下面两层意思,或者更多:

> We decided that I should study why they disagreed.
> I decided that you should study why he disagreed.

作者本人或许知道谁在做什么,读者可能不知道,所以通常需要帮助。

有时省略人物是为了使文章更具普遍性:

> Research strategies that look for more than one variable are of more use in understanding factors in psychiatric disorder than strategies based on the assumption that the presence of psychopathology is dependent on a single gene or on strategies in which only one biological variable is studied.

当我们试着修改得更清晰时,我们必须虚构一个人物,然后决定对他们如何称呼。我们是选用 **one** 或者 **we**,还是将之命名为类属名词"doer"?

> √ If *one/we/researchers* are to understand what causes psychiatric disorder, *one/we/they* should use research strategies that look for more than one variable rather than assume that a single gene is responsible for a psychopathology or adopt a strategy in which *one/we/they* study only one biological variable.

对大多数人来说，one 似乎有点呆板，而 we 又可能存在歧义，因为它可以只指作者，或者指作者和其他人但不包括读者，或指读者和作者但不包括其他人，或指任何人。如果没有直接指定读者，使用 you 也是不合适的。

如果既不用名词化的词，也不用模糊代词，那就不得不使用**被动语态**（我稍后对其进行讨论）：

> To understand what makes patients vulnerable to psychiatric disorders, strategies that look for more than one variable SHOULD BE USED rather than strategies in which a gene IS ASSUMED a gene causes psychopathology or only one biological variable IS STUDIED.

---

**快速提示** 向相关人员解释复杂的问题时，想象着他坐在桌子对面，尽可能使用 **you**：

Taxable intangible property includes financial notes and municipal bonds. A one-time tax of 2% on its value applies to this property.

√ **You** have to pay tax on **your** intangible property, including **your** financial notes and municipal bonds. On this property, **you** pay a one-time tax of 2%.

如果你觉得 **you** 不合适，就将其改成下面的说法：

**Taxpayers** have to pay tax on their intangible property, including **their** financial notes and municipal bonds. **They** pay...

## 把抽象名词当作"人物"

到目前为止,我所讨论的人物好像必须是活生生的人。但是故事中主要人物可以是抽象名词,包括名词化的词,只要保证这些词做故事中一系列句子的主语即可。前面的例子采用不同类的人物做主语,或许已经解决了这个问题,比如抽象名词 study:

> √ To understand what causes psychiatric disorder, *studies* should look for more than one variable rather than adopt a strategy in which *they* test only one biological variable or assume that a single gene is responsible for a psychopathology.

**Studies** 这个词指代的是虚拟人物,因为我们对这个词很熟悉,而且它做一系列动作的主语:understand, should look, adopt, test 和 assume。

把抽象名词当人物来用也会产生问题。如果我们对故事中的抽象名词和"studies"一样熟悉,那当然很清晰,但是如果大量抽象名词围绕一个不太熟悉的抽象人物,读者会觉得文章晦涩复杂,且没有必要。

比如说,大多数人对 **prospective** 和 **immediate intention** 不熟悉,所以他们读到这两个词时会觉得理解困难,尤其是它们周围还有大量抽象名词(黑体加粗的是行为词,斜体的是具体的人物):

> The *argument* **is this.** The cognitive component of

**intention** exhibits a high degree of **complexity**. **Intention** is temporally divisible into two: prospective **intention** and immediate **intention**. The cognitive function of prospective **intention** is the **representation** of a *subject's* similar past **actions**, *his* current situation, and *his* course of future **actions**. That is, the cognitive component of prospective **intention** is a **plan**. The cognitive function of immediate **intention** is the **monitoring** and **guidance** of ongoing bodily **movement**.

——迈尔斯·布兰德

如果从活生生的人的视角讲述这个故事，这篇文章会更加清晰（斜体是人物，黑体加粗的是行为词，大写的是动词）：

√ *I* ARGUE this about **intention**. It HAS a complex cognitive component of two temporal kinds: prospective and immediate. *We* USE prospective **intention** to REPRESENT how *we* HAVE ACTED in our past and present and how *we* WILL ACT in the future. That is, *we* USE the cognitive component of prospective **intention** to HELP *us* PLAN. *We* USE immediate **intention** to MONITOR and GUIDE *our* bodies as *we* MOVE them.

经过我的修改，这段文字的意义与原作者的有所不同吗？有些人认为，任何形式上的改变都会引起意义上的变化。这种情况下，作者可能只是提供观点，唯有读者才能决定这两段的意义是否一致，因为到头来，文章的思想究竟是什么，还得由那些细心的、有能力的读者来决定。

> **要点** 大多数读者希望句子里由活生生的人做主语。但有时不得不使用一些抽象词语。此时，使这些抽象词语做故事中一系列动词的主语，从而将其变成虚拟的人物。如果读者对这些抽象名词熟悉，理解起来就没有问题了。如果读者不熟悉，那就不要在这些抽象名词周围再使用其他大量抽象的、名词化的词。对一篇抽象的文章进行修改时，如果主语是一个抽象概念，那么你会不明所以。此时，请使用一个一般性的词语来表示做该动作的人，例如 researchers、social critics、one 等等。如果都不合适，就尝试一下 we。但事实是，与许多其他语言不同，英语没有一个很好的词来表示类属名词。

## 练习 4.1

诊断并修改下列句子。观察前六七个词（忽略简短的引导短语）。对其进行修改，使得每个特定的动词都有一个特定的人物做主语。必要时，需要虚构人物，可以选用 we、I，或其他合适的词。

1. Contradictions among the data require an explanation. [ we ]

2. Having their research taken seriously by professionals in the field was hard work for the students. [ student researchers ]

3. In recent years, the appearance of new interpretations about the meaning of the discovery of America has led to a reassessment of Columbus's place in Western history. [ historians ]

4. Resistance has been growing against building mental health facilities in residential areas because of a belief that the few examples of improper management are typical. [ residents ]

5. A decision about forcibly administering medication in an emergency room setting despite the inability of an irrational patient to provide legal consent is usually an on-scene medical decision. [ medical professionals ]

6. The performance of the play was marked by enthusiasm, but there was a lack of intelligent staging.

7. Despite the critical panning of the latest installment of the series, the love of the loyal fans was not affected.

8. Tracing transitions in a well-written article provides help in efforts at improving coherence in writing.

9. The rejection of the proposal was a disappointment but not a surprise because our expectation was that a political decision had been made.

10. With the decline in network television viewing in favor of online streaming video, awareness is growing at the networks of a need to revise programming.

## 人物和动词的被动式

比起其他建议，大家记得最清楚的一条建议可能是使用**主动语态而不是被动语态**。这一点儿都没错，不过也有例外。

使用主动语态写作时，会倾向于：

**施事者**或动作执行者做主语

**受事者**或动作接受者做**直接宾语**：

|  | 主语 | 动词 | 宾语 |
|---|---|---|---|
| 主动式： | I | lost | the memory |
|  | character/agent | action | goal |

如果**过去分词**前面有 **be** 动词（正如这里使用的）的相关形式，动词就要使用被动语态。被动语态从两点上有别于主动语态：

1. 由主语作为动作接受者。
2. 施事者或动作发出者放在由介词 **by** 引出的短语后，或者完全省略施事者。

|  | 主语 | be+ 动词 | 介词短语 |
|---|---|---|---|
| 被动式： | The money | was lost | [ by me ] . |
|  | goal | action | character/agent |

然而，主动式和被动式两个术语是有歧义的，因为它们既可以指两个语法结构也可以指读完一个句子后的**感受**。如果一个句子平淡无趣，就认为它是被动式的，不管它的动词是否为被动式。例如，试比较下面两个句子：

We can manage the problem if we control costs.

Problem management requires cost control.

从语法角度看，两个句子都是主动语态，但是第二个句子**觉得像被动**，原因有三：

两个行为词（**management** 和 **control**）都不是动词，二者都被名词化了。
主语是抽象词 **problem management**。
句子缺少活生生的人物。

要想知道为什么对这两个句子会有这种不同的反应，就要将主动式与被动式的术语意义、语法意义和修辞意义、印象意义区别开来。下面将讨论语法上的被动语态。

**在主动式与被动式之间做选择**

一些评论家告诉我们要尽量避免使用被动式，因为被动式要加新词，而且通常省略施事者，即"动作执行者"。但有时被动式是更好的选择。在主动式与被动式间做选择前要先回答三个问题：

**1. 读者一定要知道谁是动作执行者吗？** 通常我们不标明谁是动作的执行者，因为我们不知道，或者读者对此不关心。例如，在下列这些句子中，我们会很自然地选择使用被动式：

√ The president WAS RUMORED to have considered resigning.

√ Those who ARE FOUND guilty can BE FINED.

√ Valuable records should always BE KEPT in a safe.

如果不知道是谁散播的谣言，我们就不能标明；也没有人质疑究竟是谁发现人们有罪并对其进行罚款；也没有人质疑谁对档案安全负责，所以这时被动式就是正确的选择。

当然，有时作者不想让读者知道谁是动作的执行者，尤其是作者本人是施事者时，就会选择使用被动式。例如：

Because the test was not completed, the flaw was uncorrected.

我将在第 12 课讨论作者有意使用"无人称"的现象。

**2. 主动句或被动句有助于读者更流畅地往下阅读吗？**阅读新信息之前，句子的开头提供已知的语境。如果句子开头就是新的或意想不到的信息，读者会感到困惑不解。例如，下面这个段落中，在我们回忆前一句以获取更多熟悉的信息之前，第二个句子的主语提供的是新而复杂的信息（黑体加粗部分）：

We must decide whether to improve education in the sciences alone or to raise the level of education across the whole curriculum. **The weight given to industrial competitiveness as opposed to the value we attach to the liberal arts**（新信息）WILL DETERMINE（主动式）our decision.（已知信息）

在第二个句子中，动词 determine 是主动式。但如果换成被动式读起来会更容易，因为被动式将简洁熟悉的信息放在了前面，将新的复杂信息放在了后面，我们更喜欢下列顺序：

> √ We must decide whether to improve education in the sciences alone or raise the level of education across the whole curriculum. Our decision（已知信息）WILL BE DETERMINED（被动式）**by the weight we give to industrial competiveness as opposed to the value we attach to the liberal arts**.（新信息）

我将在第五课详细讨论如何安排已知信息和新信息的顺序。

3. 所采用的主动式或被动式是否给读者一个更连贯合适的视角。下面这篇文章的作者站在同盟国的立场报道二战后的欧洲。在此过程中，她使用主动式使同盟国成为一系列动作的主语：

> √ By early 1945, *the Allies* HAD essentially DEFEATED（主动语态）Germany; all that remained was a bloody climax. *American, French, British, and Russian forces* HAD BREACHED（主动语态）its borders and WERE BOMBING（主动语态）it around the clock. But *they* HAD not yet so DEVASTATED（主动语态）Germany as to destroy its ability to resist.

如果她想从德国的角度来解释这段历史，就会使用被动式，从而使德国成为主语 / 人物：

> √ By early 1945, *Germany* HAD essentially BEEN DEFEATED;（被动语态）all that remained was a bloody climax. *Its borders* HAD BEEN BREACHED,（被动语态）and *it* WAS BEING BOMBED（被动

语态）around the clock. *It* HAD not BEEN SO DEVASTATED,（被动语态）however, that *it* could not RESIST.（主动语态）

一些作者没有明显的理由就从一个人物转换到另一个人物。但是一定要避免下面这些句子：

> By early 1954, *the Allies* had essentially defeated Germany. *Its borders* had been breached, and *they* were bombing it around the clock. *Germany* was not so devastated, however, that *the Allies* would meet with no resistance. Though *Germany's population* was demoralized, *the Allies* still attacked German cities from the air.

选定一个视角，文章中一定要一以贯之。

---

**要点** 许多作者使用被动式太过频繁，但被动式的确有重要的用途。在下列这些语境下使用被动式：

不知道动作执行者是谁，读者不关心或不想让读者知道动作的执行者；

想把长而复杂的信息放在句尾，尤其是这样做的同时，还能把更简短更熟悉的信息放在句首，从而有助于理解。

想让读者的注意力集中在一个或另一个人物身上。

# 练习 4.2

将下列动词主动式变为被动式，被动式变为主动式。看看哪些句子得到了改善，哪些没有？（在前两个句子中，能将主动式变为被动式的动词已用斜体标出，已经是被动式的已用黑体加粗。）

1. Independence is **gained** by those on welfare when skills are **learned** that the marketplace *values*.

2. Different planes of the painting are **noticed**, because their colors are **set** against a background of shades of gray that are **laid** on in layers that cannot be **seen** unless the surface is **examined** closely.

3. In this article, it is argued that the Vietnam War was fought to extend influence in Southeast Asia and was not ended until it was made clear that the United States could not defeat North Vietnam unless atomic weapons were used.

4. Science education will not be improved in this nation to a level sufficient to ensure that American industry will be supplied with skilled workers and researchers until more money is provided to primary and secondary schools.

## 客观的被动式与 I/we

一些学者派头十足的作家称不应该用第一人称做主语，因为要从客观的角度写作，如下例：

> Based on the writers' verbal intelligence, prior knowledge, and essay scores, their essays **were analyzed** for structure and

evaluated for richness of concepts. The subjects **were** then **divided** into a high-or low-ability group. Half of each group **was** randomly **assigned** to a treatment group or to a placebo group.

与此相反，学术和科学界的作者经常使用主动式和第一人称 **I**、**we**。下面这些段落引自一些权威期刊：

√ This paper is concerned with two problems. How can **we** best handle in a transformational grammar certain restrictions that..., To illustrate, **we** may cite..., **we** shall show...

√ Since the pituitary-adrenal axis is activated during the acute phase response, **we** have investigated the potential role... Specifically, **we** have studied the effects of interleukin-1...

以下是引自著名杂志《科学》上一些连续句子的开头几个词：

√ **We** examine..., **We** compare...,**We** have used..., Each has been weighted..., **We** merely take..., They are subject..., **We** use..., Efron and Morris describe..., **We** observed..., **We** might find...

——约翰·P. 吉尔伯特、巴克南·麦克皮克、弗雷德里克·莫斯特勒，《外科和麻醉学中的统计与伦理》

学术文章的作者也并不总是避免使用第一人称的 **I** 和 **we**。

## 被动式、人物和元话语

学术文章的作者用第一人称写作时，是按照一定方式进行的。

观察上述文章中的动词,可分为如下两类:

一些指研究活动的词:examine, observe, measure, record, use。这些词通常用被动式:The subjects were observed...

另外一些词既不指主题也不指研究,而是指作者自己的写作与思考:cite, show, inquire。这些词通常用主动式和第一人称:We will show... 这就是**元话语**的例子。

元话语并不是指描述作者思想的语言,而是一种关于作者、读者和写作的语言:

作者的思考和写作行为:We/I will explain, show, argue, claim, deny, suggest, contrast, add, expand, summarize...

读者的行为:consider now, as you recall, look at the next example...

写作的逻辑和形式:first, second; to begin; therefore, however, consequently...

元话语常常出现在引言中,作者说明写作意图:**I claim that..., I will show..., We begin by...** 还有就是在结尾部分进行总结:**I have argued..., I have shown...** 这些话语最大的特点就是只有作者本人可以这样说。

另一方面,学者派头十足的作家在研究中通常不使用第一人称来描述特定动作或一些大众化的动作:**measure, record,**

**examine, observe, use**。这些词通常采用被动形式：**The subjects were observed...** 我们很少见到下面这样的文章：

> To determine if monokines elicited an adrenal steroidogenic response, I ADDED preparations of...

大多数作者会用被动形式的 **were added** 来说明一个除了作者外任何人都可以有的行为：

> To determine if monokines elicited a response, **preparations**... WERE ADDED.

不过，像那样的被动句也会带来问题：作者省略了一个修饰语。当开头短语的**隐性**主语与前后从句的**显性**主语不一致时，就省略一个修饰语。在该例中，**不定式动词 determine** 的隐性主语是 **I** 或 **we**：I determine or we determine.

> [ So that **I** could ] determine if monokines elicited a response, preparations WERE ADDED.

但是隐性主语 **I** 与从句中**显性**主语 preparations 不一致。当隐性主语与显性主语不一致时修饰语就被省略了。科学文章的作者经常使用这种句型，以致这种用法在该领域已经成了标准用法。

或许我要说明这种非人称的"科学的"风格是一种现代化的发展。伊萨克·牛顿爵士在《光与颜色的新理论》中，使用第一人称生动地描述了一个实验：

I procured a triangular glass prism, to try therewith the celebrated phenomena of colors. And for that purpose, having darkened my laboratory, and made a small hole in my window shade, to let in a convenient quantity of the sun's light, I placed my prism at the entrance, that the light might be thereby refracted to the opposite wall. It was at first a very pleasing diversion to view the vivid and intense colors produced thereby.

> **快速提示** 一些老师严禁学生在写作中使用 **I**，并不是因为这样用不对，而是因为没有经验的作者才会在很多句子中都用 **I think..., I believe...** 等等来引导。另外一些老师禁止学生使用 **I**，是因为他们不想让学生以叙述者的口吻来表达自己的想法：**First I read..., Then I considered...** 在这两种情况下，一定要听从老师的建议。

> **要点** 一些作者通过使用被动语态来避免第一人称，但是省略了 **I** 和 **we**，并不能使研究人员的思想更加客观。我们知道，在这些非人称句子背后，仍然是人的行为、想法和写作。事实上，第一人称的 **I** 和 **we** 与作者独有的行为动词连用的现象，在学者们的写作中是很常见的。

## 练习 4.3

下列 1 至 4 句中的动词是被动式,但其中两个可以用主动式,因为它们是第一人称主语的元话语。修改这些可变为主动式的词,然后浏览每一个句子,将所有名词化的词改为动词。

1. It is believed that a lack of understanding about the risks of alcohol is a cause of student bingeing.

2. The model has been subjected to extensive statistical analysis.

3. Success in exporting more crude oil for hard currency is suggested here as the cause of the improvement of the Russian economy.

4. The creation of a database is being considered, but no estimate has been made in regard to the potential of its usefulness.

5 至 8 句的动词是主动式,但一些应该为被动,因为它们不是元话语动词。修改这些可变为被动的词,如有需要还应进行其他修改。

5. In Section IV, I argue that the indigenous peoples engaged in overcultivation of the land, leading to its exhaustion as a foodproducing area.

6. Our intention in this book is to help readers achieve an understanding not only of the differences in grammar between Arabic and English but also the differences in worldview as reflected by Arabic vocabulary.

7. To make an evaluation of changes in the flow rate, I made a comparison of the current rate with the original rate on the basis of figures I had compiled with figures that Jordan had collected.

8. We performed the tissue rejection study on the basis of methods developed

with our discovery of increases in dermal sloughing as a result of cellular regeneration.

## 练习 4.4

———⁓∽⁓———

下列句子中，在你认为能够改善的地方将被动式改为主动式，将主动式改为被动式。必要时创造相关人物。（有不同答案）

1. The author's impassioned narrative style is abandoned and a cautious treatment of theories of conspiracy is presented. But when the narrative line is picked up again, he invests his prose with the same vigor and force.

2. These directives are written in a style of maximum simplicity as a result of an attempt at more effective communication with employees with limited reading skills.

3. The ability of the human brain to arrive at solutions to human problems has been undervalued because studies have not been done that would be considered to have scientific reliability.

4. Many arguments were advanced against Darwinian evolution in the nineteenth century because basic assumptions about our place in the world were challenged by it. No longer were humans defined as privileged creatures but rather as a product of natural forces.

## 练习 4.5

———⁓∽⁓———

下面文章节选自一所公立大学校长写给学生家长的信。除了第一段中第二个单词 you 之外，为什么会显得如此客观？为什么最后一部分显得更加主观？对两部分进行修改，为第一部分每个动作找出施事者，将第二部分所有人物省略。现在两者有什么区别？后者得到改善了吗？这个练习提出故意误导的问题，我将在十二课进行讲解。

As you probably have heard, the U of X campus has been the scene of a number of incidents of racial and sexual harassment over the last several weeks. The fact that similar incidents have occurred on campuses around the country does not make them any less offensive when they take place here. Of the ten to twelve incidents that have been reported since early October, most have involved graffiti or spoken insults. In only two cases was any physical contact made, and in neither case was anyone injured.

U of X is committed to providing its students with an environment where they can live, work, and study without fear of being taunted or harassed because of their race, gender, religion, or ethnicity. I have made it clear that bigotry and intolerance will not be permitted and that the U of X's commitment to diversity is unequivocal. We are also taking steps to improve security in campus housing. We at the U of X are proud of this university's tradition of diversity...

## 名词 + 名词 + 名词

另外一种文体选择并不直接涉及人物及行为。在此，我对它加以讨论，是因为它不能满足读者的期待：思想的形式和符合语法的表达一定要相对称。那就是长长的复合名词短语：

> Early *childhood thought disorder misdiagnosis* often results from unfamiliarity with recent *research literature* describing such

conditions. This paper is a review of seven recent studies in which are findings of particular relevance to *pre-adolescent hyperactivity diagnosis* and *to treatment modalities involving medication maintenance level evaluation procedures.*

正如许多常见的短语 **stone wall**、**student center**、**space shuttle** 及其他短语，用一个名词去修饰另外一个名词是行得通的。

但是如果是一长串名词，则会给人一种笨重感，所以要避免这样用，尤其是一些自己发明的词。一定要修改那些自己发明的复合名词，尤其要修改包含着名词化了的复合名词。请调整下列单词的顺序，找到合适的连词将其连接起来：

| 1 | 2 | 3 | 4 | 5 |
|---|---|---|---|---|
| early | childhood | thought | disorder | misdiagnosis |
| misdiagnose | disordered | thought | in early | childhood |
| 5 | 4 | 3 | 1 | 2 |

重新组合后如下：

Physicians misdiagnose[5] disordered[4] thought[3] in young[1] children[2] because they are unfamiliar with recent literature on the subject.

但是，如果长串的复合名词包含着一个技术术语，那么就需要保留该术语，然后拆分其他部分：

Physicians misdiagnose[5] **thought disorders**[3,4] in young[1] children[2] because they are unfamiliar with recent literature on the subject.

## 练习 4.6

---·~·---

对下列句子中的复合名词短语进行修改：

1. Diabetic patient blood pressure reduction may be brought about by renal depressor application.

2. The goal of this article is to describe text comprehension processes and recall protocol production.

3. On the basis of these principles, we may now attempt to formulate narrative information extraction rules.

4. This paper is an investigation into information processing behavior involved in computer human cognition simulation.

5. Enforcement of guidelines for new automobile tire durability must be a Federal Trade Commission responsibility.

6. The Social Security program is a monthly income floor guarantee based on a lifelong contribution schedule.

## 清晰与专业领域的写作观念

每个团体组织都希望成员表现出接受本组织独特的观念，进而接受本组织的价值观。学徒期间的银行家不仅要学习如何看起来像一个银行家,并像银行家那样思考,还要学习如何像银行家一样讲话和写作。很多情况下,有抱负的专业人士尽量用尽可能复杂的技术语言写作,以求加入该领域的圈子。他们在这样做的同时,采取了一种排他的写作风格,这种风格侵蚀了公民社会所依赖的信任,尤其在这样一个信息与专业知识变成了权力与控制工具的世界里。

诚然,有些研究对外行读者来说永远也不会显得清晰,但这种情况比许多研究人员想象得要少。下面这段话节选自塔尔科特·帕森斯的作品。他是一位社会科学家,因在该领域有重大影响而受到尊敬,同时也因其文章晦涩难懂而遭到讥讽。

> Apart from theoretical conceptualization there would appear to be no method of selecting among the indefinite number of varying kinds of factual observation which can be made about a concrete phenomenon or field so that the various descriptive statements about it articulate into a coherent whole, which constitutes an "adequate", a "determinate" description. Adequacy in description is secured insofar as determinate and verifiable answers can be given to all the scientifically important questions involved. What questions are important is largely determined by the logical structure of the generalized conceptual scheme which, implicitly or explicitly, is employed.

加以修改,就可以使受过良好教育的读者读起来比较清晰:

Without a theory, scientists have no way to select from everything they could say about a subject only that which they can fit into a coherent whole that would be an "adequate" or "determinate" description. Scientists describe something "adequately" only when they can verify answers to all the questions they think are important. They decide what questions are important based on their implicit or explicit theories.

甚至还可以更加简洁：

Whatever you describe, you need a theory to fit its parts into a whole. You need a theory to decide even what questions to ask and to verify their answers.

我的两个版本删去了帕森斯文章中的一些无关紧要的东西，最后一个版本甚至删除了一些内容。他那复杂的写作实在是折磨人，使所有的读者不明所以，但是那些专门喜欢受虐的读者除外。大多数读者会接受这样折中式的改动。

> **要点** 不管读还是写风格复杂的文章，我们都必须明白：为了精确表达复杂的思想，该文章是否必须写得那么复杂。艰涩的文风很容易使复杂思想变得更加难懂，这是没有必要的。爱因斯坦说过，任何事都要力求简单，但不能过分。同样地，写作风格达到必要的复杂程度即可，**无需过之**。

> 阅读时，如果发现其复杂程度超出了应有的范围，就找到人物与行为词，这样能将作者给你带来的不必要的困惑解开。
>
> 写作时，如果因为无端的复杂性而感到不安，也要用同样的工具去检验。如果的确感到不安，那么就进行修改。修改过程中要遵循作家的黄金规则：**你希望别人怎么写作，你自己就怎么写。**

## 自我检测

### 练习 4.7

浏览一页自己的文章，圈出所有名词化了的词，把所有主动动词和被动动词做上标记。解释使用每一个名词化的词和每一个被动式的词的具体原因。如果没有理由必须使用就加以修改。

### 练习 4.8

从你所在领域的主要著作中选取一段文章。与同事一起分析其专业特征。它使用的是何种主语？它是怎样平衡主动语态与被动语态的？名词化了的词是怎样用的？它是怎样使用元话语的，以及使用的频率？试着区别该文章的特征与该领域的专业特征。现在开始修改你自己的一篇文章，使其更接近专业水平。

总结你为什么不得不这样修改?

## 总结

1. 读者认为,如果句子主语指代人物,动词指代动作,那么这样的文章是清晰的文章。

| 固定格式<br>(Fixed) | 主语<br>(Subject) | 动词<br>(Verb) | |
|---|---|---|---|
| 变体<br>(Variable) | 人物<br>(Character) | 动作<br>(Action) | |

2. 如果讲故事时用抽象的名词化的词语做主要人物和主语,那就要尽量少用其他名词化的词:

*A nominalization* is a **replacement** of a verb by a noun, often resulting in **displacement** of characters from subjects by nouns.

√ When a *nominalization* REPLACES a verb with a noun, it often DISPLACES characters from subjects.

3. 如果动作的执行者是显而易见的,就使用被动语态:

The voters REELECTED the president with 54% of the vote.

√ The president WAS REELECTED with 54% of the vote.

4. 如果使用被动语态能将长串主语换成短的,就采用被动语态:

Research demonstrating the soundness of our reasoning and the need for action SUPPORTED this decision.

√ This decision WAS SUPPORTED BY research demonstrating the soundness of our reasoning and the need for action.

5. 如果使用被动语态能呈现出一系列连贯的主语，就采用被动语态：

√ By early 1945, *the Axis* nations had BEEN essentially DEFEATED; all that remained was a bloody climax. *The German borders* had BEEN BREACHED, and both *Germany and Japan* were being bombed around the clock. *Neither country*, though, had BEEN SO DEVASTATED that *it* could not RESIST.

6. 如果是元话语动词，就采用主动语态：

The term of the analysis must BE DEFINED.

√ We must DEFINE the terms of the analysis.

7. 如果可能，请重写长串复合名词短语：

We discussed the **board**[1] **candidate**[2] **review**[3] **meeting**[4] **schedule**[5].

√ We discussed the **schedule**[5] of **meetings**[4] to **review**[3] **candidates**[2] for the **board**[1].

[ 第五课 ]

# 衔接与连贯

如果一个人想要传达信息,他需要从熟悉的信息写起,然后是不太熟悉的信息,这个顺序不能颠倒。从越简单的信息写起越好。作家们的通病是在开头就透露了过多的信息给读者——他们把本应写在句中的信息放在了句首,使读者研究句子的后半部分还需跳回到前半部分。这样的话,除了作者自己,其他人不可能理解其作品,因为只有作者了解主题,而其他人却没机会读到该作品。

——本杰明·富兰克林
（Benjamin Franklin）

在写作这门艺术中,有两个重要秘诀:第一个是过渡与衔接的哲学意义,或者称之为这样一门艺术—— 一种思想的逐渐推进是为了引发另外一种思想,那些一气呵成且令人印象深刻的作品都有很强的衔接性。第二个是句子间呼应的方式;写作中最有力的效果源于句子间的前后呼应,也就是说,来源于句子间的迅速转换。

——托马斯·德·昆西
（Thomas De Quencey）

## 衔接的内涵

到目前为止，似乎通过把人物和动作转换成主语和动词，文章的表述就会清晰简洁。但是仅仅单个的句子达到明晰的要求，还不能使读者感到篇章是一个有机的整体。例如，下列两段文字描述的是同一件事，但给人的感觉却不同：

1a. The basis of our American democracy—equal opportunity for all—is being threatened by college costs that have been rising fast for the last several years. Increases in family income have been significantly outpaced by increases in tuition at our colleges and universities during that period. Only the children of the wealthiest families in our society will be able to afford a college education if this trend continues. Knowledge and intellectual skills, in addition to wealth, will divide us as a people, when that happens. Equal opportunity and the egalitarian basis of our democratic society could be eroded by such a divide.

√ 1b. In the last several years, college coats have been rising so fast that they are now threatening the basis of our American democracy—equal opportunity for all. During that period, tuition has significantly outpaced increases in family income. If this trend continues, a college education will soon be affordable only by the children of the wealthiest families in our society. When that happens, we will be divided as a people not only by wealth, but by knowledge and intellectual skills. Such a divide will erode equal opportunity and the egalitarian basis of our democratic society.

第一段看上去有点儿没有头绪，甚至很零乱，第二段则连接得比较紧凑。

但是单词"choppy""disorganized""connected"跟"clear"一样，并不指字面上的意思，而是指这些词带给我们什么样的感受。段落（1a）中，简单的**单词**排列给人们的感觉是断断续续的，这是什么原因造成的？为什么段落（1b）读起来更流畅一些？我们的判断建立在对词序的两方面理解上：

根据每个句子的结尾和下一句的开头，我们来判断句子的顺序是否有**衔接性**。

根据一段话中每个句子的开头，我们来判断段落之内句子是否**连贯**。（这里我讨论的是段落内的连贯性。第七、八课中我将讨论整篇文章的连贯性。）

# 衔接

## 流畅的意义

第四课中我们谈到了相似的内容，即避免使用被动语态。如果总是遵循这一规则，我们会在句子（2a）中选择使用主动语态的动词，而不是像句子（2b）那样用被动语态的动词：

2a. The collapse of a dead star into a point perhaps no larger than a marble CREATES（主动语态）a black hole.

2b. A black hole **is** CREATED（被动语态）by the collapse of a dead star into a point perhaps no larger than a marble.

但是，在上下文中我们可能会选择其他的词。如下：

[1]Some astonishing questions about the nature of the universe have been raised by scientists studying black holes in space.[2a] **The collapse of a dead star into a point perhaps no larger than a marble creates a black hole.**[3] So much matter compressed into so little volume changes the fabric of space around it in puzzling ways.

[1]Some astonishing questions about the nature of the universe have been raised by scientists studying black holes in space.[2b] **A black hole is created by the collapse of a dead star into a point perhaps no larger than a marble.**[3] So much matter compressed into so little volume changes the fabric of space

around it in puzzling ways.

在这个语境下，我们感觉使用被动语态的句子（2b）比使用主动语态的句子（2a）显得更流畅。

原因很清楚：第一句话的最后四个单词指明了一个很重要的人物——**black hole in space**. 但是在句子（2a）中，我们接下来看到的是 **collapsed stars** 和 **marbles**，这样使句子所提供的信息看上去很唐突：

> [1]Some astonishing questions about the nature of the universe have been raised by scientists studying <u>black holes in space.</u>[2a] <u>The collapse of a dead star into a point perhaps no larger than a marble</u> creates...

如果在第一句后面使用了被动语态的句子（2b），我们会感觉句子间连接更流畅一些。因为句子（2b）开头的词正是第一句句尾的词：

> [1]... studying black holes in space.[2b] A black hole is created by the collapse of a dead star into **a point perhaps no larger than a marble**.[3] **So much matter compressed into so little volume** changes the fabric of space around it in puzzling ways...

同样需要注意的是，被动语态使得放在句子（2b）末尾的词与第三句的开头的词连接在了一起：

[1]... black holes in space.[2b] A black hole is created by the collapse of a dead star into **a point perhaps no larger than a marble.**[3] **So much matter compressed into so little volume** changes the fabric of space around it in puzzling ways.

> **要点** 当一个句子句尾的几个单词所提供的信息出现在下句的句首时,这些句子间是有**衔接性**的。这就是所谓的表达流畅。事实上,这也是为什么需要被动语态出现在语言中的最主要原因:我们通过使用被动语态排列句子,从而使得句子能够衔接流畅。

## 诊断与修正:以旧信息引出新信息

在句子中,新鲜的、陌生的信息出现之前,读者更喜欢先看到已知的、熟悉的信息。所以:

**1. 以读者熟悉的信息作为句子的开头。**读者获得已知信息的途径有二:其一,他们记得刚刚读过的句子中的词。这就是为什么上述黑洞例子中句子(2b)的开头与第一句句尾一致,以及为什么第三句的开头与句子(2b)的末尾一致。其二,读者会把与主语的相关知识加入句子中。例如,像下面第四句这样的开头,我们就不会感到奇怪:

... changes the fabric of space around it in puzzling ways.

⁴**Astronomers have reported** that...

单词 **Astronomers** 并没有出现在前面的句子中。但是，由于我们读到的文章是有关于空间的，所以其中提到天文学家时，也不会感到奇怪。

**2. 以读者无法预知的信息作为句子的结尾。** 在读到了简单熟悉的信息之后，读者总是期望能读到新的复杂信息。

当别人没有遵循以旧引新的原则，而你遵循了，你就能轻易地觉察到。因为，你对自己的观点进行了加工，所以你很熟悉这些观点。但是在自己的作品中区别新旧信息是很难的。不得不尝试一下，因为读者想在句首看到他们熟悉的**信息**，然后再转向新的信息。

在所写的每个句子排列中，作者不得不维持句子的清晰原则和段落衔接原则之间的平衡。**但在权衡的过程中，要优先考虑如何使读者产生一种衔接流畅的感觉。** 更好的是将以旧引新原则和以人物为主语原则二者结合起来使用。一旦作者提到主要人物，读者就会将其视为熟悉的信息。所以，当把人物放在前面时，熟悉的信息也就会在前面了。

> **要点** 到目前为止,我们已确定了三个有关清晰性的规则。
>
> 其中两个是关于句子的:
>
> **主要人物做主语。**
>
> **主要动作用动词表达。**
>
> 第三个规则也是关于句子的,但它同时阐释了如何使句子流畅。
>
> **把已知信息放在新信息之前。**
>
> 这些规则通常互相补充,但是出现冲突时首选第三个规则。作者组织新旧信息的方式决定了读者如何评价其作品的连贯性。并且对读者来说,整个篇章的**连贯性**高于单个句子的**清晰性**。

## 练习 5.1

修改下列段落,通过把已知信息放在句首来增加流畅性。第一段中,黑体标出的是我认为的已知信息。

1. Two aims—the recovery of the American economy and the modernization of America into a military power—were **in the president's mind when he assumed his office**. The drop in unemployment figures and inflation, and the increase in the GNP testifies to **his success in the first**. But our increased involvement in international conflict without any clear set of political goals indicates **less success**

with the second. Nevertheless, increases in the military budget and a good deal of saber rattling **pleased the American voter**.

2. The components of Abco's profitability, particularly growth in in Asian markets, will be highlighted in our report to demonstrate its advantages and versus competitors. Revenue returns along several dimensions—product type, end-use, distribution channels, etc.—will provide a basis for this analysis. Likely growth prospects of Abco's newest product lines will depend most on its ability in regard to the development of distribution channels in China, according to our projections. A range of innovative strategies will be needed to support the introduction of new products.

---

快速提示 　作者常常在句子中用 **this, these, that, those, another, such, second** 或者 **more** 指代某些事物。如果作者想使用这类暗示，尽量把它们放在句首或者接近句首处：

How to calculate credits for classes taken in a community colleges is **another** issue that we must consider.

√ **Another** issue that we must consider is how to calculate credits for classes taken in a community college.

---

## 连贯性

### 整体性的意义

如果能够衔接流畅，作者就能使读者初步感受到文章的紧凑性。但是，只有当读者感觉到文章**连贯性**的时候他们才会认为该作者文笔不错。因为相似的发音,人们很容易混淆 cohesion(衔接)和 coherence(连贯)这两个词。

当两个句子像两块拼图板连接在一起时,这样的方式称为**衔接**(回想前文提到的有关黑洞的句子)。

当作品中所有句子像拼图板拼凑成图画时,这样的方式称为**连贯**。

下面一段话衔接很流畅,因为句子与句子之间没有跳跃:

Sayner, Wisconsin, is the snowmobile capital of the world. The buzzing of snowmobile engines fills the air, and their tank-like tracks crisscross the snow. The snow reminds me of Mom's mashed potatoes, covered with furrows I would draw with my fork. Her mashed potatoes usually make me sick—that's why I play with them. I like to make a hole in the middle of the potatoes and fill it with melted butter. This behavior has been the subject of long chats between me and my analyst.

尽管单个句子之间有衔接,但是整个篇章却并不连贯。(整段话是由六个作者写就的,其中一个写了第一句话,其他五个人依次加上了一句,他们只了解紧挨的那句话而不理解全文。)这段话之所以不连贯,有三个原因:

1. 句子主语完全不相关。

2. 句子间没有共同的主题或观点。

3. 整段话中没有一句话能概括该段主旨。

我会在第六课中探讨第二点，在第八课中探讨第三点。那么本课接下来的探讨集中在第一点上，即共同主语。

**主语、话题和连贯**

500 年来，英语老师从两个方面给主语下了定义：

1. 动作的"**执行者**"。
2. 句子大意，即**主题**。

在第三课和第四课中，我们了解到为什么第一条定义行不通：很多句子的主语并不是动作执行者。例如，主语有时候是个动作：The **explosion** was loud. 有时候，主语是一种定性：**Correctness** is not writing's highest virtue. 有时候主语只是一个**语法形式**：It was a dark and stormy night.

但是第二个定义也有缺陷：**有时候主语传达了句子的大意**。之所以有缺陷是因为主语通常不传达句子的主要观点，那是其他部分"讨论"的内容。这种"主题化"的作用可能由句子其他部分来承担。

例如，下列句子的**主要主语**并没有指称主题。

这句的主要主语是 **it**，但是句子的主题是 **your claim**，是介词 for 的宾语：

*It* is impossible for **your claim** to be proved.

这句的主语是 **I**，但是主题是 **this question**，是介词 **to** 的宾语：

In regard to **this question**, *I* believe more research is needed.

这句的主语是 **it**，但是主题是 **our proposal**，是一个从句中动词的主语：

*It* is likely that **our proposal** will be accepted.

这句的主语是 **no one**，但是主题是 **such results**，是一个被放到句首表示强调的直接宾语：

**Such results** *no one* could have predicted.

> **快速提示** 当开始读一篇难懂的文章时，先快速浏览找到其中的主要人物。然后在细读之前思考一下这些人物。关于他们，你了解什么？你能联想到哪些其他的与之有关的观点？你期望从中读到什么？阅读的时候大脑中的人物形象越鲜明，你就越能理解他们的故事。

## 诊断和修改：话题

正如清晰性中的其他问题一样，仅仅自己阅读是无法预知读者如何评价作品的流畅程度的，因为作者对自己的作品过于了解。作者必须更客观地分析作品。下面这段话看上去不连贯，没有中心，甚至杂乱无章：

> Consistent ideas toward the beginnings of sentences help readers understand what a passage is generally about. A sense of coherence arises when a sequence of topics comprises a narrow set of related ideas. But the context of each sentence is lost by seemingly random shifts of topics. Unfocused paragraphs result when that happens.

下面是如何诊断并修改类似的段落：

## 1. 诊断

a. 用下划线标出段落中每句话的前七个或八个词，直到遇见动词。

b. 如果可以的话，用下划线标出每个从句中的前五个或六个单词。

> Consistent ideas toward the beginnings of sentences, especially in their subjects, help readers understand what a passage is generally about. A sense of coherence arises when a sequence of topics comprises a narrow set of related ideas. But the context of each sentence is lost by seemingly random shifts of topics. Unfocused, even disorganized paragraphs result when that happens.

## 2. 分析

　　a. 划线的词语是否构成了一小组相关观点？即使**作者**明白它们是如何联系在一起的，那么读者明白吗？就上段话而言，答案是否定的。

　　b. 划线的词语指明了最主要的人物吗？是真实的还是抽象的？显然，答案也是否定的。

## 3. 改写

　　a. 在大部分（不一定是所有的）句子中，用主语来指称句子的主题。

　　b. 确定读者熟悉这些语境中的主题。

下面一段话是修改过的，黑体的词表示新的主题：

> **Readers** understand what a passage is generally about when **they** see consistent ideas toward the beginnings of sentences, especially in their subjects. **They** feel a passage is coherent when **they** read a sequence of topics that focuses on a narrow set of related ideas. But when **topics** seem to shift randomly, **readers** lose the context of each sentence. When **that** happens, **they** feel they are reading paragraphs that are unfocused and even disorganized.

现在主语形成了一系列有力的话题：readers, they, they, they, topics, readers, that, they [ readers ]。

> **快速提示** 如果准备开始新的一章,首先列出那些打算写的人物。这不止包括有血有肉的人物形象,也包括一些重要的概念。**起草前**,想一想每个人物。在列表上试着勾勒出这一人物或者事物。至于那些概念,想一想能联想到的与之有关的观点。起草过程中,试着把这些人物放到大部分句子的主语中。如果在几个句子中没有提到其中的一个人物,那可能就是跑题了。

## 开门见山

句子开个好头是很难的。读者总是希望快速进入主题,但是他们往往受到作者的阻碍。这就叫作"清嗓子"。它常常以元话语(参见109—112页)开头来与前一句连接,用 **and**、**but**、**therefore** 等词语过渡:

  And therefore...

然后添加另一类元话语来表达作者对后文的态度,比如 **fortunately**、**perhaps**、**allegedly**、**it is important to note**、**for the most part**,或者 **in a manner of speaking**:

  And therefore, it is important to note...

接着我们指出时间、地点或者方式:

  And therefore, it is important to note that, in Eastern states since 1980...

之后，我们才进入主题：

> And therefore, it is important to note that, in Eastern states since 1980, **acid rain** has become a serious problem.

如果以这样的句子开始，读者不仅要花费时间来了解每个句子的内容，还需要找到整篇文章的主旨。如果发现一个句子中主语之前有很多词语，那么这句话需要如此修改：

> √ Since 1980, therefore, **acid rain** has become a serious problem in the Eastern states.

> **要点** 写作之前，指出要写的有关内容，这些就是**主题**。主题要用简短、具体、熟悉的词概括，它们多半是故事中的主要人物。大部分主语应该与主题有关。更重要的是一定要保持一致：主题应该能够告诉读者整篇文章在**讲什么**。

## 练习 5.2

修改下列段落，使它们连成话题链。找出文章中"发表意见"的那些词，并把这些词作为大部分句子的主语。第一段中，黑体词可以作为一致的主语/主题。

1. **Vegetation** covers the earth, except for those areas continuously covered with ice or utterly scorched by continual heat. Richly fertilized plains and river valleys are places where **plants** grow most richly, but also at the edge of perpetual snow in high mountains. The ocean and its edges as well as in and around lakes and swamps are **densely vegetated**. The cracks of busy city sidewalks have **plants** in them as well as in seemingly barren cliffs. Before human existed, the earth was covered with **vegetation**, and the earth will have **vegetation** long after evolutionary history swallows us up.

2. The power to create and communicate a new message to fit a new experience is not a competence animals have in their natural states. Their genetic code limits the number and kind of messages that they can communicate. Information about distance, direction, source, and richness of pollen in flowers constitutes the only information that can be communicated by bees, for example. A limited repertoire of messages delivered in the same way, for generation after generation, is characteristic of animals of the same species, in all significant respects.

3. The importance of language skills in children's problem-solving ability was stressed by Jones (1985) in his paper on children's thinking. Improvement in nonverbal problem solving was reported to have occurred as a result of improvements in language skills. The use of previously acquired language habits for problem articulation and activation of knowledge previously learned through language are thought to be the cause of better performance. Therefore, systematic practice in the verbal formulation of nonlinguistic problems prior to attempts at their solution might be an avenue for exploration in the enhancement of problem solving in general.

# 两个限制条件

## 所谓的"千篇一律"

这一点与"开头的句子要灵活多样"这一建议相矛盾。此建议不太实用,尤其是在变换主语以使句子显得灵活的时候。在自己的文章中,如果看到几个句子的主题相同,你会感觉文章很单调乏味、千篇一律。但是读者可能不太注意这些,因为他们更关注的是你的思想。

另一方面,如果发现在相同的情境下,使用相同的词语表达同一主题,你可能需要修改。下面这段话并没有过分地追求一致性:

"**Moral climate**" is created when an objectivized moral standard for treating people is accepted by others. **Moral climate** results from norms of behavior that are accepted by society whereby if people conform they are socially approved of, or if they don't they are shunned. In this light, **moral climate** acts as a reason to refrain from saying or doing things that the community does not support. **A moral climate** encourages individuals to conform to a moral standard and apply that standard to their own circumstances.

在这段话中,可以稍微变化一些词来指代一个重复的主题:

"**Moral climate**" is created… . **This climate** results… . In this light, **morality** acts… . **A moral climate** encourages… .

注意，大部分作者过于频繁地变换主题，这是不可取的。

## 貌似连贯

一些作者试着用诸如 **thus**、**therefore**、**however** 等连词来连接句子，使文章看似连贯。但是他们忽略了这些句子在逻辑上的联系。例如：

> Because the press is the major medium of interaction between the president and the people, how it portrays him influences his popularity. **Therefore**, it should report on the president objectively. Both reporters and the president are human, **however**, subject to error and favoritism. **Also**, people act differently in public than they do in private. **Hence**, to understand a person, it is important to know the whole person, his environment, upbringing, and education. **Indeed**, from the correspondence with his family, we can learn much about Harry S. Truman, our thirty-third president.

有经验的作者也使用这些连词，但他们更看中的是逻辑上的流畅性。他们小心翼翼地使用 **and**、**also**、**moreover**、**another** 等，以及表达简单意思的词，如 **Here's one more thing**。如果要反驳或者证明刚刚说的事情，就需要使用 **but** 或者 **however**，还可以使用 **therefore** 或者 **consequently** 来引导一连串的原因。但是一页之内，不能太频繁地使用这类词。如果句子是衔接在一起的，它们构成的段落也是连贯的，那么就无需用这些词。

# 自我检测

## 练习 5.3

———⁕———

第四课中（104—107 页）我讨论过，可以通过变换句子中那些作为主语的人物／话题来改变视角：

By early 1945, *the Allies* had essentially defeated *Germany*...

By early 1945, *Germany* had essentially been defeated *by the Allies*...

第一个版本是站在联军的立场写的，第二个是站在德国的立场。

用自己作品中的一段话练习视角的转换。首先，圈出那些指称人物／话题的词语。然后在每个从句的主语下划线。应该能够看到，一些人物／话题大多都是作为主语出现的，但其他的则是出现在句子的其他部分（比如出现在动词后）。用出现在动词后做主语的人物／话题来修改句子，把做主语的人物／话题移到动词后。你能发现文章的意思或整体感觉上有什么变化吗？

## 练习 5.4

———⁕———

作者常常违背以旧信息引出新信息的规则，因为他们太了解自己的作品了：对于他们来说，所有的事情都是已知信息。所以作者需要和读者一起来分析作品中新旧信息的转换是否流畅。让读者通读一段，然后划出每一条新信息。如果划线部分在句子开头，那么就需要修改。以此类推。

## 练习 5.5

———

作者用 also, furthermore, moreover, another, but, however, although, nevertheless 和 consequently 这样的连词和过渡词来帮助读者明白想法之间的联系。但这类词并不能够真正使段落连贯。当作者努力表达自己的思想时，他们可能会使文章貌似连贯，实则零乱。挑一篇自认为难懂的文章，让读者找出那些给人假相的地方。让读者圈出那些看似有逻辑，实则没意义的连接词，然后做必要的修改。

## 总结

我们可以把以旧引新规则和主题一致规则同第三课和第四课中的人物做主语、动词表达动作的规则结合起来（我会在第六课完成下面的表格）：

| | | | |
|---|---|---|---|
| 固定格式<br>（Fixed） | 话题<br>（Topic） | | |
| 变量<br>（Variable） | 已知信息<br>（Familiar） | 新信息<br>（New） | |
| 固定格式<br>（Fixed） | 主语<br>（Subject） | 动词<br>（Verb） | |
| 变量<br>（Variable） | 人物<br>（Character） | 行动<br>（Action） | |

本课中提到的规则如下：

1. 句子开头的主语能够表达读者所熟悉的信息（黑体词）；在句尾给出新的、陌生的信息（斜体词）：

The *number of dead in the Civil War* exceeded **all other wars in American history** combined. A reason for *the lingering animosity between North and South* today is **the memory of this terrible carnage**.

√ Of **all the wars in American history**, none has exceeded the Civil War in *the number of dead*. **The memory of this terrible carnage** is one reason for the *lingering animosity between North and South today*.

2. 通过一系列句子，使话题简短且保持恰当的一致性。

**Competition by Asian companies with American companies in the Pacific** is the first phase of this study. **Labor costs and the ability to introduce new products quickly in particular** are examined. **A plan that will show American industry how to restructure its facilities** will be developed from this study.

√ In the first phase of this study, **we** examine how **Asian companies** compete with American companies in the Pacific region. **We** examine in particular their labor costs and ability to introduce new products quickly. **We** develop from this study a **plan** that will show **American industry** how to restructure its facilities.

[ 第六课 ]
# 强 调

文章的开头和结尾要彼此呼应。
——德国谚语
（German Proverb）

文章的开头预示着文章的结尾。
——T. S. 艾略特
（T. S. Eliot）

漂亮的结尾才会写就漂亮的文章。
——威廉·莎士比亚
（William Shakespeare）

## 句子结尾的内涵

如果写出的句子里,中心人物作为主语/主题,并且它们和主要动词连接在一起,那么该句的其余部分也很可能正确,并且在这一创作过程中,整个段落都会是一气呵成的。但是,如果句子开头的几个词需要特别关注,那么也要关注句子最后的几个词。如何结束一个句子,不单单左右着读者对单个句子的清晰性和力度的判断,同时也影响着对句子之间的连贯性和连接性的判断。

如果读者在句子的前九个或十个单词中形成惯性,那么他们很容易读懂下面这样复杂的材料。对比下面两段:

1a. A sociometric and actuarial analysis of Social Security revenues and disbursements for the last six decades to determine changes in projecting deficits is the subject of this study.

√ 1b. In this study, we analyze Social Security's revenues and disbursements for the last six decades, using sociometric and actuarial criteria to determine changes in projecting deficits.

正如在(1a)中,我们既要费劲地理解它的专业术语,同时还要搜肠刮肚地琢磨一个长达二十二个词的主语。但是在(1b)中,句子的开头五个词后就是主语和谓语,而跟在十二个词后就是一个术语（sociometric），这会让我们放慢阅读速度。因此，我们有足够的耐力去弄明白句子结尾的复杂性。

## 复杂的语法

下面两个句子，你更喜欢哪一句？

2a. Lincoln's claim that the Civil War was God's punishment of both North and South for slavery appears in the last part of the speech.

2b. In the last part of this speech, Lincoln claims that God gave the Civil War to both North and South as a punishment for slavery.

大部分读者偏爱（2b），因为它以一个简洁而短小的介绍性短语开始，后面接着一个词的主语和一个特殊的动词，之后跟着复杂的语法结构。我们会在第五课探讨这个问题。

## 复杂的意义

另一种复杂性体现在词的意义上，尤其是专业词汇方面。比较下面两段：

3a. The role of calcium blockers in the control of cardiac irregularity can be seen through an understanding of the role of calcium in the activation of muscle cells. The regulatory proteins actin, myosin, tropomyosin, and troponin make up the sarcomere.

The energy-producing, or ATPase, protein myosin makes up its thick filament, while actin, tropomyosin, troponin make up its thin filament. Interaction of myosin and actin triggers muscle contraction.

√ 3b. When a muscle contracts, it uses calcium. If we can understand how calcium affects muscle contraction, we can explain how the drug called "calcium blockers" control cardiac irregularity. The basic unit of muscle contraction is the sarcomere. It has two filaments, one thin and one thick. Those filaments consist of four proteins that regulate contraction: actin, tropomyosin, and troponin in the thin filament and myosin in the thick one. Muscles contract when a protein in the thin filament, actin, interacts with the protein in the thick filament, myosin, an energy-producing or ATPase protein.

两段都用了相同的术语，但对于那些不懂肌肉的化学构成的人来说，（3b）显得更清晰些。

这两段有两个方面不同。首先，（3a）中的信息是隐含的，而（3b）陈述得很清晰。其次，注意（3a）中几乎所有的专业词是怎样用在句子的开头的，而熟悉的词集中在句子末尾：

3a. The role of **calcium blokers** in the control of **cardiac irregularity** can be seen through an understanding of the role of calcium in the activation of muscle cells.

The **regulatory proteins actin, myosin, tropomyosin, and troponin** make up the **sarcomere**.

The **energy-producing, or ATPase, protein myosin** makes up its thick filament, while **actin, tropomyosin, and troponin** make up its thin filament.

**Interaction of myosin and actin** triggers muscle contraction.

在（3b）中，这些术语出现在句子的结尾：

... uses **calcium**.

... "calcium blockers" control **cardiac irregularity**

... is the **sarcomere**.

... **actin, tropomyosin, and troponin** in the thin filament and **myosin** in the thick one.

... myosin, an **energy-producing or ATPase protein**.

使用陌生术语引导的方式写作更适合给专业的读者阅读。在下面选自《新英格兰医学学报》的段落中，为了把术语置于结尾，作者刻意地使用了元话语：

The incubation of peripheral-blood lymphocytes with a lymphokine, interleukin—2, generates lymphoid cells that can lyse fresh, noncultured, natural-killer-cell-resistant tumor cells but not normal cells. *We term these cells* **lymphokine-activated killer (LAK) cells**.

> **要点** 读者希望作者合理组织句子,从而帮助他们解决两类难题:
>
> 长而复杂的短语和从句
> 新的知识,尤其是陌生的专业术语
>
> 一般来说,句子应该用相对短的成分开始:一个短的引导性短语或从句,它跟随着一个短且具体的主语,以及一个表示特别动作的动词。在动词之后,如果结构合理,句子可以继续延伸几行(见第十课和第十一课)。一般原则是:不要让读者从难到易地阅读,而是从易到难进行。

## 另一个新术语:重读

上一课中,我们讨论过句子的前几个词是极其重要的,即它陈述了该句的**核心内容**。句子的最后几个词也非常重要,因为它们受到特别的关注。你会感觉到,当声音将在句尾处升高时,是为了凸显一个音节比其他的更强烈。

  ... more strongly than the ó-thers.

默读时,我们也会有同样的经历。

我将句子中着重强调的部分称为**重读**。将重要的部分放在重读的位置上,有助于读者听明白文章的主要观点,因为如果句子用无足轻重的词结束,那它就显得没有力量了。

Global warming could raise sea levels to a point where much of the world's low-lying coastal areas would disappear, **according to most atmospheric scientists.**

√ According to most atmospheric scientists, global warming could raise sea levels to a point where much of the world's low-lying coastal areas **would disappear.**

在第四课和第五课，我了解到不同的主语或主题是怎样表达出不同观点的（见 104—107 页，134—137 页）。通过合理安排句子的结尾，能实现不同风格的效果。

对比下面这些段落。一个是指责美国总统在对伊朗核武力控制上态度软弱。另一段经过修改，则强调了伊朗的责任。从句子的结尾，就可以辨别出它们的不同：

1a. The administration has blurred an issue central to nuclear arms control, **the issue of verification.** Irresponsible charges, innuendo, and leaks have submerged **serious problems with Iranian compliance.** The objective, instead, should be not to exploit these concerns in order to further poison our relations, repudiate exsiting agreements, or, worse still, terminate arms control altogether, but **to insist on compliance and clarify questionable behavior.**

1b. The issue of verification—so central to nuclear arms control—has been **blurred by the administration.** Serious problems with Iranian compliance have been submerged in irresponsible charges, innuendo, and leaks. The objective, instead, should be to clarify questionable behavior and insist on compliance—not to exploit these concerns in order to **further poison our relations, repudiate existing agreements, or, worse still, terminate arms control altogether.**

> 要点　正如我们要从句子的前几个词找到作者的立场一样，要找到句子的重点部分，则要参照句子后面的几个词。可以修改句子的末尾，从而特别强调几个你希望读者听到的词，让他们注意到其特别的意义。

## 诊断和修改：重读

如果句子的主语和主题已经安排得恰如其分，那么在默认的情况下，可以将希望得到强调的词放在句子结尾。为了验证，你可以大声地朗读，当读到句子倒数第三个或第四个词时，就像在演讲中重读这些词一样用力地拍手。如果拍手时重读的词并不是值得特别强调的，就请查找值得重读的词。然后，把它们置于句子的结尾附近。下面是一些方法：

### 三个修改策略

**1. 删减结尾**

Sociobiologists claim that our genes control our social

behavior in the way we act in situations we are in every day.

由于 social behavior（社会行为）就意味着 the way we act in situations...，所以我们要将 behavior 之后所有的词删掉。

√ Sociobiologists claim that our genes **control our social behavior.**

**2. 将无足轻重的观点放在句子左边。**

The data offered to prove EPS are weak, **for the most part.**

√ **For the most part**, the data offered to prove EPS are **weak.**

应特别注意：避免使用虎头蛇尾的元话语结尾。

Job opportunities in computer programming are getting scarcer, **it must be remembered.**

√ **It must be remembered** that job opportunities in computer programming are getting scarcer.

**3. 将新的信息放在句子右边。处理重读时，一个很常见的方法是把新的信息放在句子的结尾处。**

**Questions about the ethics of withdrawing intravenous feeding** are *more difficult* [ than something just mentioned ].

√ *More difficult* [ than something just mentioned ] are **questions about the ethics of withdrawing intravenous feeding.**

## 六种强调右边部分的句法

有一些句法结构,允许合理安排句子中强调的新信息。(你只能读他们中的一个)

1. **There 句型的转换**　一些编辑在使用 there is /there are 结构时很是受挫,然而这个句型却能把主语放到句子右边,从而达到强调目的。对比下面句子:

**Several syntactic devices** let you manage where in a sentence you locate units of new information.

√ *There are* **several syntactic devices** that let you manage where in a sentence you locate units of new information.

经验丰富的作者通常会用 **there** 句型开始一个段落,从而引出下文出现的新主题和新观点。

2. **被动语态(这是不得已的选择)**　被动句里,主语和宾语之间可以自如地切换。对比下面句子:

Some claim that **our genes** influence(主动语态)aspects of behavior that we think are learned. **Our genes**, for example, seem to determine...

√ Some claim that aspects of behavior that we think are learned are in fact influenced(被动语态)**by our genes**. **Our genes**, for example, seem to determine...

正是语言中存在着被动语态,因此我们可以合理安排新旧信息。

3. **What 句型的转换**　这是另一种方法：将句子中的一部分转换到句子右侧，从而达到强调的效果：

We need a monetary policy that would end fluctuations in money supply, unemployment, and inflation.

√ **What** we need **is** a monetary policy that would end fluctuations in money supply, unemployment, and inflation.

4. **It 句型的转换**　如果主语是由较长的名词从句构成，你可以把它移到句子结尾处，然后将 It 放在句首：

**That oil prices would be set by OPEC** once seemed inevitable.

√ *It* once seemed inevitable **that oil prices would be set by OPEC.**

5. **Not only X, but (also) Y (as well) 句型**　在下面一组句子中，注意 but 是如何强调句子最后部分的：

We must clarify these issues and **develop trust**.

√ We must *not only* clarify these issues, *but* also **develop trust.**

6. **代词替换和省略**　这有一个关键点：如果把前面已经使用过的词放在句子结尾处，句子会结束得很平淡，因为在我们意识里，以前听到的观点在结尾处已被淡化了。如果大声地逐句朗读，你就会听出来它们是如何被淡化的。为了避免这种平白，你可以改写，或者用代词替换句子结尾处重复出现的词。例如：

A sentence will seem to end flatly if at its end you use a word that you used just a few words before, because when you repeat that word, your voice **drops**. Instead of repeating the noun, use a **pronoun**. The reader will at least hear emphasis on the word just **before** *it*.

有时，可以删掉前面重复出现的词：

It is sometimes possible to represent a complex idea in a simple sentence, but more often you cannot.

一篇散文的特征之一就是，作者总能灵活运用一些修辞手法来结束句子。我将会在十一课讨论这些修辞用法。

> **快速提示** 大声地朗读句子，就可以轻松地检查出是否强调了正确的词：朗读到最后几个单词时，提高你的声音并且用手轻拍桌子。如果强调了错误的单词，你的声音和桌子的击打声会让你感觉到错误：
>
> It is sometimes possible to represent a complex idea in a simple sentence, but more often you cannot represent it in that kind of sentence.
>
> 如果强调了正确的词，你的声音和击打桌子声会使你感觉很舒服：
>
> It is sometimes possible to represent a complex idea in a simple sentence, but more OFTEN you CANNOT.

# 练习 6.1

修改下面这些句子，使它们强调正确的词。在前三句中，我把我认为应该被强调的词标成了黑体。然后删除冗长的词和名词化的词。

1. The President's tendency **to rewrite the Constitution** is the biggest danger to the nation, in my opinion, at least.

2. A new political philosophy that could affect our society **well into the twenty-first century** may emerge from these studies.

3. There are **limited** opportunities for faculty to work with individual students in large American colleges and universities.

4. Building suburban housing developments in floodplains has led to the existence of extensive and widespread flooding and economic disaster in parts of our country in recent years, it is now clear.

5. The teacher who makes an assignment of a long final term paper at the end of the semester and who then gives only a grade and nothing else such as a critical comment is a common object of complaint among students at the college level.

6. Renting textbooks rather than buying them for basic required courses such as mathematics, foreign languages, and English, whose textbooks do not go through yearly changes, is feasible, however, economically speaking.

# 练习 6.2

修改下面的句子,使它们用恰当的话题开头,用合适的重读结尾。

1. The story of King Lear and his daughters was a popular one during the reign of Queen Elizabeth. At least a dozen available books offered the story to anyone wishing to read it, by the time Elizabeth died. The characters were undeveloped in most of these stories, however, making the story a simple narrative that stated an obvious moral. When he began work on *lear*, perhaps his greatest tragedy, Shakespeare must have had several versions of this story available to him. He turned the characters into credible human beings with complex motives, however, even though they were based on the stock figures of legend.

2. Whether the date an operation intends to close down might be part of management's "duty to disclose" during contract bargaining is the issue here, it would appear. The minimization of conflict is the central rationale for the duty that management has to bargain in good faith. In order to allow the union to put forth proposals on behalf of its members, companies are obligated to disclose major changes in an operation during bargaining, though the case law is scanty on this matter.

3. Athens' catastrophic Sicilian Invasion is the most important event in Thucydides' *History of the Peloponnesian War*. Three-quarters of the history is devoted to setting up the invasion because of this. Through the step-by-step decline in Athenian society that Thucydides describes, we can see how he chose to anticipate the Sicilian Invasion. The inevitability that we associate with the tragic drama is the basic reason for the need to anticipate the invasion.

## 话题、强调、主题和连贯性

某些句子的重读有更多的功能,其中之一便是有助于读者考虑整个篇章的连贯性。正如我们在第五课看到的,读者通常把最清晰的话题——出现在句子前面的简短的名词短语当作句子主语。这也是大多数人认为下面这一段话没有重点的原因,它的句子开头似乎太过盲目,缺乏一致性的观点:

1a. Great strides in the early and accurate diagnosis of Alzheimer's disease have been made in recent years. Not too long ago, senility in an older patient who seemed to be losing touch with reality was often confused with Alzheimer's. Genetic clues have become the basis of newer and more reliable tests in the last few years, however. The risk of human tragedy of another kind, though, has resulted from the increasing accuracy of these tests: predictions about susceptibility to Alzheimer's have become possible, long before the appearance of any overt symptoms. At that point, an apparently healthy person could be devastated by such an early diagnosis.

如果修改这段话,使它的各个话题保持协调,那么整个篇章也就显得更加连贯(主题用黑体字):

√ 1b. In recent years, **researchers** have made great strides in the early and accurate diagnosis of Alzheimer's disease. Not too long ago, when **a physician** examined an older patient who seemed out of touch with reality, **she** had to guess whether the **person** was senile or had Alzheimer's. In the past few years, however, **physicians** have been able to use new and more reliable tests focusing on genetic clues. But in **the accuracy of these new tests** lies the risk of another kind of human tragedy: **physicians** may be able to predict Alzheimer's long before its overt appearance, but **such an early diagnosis** could psychologically devastate an apparently healthy person.

现在这段话有两个重点:"researchers/physicians"和"testing/diagnosis"。

但是，进一步的修改会使篇章更加连贯，修改的原则是:

> 把关键词放在第一句的重读位置上，来强调重要的观点，以让重要的观点统领下文。

（1b）中的第一句强调的是诊断领域的进步: ... **the early and accurate diagnosis of Alzheimer's disease.** 但是文章的主题不是讨论诊断的，而是讨论它的风险。然而，统领全文的概念直到篇幅过半才出现。

如果关键的信息出现在第一句，具体地说，是**在句子结尾处，即强调的部分**，读者就能更好地抓住文章的重点。读者之所以读开篇句，或者段落的前两句，是为了发现文章的主要概念，这些概念也会在下文中不断重复。具体地说，读者会在开场句、引导句和框架句中的最后几个词中寻找这些概念。

下面为（1b）设计了新的开篇句，它有助于读者把重点放在关键概念上，而不只是"Alzheimer's"和"new diagnoses"，还有"new problem"和"informing those most at risk"：

> In recent years, researchers have made great strides in the early and accurate diagnosis of Alzheimer's disease, but those **diagnoses** have raised **a new problem** about informing those most at risk who show no symptoms of it.

我们可以将这些贯穿整个篇章的关键概念称之为主题。

再一次观察下面段落中被强调的单词：

黑体字都与检测有关。
斜体字都与精神状态有关。
大写字都与新问题有关。

每一个概念都出现在新开篇句的末尾处，尤其涉及新问题的主题。

√ 1c. In recent years, researcher**s** have made great strides in the early and accurate **diagnosis** of *Alzheimer's disease*, but those **diagnoses** have raised A NEW PROBLEM about INFORMING THOSE MOST AT RISK WHO SHOW NO SYMPTOMS OF IT. Not too long ago, when a physician examined an older patient who seemed *out of* *touch with reality*, she had to **guess** whether that person had *Alzheimer's* or was *only senile*. In the past few years, however, physicians have been able to use **new and more reliable tests** focusing on genetic clues. But in the accuracy of these **new tests** lies the RISK OF ANOTHER KIND OF HUMAN TRAGEDY: physicians may be able to **predict** *Alzheimer's* long before its overt appearance, but such an early **diagnosis** could PSYCHOLOGICALLY DEVASTATE AN APPARENTLY HEALTHY PERSON.

不单单是一个理由,而是三个理由将整个篇章"黏合"在一起:

它的话题一直在强调医生和诊断。

贯穿段落的是一串词,它们的重心一直在(1)检测,(2)精神状态和(3)新问题,这三个主题上。

同样重要的是,开篇句通过在结尾的强调,从而帮助我们注意到这些主题。

**再次强调,将打算让那些在段落剩余部分中出现的主题词放在引导句的末尾处。这个规则适用于引导平淡冗长的句子(两或三句的引导句、过渡句和其他有不同句型的段落)中。它也适用于那些引导任何长度的篇章,甚至整个文本。**

**要点** 依靠贯穿整个篇章的观点来创造一种连贯性。可以使用以下两种方法帮助读者辨识那些主要概念:

重复那些作为句子话题的人物,通常就是句子的主语。重复篇章、名词、动词和形容词中用作主题的其他因素。

如果你在引导段落的句子中强调这些主题,读者可能会注意它们。

**快速提示** 对于一段超过五、六句的段落,在你认为最能引导或者概括段落的句子下面划线。如果不能迅速地划出来,你的段落可能就有问题。如果你可以,请划出、圈出引导部分的重点词。这些词听起来应该像这个段落的标题。如果它们不像,你的读者可能就会有困惑。在第八课,我们会继续探讨这个话题。

## 自我检测

### 练习6.3

———❦———

大声朗读你著作中的一页,在读到句子末尾时(正如156页快速提示中建议的那样)提高声音,轻拍手。你注意到了什么?强调错误单词的频率是多少?强调正确单词的频率又是多少?你察觉到什么规律了吗?如果你无意地强调了错误的单词，你的意义会怎样改变？

## 练习 6.4

请读者用 152—153 页中的三个修改策略（删掉结尾，将无足轻重的观点放到句子左边，或者将新信息放到句子右边）去修改你的作品中至少四到五个句子。

- 在修改句子结尾时，读者有没有删掉你认为必要的材料？
- 你的读者有没有把你认为是重要的观点当作是无足轻重的？
- 你对于读者划分的"新信息"感到惊讶吗？

哪一种修改方式提高了你的写作，而哪一个没有提高？为什么？

## 总结

我们可以把这一课的规则和其他的规则整合到一起。

| 固定格式<br>（Fixed） | 话题<br>（Topic） | | 重读<br>（Stress） |
|---|---|---|---|
| 变量<br>（Variable） | 简短，简单句，熟悉的信息<br>（Short, simple, familiar） | | 长句，复杂句，新信息<br>（Long, complex, new） |
| 固定格式<br>（Fixed） | 主语<br>（Subject） | 动词<br>（Verb） | |
| 变量<br>（Variable） | 人物<br>（Character） | 行动<br>（Action） | |

1. 用一个句子的结尾去引导较长的、复杂的，或者是其他难以处理的材料，尤其是陌生的专业术语和新的信息。

**A determination of involvement of lipid-linked saccharides in the assembly of oligosaccharide chains of ovalbumin *in vivo*** was the principal aim of this study. **In vitro and *in vivo* studies utilizing oviduct membrane preparations and oviduct slices and the antibiotic tunicamycin** were undertaken to accomplish this.

√ The principal aim of this study was to determine how **lipid-linked saccharides are involved in the assembly of oligosaccharide chains of ovalbumin *in vivo***. To accomplish this, studies were undertaken *in vitro* and *in vivo*, **utilizing the antibiotic tunicamycin on preparations of oviduct membrane and on oviduct slices.**

2. 将重读位置放在句子结尾处，以强调那些希望让读者听到的、一直在他们的脑海中被强调的词：

The administration has blurred an issue central to arms control, **the issue of verification.** Irresponsible charges, innuendo, and leaks have submerged **serious problems with Iranian compliance.**

The issue of verification—so central to arms control—has been **blurred by the administration.** Serious problems with Iranian compliance have been submerged in **irresponsible charges, innuendo, and leaks.**

3. 让下文即将出现的主题词出现在开篇句的重读位置：

In recent years, researchers have made great strides in the early and accurate **diagnosis** of *Alzheimer's disease*, but those **diagnoses** have raised A NEW PROBLEM about INFORMING THOSE MOST AT RISK WHO SHOW NO SYMPTOMS OF IT. Not too long ago, when a physician examined an older patient who seemed out of touch with reality, she had to **guess** whether that person was senile or had *Alzheimer's*. In the past few years, however, they have been able to use **new and more reliable tests** focusing on genetic clues. But in the accuracy of these **new tests** lies the RISK OF ANOTHER KIND OF HUMAN TRAGEDY: physicians may be able to **predict** *Alzheimer's* long before its overt appearence, but such an early **diagnosis** could PSYCHOLOGICALLY DEVASATE AN APPARENTLY HEALTHY PERSON.

## 总结：第二部分

简单的英语句子比句子单词的总和要有意义得多；因为句子是多个系统的集合。

| 固定格式<br>（Fixed） | 话题<br>（Topic） | | 重读<br>（Stress） |
|---|---|---|---|
| 变量<br>（Variable） | 简短，简单句，熟悉的信息<br>（Short, simple, familiar） | | 长句，复杂句，新信息<br>（Long, complex, new） |
| 固定格式<br>（Fixed） | 主语<br>（Subject） | 动词<br>（Verb） | |
| 变量<br>（Variable） | 人物<br>（Character） | 行动<br>（Action） | |

读者一直喜欢的，也是作者要千方百计实现的：

1. 他们希望快速找到主句的主语，这样避免了阅读更多较长的、复杂的短语和从句。

2. 他们希望能在主语之后迅速地找到动词，像下面这样做：

a. 保持主语的简短，如果可以的话，就能塑造一个活生生的人物。

b. 用熟悉的信息开始句子。

3. 他们希望动词指称具体的动作，所以不要用抽象的词来表示动作。

4. 越陌生、越复杂、越难理解的信息应该放在句子的末尾处，因为在句子结尾处，读者更容易处理复杂信息。

5. 如果一连串句子都由不同主语开始，读者就会感到迷糊。因此，用一些可以定义**篇章大意**的话题来贯穿始末。

6. 如果把篇章的观点和一些关键概念联系起来的话，读者理解篇章的观点就会比较容易,因此就要把指示文章重要观点的主题串在一起。

总之,写的句子要迅速地出现简短、具体、熟悉的主语,将主语和表达特殊动作的动词连接在一起,并且保持主语的一致性。读者不仅希望在主句中读到这样的句型,而且也希望在每一个从属句中能够读到。

# 第三部分 形式的简洁

良好的开端,等于成功的一半。

——柏拉图

（Plato）

[ 第七课 ]

# 动 机

问题设置得好,才能解决得顺利。

——约翰·杜威

(John Dewey)

就我的经验而言,看清问题比解决问题更难。

——查尔斯·达尔文

(Charles Darwin)

提出一个问题往往比解决一个问题更重要,因为解决问题也许仅是一个数学或实验技巧而已。而提出新的问题,却需要有创造性的想象力,而且标志着科学的真正进步。

——阿尔伯特·爱因斯坦

(Albert Einstein)

## 动机的内涵

在第二部分,我着重讲了句子和段落的特征,以便使读者的思路更加清晰、连贯,更容易理解。但是,对较大的语篇单位(段落、结构和整篇文章)大书特书,也会对读者关于简洁、连贯和理解的概念造成影响。在第三部分我要讲的就是这些。我首先讨论的是如何写前言。前言写得恰当,读者才能够清楚、连贯地理解下文。

我们如果深入地探讨一个话题,即便再难,也愿意将手头所有的相关资料通读一遍。我们不仅要绞尽脑汁地解读那些高度凝炼的句子,而且还要用已有的知识填补空白,纠正逻辑上的错误,厘清混乱的结构关系。拥有这类读者的作者,与其他作者相比他的优势很明显。

但是大部分作家并不是那么幸运。他们常常面对的读者并不是那么投入或者对该领域不甚了解。如此一来,作家们就不得不以下面两种方式来做准备:

    作家必须激发读者的积极性,使他们愿意认真地读作品。
    作家必须让读者有所期待,这样就能使他们更熟练地阅读作品。

如果我们要阅读的**话题**不仅重要而且有趣,比如从找到一份好工作到探讨生命的起源,那么我们读书的时候会十分认真。

## 在导言部分陈述问题

从计划写作那一刻开始,不要把这项任务当成只是围绕某一话题而展开的写作,或者只将之当成传递你所感兴趣的信息。而是要提出一个**读者**希望被解决的问题。然而,这一问题可能是读者不曾留意或不曾了解的。如果是这样的话,你就会面临一个挑战:你必须事先准备好回答他们偏向提出的"那又怎样"的问题。你要在导言部分将该问题交代清楚,一步到位。这里,你必须激发读者把你提出的问题看作他们自己的问题。

例如,读下面这一导言(所有这些例子都比标准句短很多)。

1a. When college students go out to relax on weekend, many now "binge", downing several alcoholic drinks quickly until they are drunk or even pass out. It is a behavior that has been spreading through colleges and universities across the country, especially at large state universities. It once was done mostly by men, but now even women binge. It has drawn the attention of parents, college administrators, and researchers.

这一导言只提出了一个话题:它没有激励我们去关注它。除非读者已经对此事感兴趣,否则他会感觉无所谓,**那又怎样?谁会关心大学生饮酒过量的事情?**

将下面这个导言与上一个对比会发现：它告诉我们为什么狂欢放纵不仅仅是一个有趣的话题而是一个值得关注的问题：

> 1b. Alcohol has been a big part of college life for hundreds of years. From football weekends to fraternity parties, college students drink and often drink hard. But a new kind of drinking known as "binge" drinking is spreading through our colleges and universities. Bingers drink quickly not to be sociable but to get drunk or even to pass out. Bingeing is far from the harmless fun long associated with college life. In the last six months, it has been cited in at least six deaths, many injuries, and considerable destruction of property. It crosses the line from fun to reckless behavior that kills and injures not just drinkers but those around them. We may not be able to stop bingeing entirely, but we must try to control its worst costs by educating students in how to manage its risks.

虽然简短，但是（1b）包含了大部分导言所涵盖的三部分。每一部分对激励读者阅读起到了一定的作用。这三部分是：

共时语境——问题——方法/要点/主张

> Alcohol has been a big part of college life... drink hard.（共时语境）But a new kind of drinking known as "binge" drinking is spreading... kills and injures not just drinkers but those around them.（问题）We may not be able to stop bingeing entirely, but

we must try to control its worst costs by educating students in how to manage its risks.（方法／要点／主张）

## 第一部分：建立一个共时语境

大部分作品都以共时语境开篇，例如（1b）：

> Alcohol has been a big part of college life for hundreds of years. From football weekends to fraternity parties, college students drink and often drink hard.（共时语境）But a new kind of drinking known as "binge"...

这一共时语境提供了历史背景，不过可能只是一件近来发生的事件、一种普遍的信仰，或者其他能够使读者想起他们所知道的、所经历过的或者已经接受的任何事情。

> 事件：A recent State U survey showed that 80% of first-year students engaged in underage drinking in their first month on campus, a fact that should surprise no one.（共时语境）But what is worrisome is the spread among first-year students of a new kind of drinking known as "binge"...

> 信仰：Most students believe that college is a safe place to drink for those who live on or near campus. And for the most part they are right.（共时语境）But for those students who get caught up in the new trend of "binge" drinking,...

各种形式的共时语境对于激励读者去阅读起着特殊作用，在（1b）中，我想让读者在思考滥饮问题时，将之放在似乎不存在任何争议的语境中，那我就能顺理成章地提出质疑了。实际上，我有意在诱导读者，让他们认为自己了解整个故事，但事实并非如此。"但是"这个词标志着接下来的限制条件：

> ... drink and often drink hard.（共时语境）BUT a new kind of drinking known as "binge" drinking is spreading...

换句话说，大学饮酒看似是没有问题的，但事实并非如此。"but"所引起的诧异激励着读者继续阅读。

许多有经验的作者经常不设置共时语境，而以一个看似正确的事实开头，然后论证它的合理性，或者予以否定。读者可以在报纸、杂志尤其是学术期刊上看到无数个这样的例子。在这里，开篇的语境可以是一句话或者两句话。在期刊中，也可以是长达几段的文献综述。文献综述是一项研究者已做的调查，作者将会对此进行证明或修正。

不是每一篇文章的开篇都设置了共时语境。一些文章直接跳到导言的第二部，即陈述问题。

## 第二部分：陈述问题

如果作者以共时语境来开篇，她通常会用 but 或者 however 这样的词引出问题：

> Alcohol has been a big part of college life for hundreds

of years. From football weekends to fraternity parties, college students drink and often drink hard.（共时语境）**But** a kind of drinking known as "binge" drinking is spreading through our colleges and universities. Bingers drink quickly not to be sociable but to get drunk or even to pass out. Bingeing is far from the harmless fun long associated with college life. In the last six months, it has been cited in at least six deaths, many injuries, and considerable destruction of property. It crosses the line from fun to reckless behavior that kills and injures not just drinkers but those around them.（问题）We may not be able to…

**问题的两个部分**　为了让读者思考所提出的问题，文章必须包含以下两个部分：

第一部分设置某种**情境**：恐怖主义、学费增长、酗酒等可能会引起麻烦的潜在的任何事情。

第二部分陈述该情境产生的**让人难以忍受的结果**，这是读者不愿付出的**代价**。

激励读者阅读的正是这样的代价。由于此代价会使读者感到不快，所以他们希望根除或至少减轻这一代价。恐怖主义的代价是伤亡；学费增长的代价意味着掏更多的钱。如果学费增长没有让父母和学生感到不快，那么它就不是问题了。

如果对读者的质疑稍加思考，你就能够确定该问题将会产生

什么样的后果了。下面就要回答读者的质疑,同时也就发现了该问题所产生的后果:

> But a kind of drinking known as "binge" drinking is spreading through our colleges and universities. Bingers drink quickly not to be sociable but to get drunk or even to pass out.(条件)So what? **Bingeing is far from the harmless fun long associated with college life. In the last six months, it has been cited in at least six deaths, many injuries, and considerable destruction of property. It crosses the line from fun to reckless behavior that kills and injures not just drinkers but those around them.**(条件产生的代价)

问题的条件是酗酒,代价是伤害和死亡。如果酗酒没有代价,那就不算是问题了。识别问题之前,读者要把情境和后果综合考虑。

**两类问题:实践问题和观念问题** 问题可分为两类,不同的问题以不同的方式激励读者。你需要将其分别陈述出来。

**实践**问题与某一情境相关,它要求为了解决问题而付诸**行动**。大学生酗酒,对自己造成伤害,就是一个实践性问题。

**观念**问题与我们对某事的看法有关,它要求为了解决问题而改变观念。我们不知道为什么学生会酗酒,这就是一个观念性问题。

学界外的作者提出的常常是实践问题,学界内的作者提出的常常是观念问题。

**实践问题：我们应该怎么做？** 之所以把酗酒归结为实践问题，有两个原因：第一，这一问题涉及让读者感到不愉快的明显后果。第二，为了解决这一问题，人们必须采取不同的行动。如果这些问题不能回避，我们就必须采取行动，来改变这一状况，由此来根除或者减轻问题所产生的后果。

我们通常用一两个词来指称实践问题：**癌症**、**失业**、**酗酒**。但这是一种速记的方法。这些词只是指出了**情境**，并不涉及代价。大部分情境听起来很麻烦，但是如果**任何事情**的后果让读者不快，这件事情就会成为问题的情境。但是如果中彩票会让人承受丧友或丧亲之痛，那么这件事就变成了一个实践性问题。

你可能认为诸如酗酒之类问题的后果过于明显，因而不必陈述，但是读者的看法或许与你不同。不同的读者看到的后果可能也不同：在你看到会有伤亡的地方，大学发言人可能只会想到负面新闻：**这些酗酒的学生使学校成了聚众酗酒的场所，损害了学校在家长心中的形象**。还有更多麻木的读者可能根本看不到代价：**如果大学生受伤了或者自杀了，那又怎样？跟我有什么关系？** 这样一来，你就不得不指出，如何让此类读者明白该后果会对他们产生怎样的影响。如若不能清楚描述那些**对读者产生影响**的代价，读者就没理由关心你所写的内容。

**观念问题：我们应该思考些什么？** 观念问题和实践问题一样分为两部分：情境和代价。而除此之外，这两类问题完全不同。

观念问题的情境通常指我们不知道或者不理解的事情。

我们可以把此情境用一个问题来表达：宇宙的重量是多少？为什么头发能不停地生长，而腿上的汗毛却不是如此？

观念问题的后果，不是从疼痛、苦恼或损失中感受到明显的不愉快，而是因为不理解某些重要的事情而产生的不满。

我们可以把这个后果表述为更重要的、读者却不知道的事情，正如下面这个较为宏大的问题：

Cosmologists do not know how much the universe weighs.（条件）**So what?** Well, if they knew, they might figure out something more important: Will time and space go on forever, or end, and if they do, when and how?（代价／更大的问题）

Biologists don't know why some hair keeps growing and other hair stops.（条件）**So what?** If they knew, they might understand something more important: What turns growth on and off?（代价／更大的问题）

Administrators do not know why students underestimate the risks of binge drinking.（条件）**So what?** If they knew, they might figure out something more important: Would better information at orientation help students make safer decisions about drinking?（代价／更大的问题）

正如最后一个例子谈到的那样，有时候读者也不知如何处理较为宏大的问题。但这仍然是一个观念性的问题，因为它与我们所不知道的东西相关；也因为信息而非行动，才是解决该问题的关键。

试想：对一个观念性的问题而言，你先回答一个小问题，其答案有助于回答更宏大、更重要的问题。由于小问题的重要性蕴含在大问题之中，读者因此受到激励。

如果小问题的答案不能帮助解决更大更重要的问题，那么这个小问题就没有价值。下面这一问题看上去不太可能帮助我们理解任何重要的事情：What color were Lincoln's socks when he delivered the Gettysburg Address?（林肯在葛底斯堡发表演说时穿的袜子是什么颜色？）但下面这个问题可能就有价值：How did Lincoln plan this Address?（林肯是如何设计这次演讲的？）如果我们知道这一问题的答案，我们可能会了解到更重要的信息：林肯安排事情很有创造性。

> **要点** 像读者一样，作为作者的你通常也更容易受到宏大问题的激励。但是有限的资源，如时间、资金、知识、技能、篇幅等，使你不能满意地解决问题。所以你不得不找一个你能回答的问题。当计划写论文的时候，千万要找一个合适的问题，而是要找到一个小到你能够回答的问题，但它又与另一个足够大、能引起你和读者关注的问题相关。

> **快速提示** 有的学生认为，如果老师指定了一个具体话题，他们就不需要再陈述问题了，但是他们这样想是错的。如果作业中包括 discuss（讨论）、explain（解释）或者 analyze（分析）这类词，你就需要找出作业背后隐含的问题。如果在作业中只是陈述了问题但不涉及它的意义，那么你要做的就是找到"为什么会这样"的答案。如果你在论文的开头提出了一个完整的问题，那么你的论文会更好写，也更容易被读者接受。

> **快速提示** 当阅读学术著作或者论文的时候，首先在问题陈述部分找出隐含的问题，然后找出对该问题做了回答的主要陈述部分。答案能够帮助你把注意力放在阅读上。如果你在导言部分没有找到问题，那么就去结论部分找。如果还没有找到，那就先找主要论述，然后问自己：回答的是什么问题？为什么作者告诉你某些事情，你对此理解得越透彻，就越能理解他所写的内容。

## 第三部分：陈述解决方法

解决方法是你的主要观点或者主张。实践性问题和观念性问题的解决方法不同。解决实践性问题需要采取行动：读者（或者某人）必须**改变他们所做的事情**。解决观念性问题需要获知信息：读者（或者某人）必须**改变他们的想法**。你所给出的小问题的答案有助于读者理解较宏大的问题。

**实践性问题** 为了解决实践性问题，你必须建议读者（或者某人）做些事情来改变某一状况：

... behavior that crosses the line from fun to recklessness that kills and injures not just drinkers but those around them.（问题）**We may not be able to stop bingeing entirely, but we must try to control its worst costs by educating students in how to manage its risks.**（方法／要点）

**观念性问题** 为了解决观念性问题，你必须陈述一些作者想让读者理解或者相信的事情：

... we can better understand not only the causes of this dangerous behavior but also the nature of risk-taking behavior in general.（问题）**This study reports on our analysis of the beliefs of 300 first-year college students. We found that students were more likely to binge if they knew more stories of other students bingeing, so that they believed that bingeing is far more common that it actually is.**（方法／要点）

正如达尔文和爱因斯坦所说的，提出一个好的问题是最难的，因为没有一个好的问题，就不会有一个值得支持的答案。

## 另一个部分："序曲"

你可能会想起，有人曾告诉过你用一个简练的引语、事实或者轶事开篇来"引起读者的注意"。最能引人注意的是有待解决的问题，但是醒目的开篇能够生动地把主题引到问题中。我们可以用一个音乐术语来称呼这一方法：**序曲**。自然科学和社会科学领域中几乎没有作家使用序曲。人文科学中"序曲"（意即"序言"，下文均采用这一译法）使用得比较普遍，最常见的是用在为公众写作的时候。

以下三个序言可以在酗酒狂欢论文中确立关键主题。

**1. 一条引语**

"If you're old enough to fight for your country, you're old enough to drink to it."

**2. 一个令人震惊的事实**

A recent study reports that at most colleges three out of four students "binged" at least once in the previous thirty days, consuming more than five drinks at a sitting. Almost half binge once a week, and those who binge most are not just members of fraternities but their officers.

**3. 一件解说性的轶事**

When Jim S., president of Omega Alpha, accepted a dare from his fraternity brothers to down a pint of whiskey in one long swallow, he didn't plan to become this year's eighth college fatality from alcohol poisoning.

我们可以把这三个结合起来：

It is often said that "if you're old enough to fight for your country, you're old enough to drink to it."（引文）Tragically, Jim S., president of Omega Alpha, no longer has a chance to do either. When he accepted a dare from his fraternity brothers to down a pint whiskey in one long swallow, he didn't expect to become this year's eighth college fatality from alcohol poisoning.（趣闻）According to a recent study, at most colleges, three out of four students have, like Jim, drunk five drinks at a sitting in the last thirty days. And those who drink the most are not just members of fraternities but—like Jim S.—officers.（明显的事实）

Drinking, of course, has been a part of American college life since the first college opened...（共时语境）But in recent years...（问题）

下面是导言的总体规划：

| 序言 |
| --- |
| 共时语境 |
| 问题 [情境 + 后果] |
| 方法 / 要点 / 主张 |

## 导言部分的诊断与修改

为了判断导言在多大程度上激励了读者,你必须做到以下几点:

**1. 确定你提出的是一个实践性问题还是一个观念性问题。** 你想让读者做什么,还是想让他们思考什么。

**2. 在导言之后做一个提纲。** 如果导言写得太长,你的读者就不能快速地完成阅读。这样一来,他们可能会漏读你所提出的问题和解决方法(即论文要点)。

**3. 把导言分为三部分:共时语境+问题+方法/要点/主张。** 如果你不能迅速地确定这三部分,你的导言可能会显得没有重点。

**4. 确定共时语境之后的第一句话的第一个单词是 but、however,或者此类转折词,以此来表示你质疑前面的看法。** 如果你没有明确指出共时语境和问题之间的鲜明对比,那么读者可能会忽略它。

**5. 把问题分成两部分:情境和后果。**

**5a. 情境是否与问题相符?**

如果你提出的是一个实践性问题,那么就需要一个产生明显后果的情境。

如果你提出的是一个观念性问题,那么就需要一个未知的或未被理解的情境。问题通常不应该用直接的方式提出,What causes bingeing? 而是用一种我们所不理解的态度提出:

But we don't know why bingers ignore known risks.

**5b. 后果是否恰当地回答了 So what？这样的提问？**

如果你提出的是一个实践性问题，回答 So what？这一提问时必须陈述清楚引起不快的情境所产生的明显后果。

如果你提出的是一个观念性问题，回答 So what？这一问题时必须陈述某些未知的或未被理解的重要事情。

**6. 用下划线标出方法 / 要点 / 主张**。这一部分应该放在导言结尾的重要位置，并且应该阐述清楚论文剩余部分的关键主题（第八课会有详细讲解）。

# 结论

好的导言能够激励读者，引出关键的主题、陈述要点、阐明问题的解决方法。导言写得直白，读者就能较快地把文章剩余部分读完，并且较好地理解文章。好的结尾会产生不一样的结果：作为读者最后阅读的部分，结论应该结合作者的观点、其重要性以及它的含义，以此来深入思考问题。结论比导言更多样化，但必要时可以把导言的几个部分和结论联系在一起，只是调整一下顺序：

**1. 结论开头要陈述（重述）主旨观点、论文的主张和问题的解决方法：**

Though we can come at the problem of bingeing from

several directions, the most important is education, especially in the first week of a student's college life. But that means each university must devote time and resources to it.

**2.** 如果可以的话，应该以一种新的方式来回答 **So what?** 的提问，以此来解释这个问题的重要性。如果你不能做到这一点，那么就再次陈述导言提到的观点，下面这个例子就显示了这种优势：

If we do not start to control bingeing soon, many more students will die.

If we start to control bingeing now, we will save many lives.

**3.** 再提出一个更深入的有待解决的问题。回答 **Now what**？

Of course, even if we can control bingeing, the larger issue of risk-taking in general will remain a serious problem.

**4.** 用一个与序言相呼应的轶事、引言或事实做结尾。我们用另外一个音乐术语称之为后奏（这一用法常常出现在大众写作中，很少出现在自然科学和社会科学中）：

We should not underestimate how deeply entrenched bingeing is: We might have hoped that after Jim S.'s death from alcohol poisoning, his university would have taken steps to prevent more such tragedies. Sad to say, it reported another death from bingeing this month.

写结论的方法有很多种,如果不知如何下手,不妨试试上面这种方式。

## 自我检测

### 练习 7.1

———✥———

做这个练习时,你可以选择那些已经完成的或者未完成的作品。在每一篇选文中,区分清楚问题和方法,用横线画出情境,用括号标出后果。确定这一问题是实践性问题还是观念性问题,然后把观念性问题改写成实践性问题,把实践性问题改写成观念性问题。你需要对哪部分进行修改?和其他方式比起来,用这种方式重写问题更简单?为什么?

### 练习 7.2

———✥———

相比导言其他部分,作者在做问题陈述时更费力,尤其是从事学术写作的作者。他们知道自己想表达什么,但是不知道其他人应该关注的原因。或者情况更糟:他们以为读者会像他们一样关注这些问题。(有时候学生认为他们不需要陈述问题,因为老师已经指定了话题,但是事实并非如此。)作者的确会纠结于这些问题。为了陈述问题,作者不仅要弄清楚他们自己的想法,

还要清楚读者的动机。这一练习会对你有所帮助。刚着手一项写作时,试尝下面的练习:

1. 在句子中写清楚话题:In this paper I am writing about _____.(比如,丁尼生的诗歌《悼念集》中的科学问题、公民联合诉讼联邦选举委员会选举筹资案的影响,再比如,哥伦比亚航天飞机的事故)。

2. 在句子中写清楚,为什么你从那么多可选范围中挑出了这一特定话题:I care about my topic because _____.(如果不能完成这句话,你需要再想想或者选另外一个的话题。如果连你自己都不知道为什么这么做的话,就别指望读者对其能给予关注了。)

3. 在句子中写清楚你的**主要观点**或者**主张**:The point I want to make about [ topic ] is that _____.

4. 在一段话中,描述一下那个会对你的想法感兴趣的人(真实的或者虚构的)。她(或者他)长得什么样?做什么工作的?个人兴趣是什么?最近两个月读了些什么书?

5. 现在,给刚才你所描述的那个人写一封简短的信,向她解释一下为什么应该关注你的论文。

在这封信中你可能会发现一些短语或想法,你可以把这些短语或想法用在问题陈述里。

## 练习 7.3

———❧———

让读者用 186—187 页上的步骤分析你所写的一个导言:

1. 确定这个问题是实践性的还是观念性的。

2. 在导言的末尾写一个提纲。

3. 把导言分成三部分：共时语境、问题和方法／要点／主张。导言中有这三部分吗？顺序是否正确？

4. 圈出那些质疑共时语境的词组（通常是 but 或者 however 这样的词）。

5. 把问题分成两部分：情境和后果。后果是否回答了 So what？这样的问题？

6. 在方法／要点／主张下划线。

如果读者在哪一步遇到了困难，做相应的修改。

## 总结

你可以用导言来促进有目的的阅读。导言中需要陈述读者想知道答案的问题。

对于实践性问题而言，重点是讲清楚问题的后果，这样读者就不会再问 So what? 而是会问 What do we do? 下面这个方案告诉我们该如何提出实践性问题：

| | |
|---|---|
| Alcohol has been a part of college life for hundreds of years. From football weekends to fraternity parties, college students drink and often drink hard.（共时语境） | 导言部分以**共时语境**开头，对接下来要证明或否定的内容进行简述。 |
| But a kind of drinking known as "binge" drinking is spreading through our colleges and universities. Bingers drink quickly not to be sociable but to get drunk or even to pass out. [ *So what?* ]（条件） | 接下来陈述问题的情境，该部分用 **but**、**however**、**on the other hand** 等词引导。然后设想一下问题的严重性（**So what?**）。 |

| | |
|---|---|
| Bingeing is far from harmless. In the last six months, it has been cited in six deaths, many injuries, and considerable destruction of property. It crosses the line from fun to reckless behavior that kills and injures not just drinkers but those around them. (代价) | 陈述这一情境所带来的后果及读者不想付出的代价,以此来解答设想的那个严重后果(**So what?**)。 |
| We may not be able to stop bingeing entirely, but we must try to control its worst costs by educating students in how to manage its risks. (解决方法) | 用问题的解决方法做结尾,这一方法一般是能够根除或至少减轻后果的**行动**。 |

就观念性问题而言,重点是讲清楚值得解决的小问题,因为这个小的问题能帮助解决一个更大更重要的问题。下面这个方案告诉我们该如何提出观念性问题:

| | |
|---|---|
| Colleges are reporting that binge drinking is increasing. We know its practical risks. We also know that bingers ignore those risks, even after they have learned about them. (共时语境) | 导言部分以**共时语境**开头,对接下来要证明或否定的内容进行简述。 |
| But we don't know what causes bingers to ignore the known risks: social influences, a personality attracted to risk, or a failure to understand the nature of the risks. [ So what? ] (条件/首先发现的,小问题) | 接下来是陈述问题的情境,该部分用 **but**、**however**、**on the other hand** 等词引导。陈述一些未知的或未被理解的事情。然后设想一下问题的严重后果(**So what?**) |

> If we can determine why bingers ignore known risks of their actions, we can better understand not only the causes of this dangerous behavior but also the nature of risks-taking behavior in general.（代价/思考后发现的，较大的问题）

> In this study, we analyzed the beliefs of 300 first-year college students to determine... We found that...（方法）

利用这一情境所产生的后果解答设想的那个 So what?，该情境是一个更大或更重要的、未知的或未被理解的问题，如果我们知道第一题的答案，可能就可以解决这一问题。

用陈述解决问题的方法结束导言，该方法是第一个问题的答案，也有助于回答第二个问题。

[ 第八课 ]

# 整体连贯

> 写作最困难的事情之一就是写第一段。我曾经花费了好几个月来写第一段，写完第一段之后，剩下的部分就很轻松地写出来了。因为第一段中解决了书中大部分的问题，确定了主题、风格、语调。
>
> ——加布里埃尔·加西亚·马尔克斯
> （Gabriel Garcia Márquez）

## 文章结构是如何影响阅读的

上一课,我阐释了必须写一个包含两个要点的导言的方法:

通过陈述读者感兴趣的问题来激励读者。

陈述下文中要表达的观点和主要概念,以此来构思文章的其他部分。

本课中,我将解释如何把上述第二点运用到文章的各部分、各小节,甚至每个段落中。与清晰(clear)这个术语一样,我们同样不能在书本中找到"连贯的"这个术语的具体所指。连贯是我们在阅读过程中形成的一种自我体验。

我们在纸面上寻找的是一些标记,它们能帮助我们了解学过的知识属于文章的哪部分,以及如何将学过的知识整合在一起。为了帮助读者这样做,可以有意地做一些标记。

### 预测主题,实现连贯

在第五课和第六课中,我们探讨了一些能够帮助读者实现段落间"局部"连贯的技巧,但是为了抓住整篇文章的连贯性,读者需要更多的技巧。为了帮助读者达到这个目的，作者可以采用一个惯用的原则：每篇文章、各个大章节及各个小节均以一小段简明且易掌握的文字开头，这个段落陈述了观点，介绍了主题，读者以此来组织文章的剩余部分。然后，在文章的主体部分，作者的工作就是支撑、展开论证或者解释在第一部分中提出的观点和主题。

为了帮助读者抓住文章整体和局部的连贯性，作者需要遵循以下原则：

**整体连贯：**

  1. 读者必须知道导言部分是在什么地方结束的，主体是从什么地方开始的。同时也要了解前一章节是在什么地方结束的，下一章节是从什么地方开始的。用一个标题来识别每个新章节的开头，这个标题包括该部分的关键主题（见下面第 5 条）。如果你所研究的领域不使用标题，在终稿时就将其删除。

  2. 在导言部分的结尾，读者会寻找陈述下文主题的要点或问题的解决方法。如果有恰当的理由把要点留在结论部分，那么你要在导言部分的结尾放一个句子，该句既保证读者会在下文读到要点，**同时**也陈述了核心思想。

  3. 在主体部分，读者会寻找出现在导言结尾的那些作为主题的概念，并用这些概念形成他们对整篇文章的理解。您要确保有规律地重复这些主题。

**局部连贯：**

4. 读者要找出一个引导大章节或者小节的部分。

5. 在这个引导性的部分结尾，读者一般要找出一句话，该句话既陈述了这一章节的**要点**，又陈述了具体的概念，这些概念会成为该部分鲜明的主题。

6. 在这一章的主体中，读者经常要找出介绍性部分结尾里作为主题的概念，并用这些概念来形成对这一章节的理解。你要确保有规律地重复这些概念。

> **快速提示** 可以把这六条原则应用在一篇较难的文章中。首先，强调问题陈述中的疑问和解答该疑问的主张（参考176—182页）。然后，在每一个章节中，强调导言、观点和主要概念。如果在该章节的导言部分没有找到这些，那就到这一章节的结尾去找。最后，通读所强调的部分。当细读这些时，脑海中会有一个整体概念，这能够帮助读者较好地理解和记住剩余部分。

由于篇幅有限，我不能用整篇文章甚至是一些篇幅长的章节来解释这六条原则。所以我会用几段文字来解释，并要求你把这些段落的结构同文章的整体部分联系起来。

例如，读下面一段话：

1a. Thirty sixth-grade students wrote essays that were analyzed to determine the effectiveness of eight weeks of training to distinguish fact from opinion. That ability is an important aspect of making sound arguments of any kind. In an essay written before instruction began, the writers failed almost completely to distinguish fact from opinion. In an essay written after four weeks of instruction, the students visibly attempted to distinguish fact from opinion, but did so inconsistently. In three more essays, they distinguished fact from opinion more consistently, but never achieved the predicted level of performance. In a final essay written six months after instruction ended, they did no better than they did in their pre-instruction essays. Their training had some effect on their writing during the instruction period, but it was inconsistent, and six months after instruction it had no measurable effect.

前几个句子引出了整篇文章的意思,但是在这几个句子中找不到下面这样的重要概念:**inconsistently, never achieved, no better, no measurable effect**。这些词在整篇文章中起着很重要的作用。更糟糕的是,直到文章结尾,我们才读到要点:training had no long-term effect(训练没有产生长期的效果)。当读文章时,我们发现文章似乎很零乱,直到结尾我们才意识到,为了掌握这段文字的内容,我们需要知道什么。但是我们却付出了许多本不该付出的努力。

比较下面这一版本:

1b. In this study, thirty sixth-grade students were taught to distinguish fact from opinion. They did so successfully during the instruction period, but the effect was inconsistent and less than predicted, and six months after instruction ended, the instruction had no measurable effect. In an essay written before instruction began, the writers failed almost completely to distinguish fact from opinion. In an essay written after four weeks of instruction, the students visibly attempted to distinguish fact from opinion, but did so inconsistently. In three more essays, they distinguished fact from opinion more consistently, but never achieved the predicted level of performance. In a final essay written six months after instruction ended, they did no better than they did in their pre-instruction essay. We thus conclude that short-term training to distinguish fact from opinion has no consistent or long-term effect.

在1（b）中，我们很快就明白了前两个句子引出了下文。从第二个句子中，我们发现了两件事情：文章的要点（划线句子）和关键词（黑体）。

1b. In this study, thirty sixth-grade students were taught to distinguish fact from opinion. <u>They did so successfully during the instruction period, but the</u> **effect was inconsistent and less than predicted**<u>,</u> and six months after instruction ended, the instruction had **no measurable effect.**（本文的要点）

这样做的结果是，我们感觉文章衔接得更好了，并且可以更好地理解文章。

试想有这样两篇文章：一篇的每一章节和整个文章的观点都写在了**结尾**（例如 1a），并且每个开头都没有引导下文要讲的重点概念。另一篇的每一个观点都写在了每段、每个章节以及整篇文章的**开头部分**（例如 1b）。哪篇文章读起来更简单易懂？当然是第二篇。那么就记住以下原则吧：

把观点性的句子放在简短的开篇部分的结尾，在读者开始读接下来更长更复杂的部分之前，确保这是读者读到的**最后一句**。

在一个段落中，开头部分可能只是一个简单的句子，所以默认为这是读者在读下文之前读到的最后一个句子。如果该文章的导言是由两句话组成的（如 1b），那么你要确保该段的要点是第二句话，这句话仍是读者在读下文之前读到的最后一句话。

至于章节部分，导言可以是一段话或者几段话。就整篇文章而言，可能需要好几段话才能把导言表述清楚。即使是在这些情况下，无论要点句子有多长，也要把它放在开头部分的结尾。在读者开始读接下来更长更复杂的部分之前确保要点句子是他们读到的最后一句话。

没有经验的作者认为，如果他们将要点从导言部分删除的话，读者可能会感到厌倦不愿再读下去了。这个想法是不对的。如果能用一个有意思的问题激励读者，读者会想知道如何来解决这一问题的。

> **要点** 要想写读者认为连贯性很强的文章，就要用简短的、容易理解的介绍性部分引出每个大章节、小节以及整篇文章。在开头部分的结尾，用一句话陈述清楚每一单元的要点和下文会提到的重要概念。这一要点性句子构成了文章的大致轮廓以及逻辑结构。如果读者没有读到这些，他们会认为文章没有连贯性。

**连贯性的另外两个要求**

如果知道了要点的话，我们就能够理解所读到的任何东西。但是为了使文章实现连贯性，我们必须了解另外两个要求。

**1. 读者必须了解，章节或整篇文章中的每句话是如何与要点相联系的。** 看下面一段文章：

> We analyzed essays written by sixth-grade students to determine the effectiveness of training in distinguishing fact from opinion. In an essay written before training, the students failed almost completely to distinguish fact and opinion. These essays were also badly organized in several ways. In the first two essays after training began, the students attempted to distinguish fact from opinion, but did so inconsistently. They also produced

fewer spelling and punctuation errors. In the essays four through seven, they distinguished fact from opinion more consistently, but in their final essay, written six months after completion of instruction, they did no better than they did in their first essay. Their last essay was significantly longer than their first one, however. Their training thus had some effect on their writing during the training period, but it was inconsistent and transient.

这些关于拼写、文章的组织结构和长度的句子在这里起什么作用？如果读者没有发现句子和要点之间的关系，他们可能会断定自己读到的东西并不连贯。

我恐怕不能给出一个简单的关联规则，因为它太抽象了。我只能罗列出一些最重要的因素。如果句子中包含以下内容，那就说明它和要点是相关联的：

背景或语境

各章节和整篇文章的要点

支撑要点的理由

支撑理由的证据、事实或者数据

对推理过程和方法的说明

对其他视角的考量

**2.** 读者必须了解文章的各个部分是如何安排的。读者不仅想看他们读到的每句话是如何与要点相联系的，还想看各部分的排列遵循什么原则。下面我们来看三类排列顺序：时间顺序、并列顺序和逻辑顺序。

**时间顺序**　这是最简单的排列顺序，按年代由远及近（或者由近及远），可用来表达叙事或者因果关系。用 first、then、finally 这类词表示时间；用 as a result、because、of that 等词表示因果关系。综述类的文章常用这类排列顺序。

**并列顺序**　如果两个或者更多章节论述的是同一观点，那么它们就是并列关系。There are three reasons why... 根据重要性、复杂性等将这些章节按顺序排列，使读者易于理解。然后用 first、second... 或者 also、another、more important、in addition 等词组标记这种关系。这就是这一部分的顺序。

**逻辑顺序**　这是最复杂的顺序：由特例到一般（或者由一般到特例），由前提到结论（或者由结论到前提），或者由肯定到否定。用 for example、on the other hand、it follows that 等词组表示逻辑关系。

> **快速提示**　作者常常以时间关系来组织文章，因为这样最简单。当初稿完成时，先通读一遍，看它是不是按照自己的想法组织起来的。如果是，想想如何进行修改。大部分读者对作者思考问题的过程并不感兴趣，他们感兴趣的是思考的结果。

## 关于段落

真正困难的是，要让所有的段落都遵循下述原则：

用一两句简短易于理解的句子开篇。

在导言部分的最后用一句话中陈述段落的**要点**（传统上来说段落的要点就是话题）。如果文章的导言只有一句话，这句话就默认为是要点句。

在观点性句子的结尾，说出贯穿全文的重要主题。

问题是，并非所有的段落都遵循这种整齐的结构，我们也能够读懂那些结构安排不恰当的段落。我们可以忽略一些起特殊作用的小段落，比如过渡段或者旁白，因为我们读（或者写）这样的段落没有问题。但是很多包含六七句话甚至更多的重要段落似乎也没有明显的设计原则。即使这样，我们仍可以从中找到引领全文的开头部分。但它可能不包括**要点**——要点可能在后文，通常在结尾处。但是第一个句子或者前两个句子引领全文，引出关键性术语。通常这就足够了。

例如，比较下面两个段落：

2a. The team obtained exact sequences of fossils—new lines of antelopes, giraffes, and elephants developing out of old and appearing in younger strata, then dying out as they were replaced by others in still later strata. The most specific sequences they reconstructed were several lines of pigs that had been common at the site and had developed rapidly. The team produced family trees that dated types of pigs so accurately that when they found pigs next to fossils of questionable age, they could use the pigs to date the fossils. But mapping every fossil precisely, the team was able to recreate exactly how and when the animals in a whole ecosystem evolved.

2b. By precisely mapping every fossil they found, the team was able to recreate exactly how and when the animals in a whole ecosystem evolved. They charted new lines of antelopes, giraffes, and elephants developing out of old and appearing in younger strata, then dying out as they were replaced by others in still later strata. The most exact sequences they reconstructed were several lines of pigs that had been common at the site and had developed rapidly. The team produced family trees that dated types of pigs so accurately that when they found pigs next to fossils of questionable age, they could use the pigs to date the fossils.

段落（2a）把要点放在了最后一句话，段落（2b）却把它放在了第一句。但是如果（2a）（关于化石搜寻者及其工作）是用一种连贯的方式表达的话，我们理解起来就没有什么大问题了。

以上只是强调了清楚、准确且有用地引出下文的重要性。如果读者在读某一章节时知道其要点，他们可以以他们的方式读几段写得并不是很好的文章。但是如果他们并不清楚这些段落是在讲什么，那么不管单个的段落写得多么好，读者都会感到无所适从。

## 清晰性基本原则

这一基本原则适用于单个句子、重要段落、章节，以及整篇文章：

读者判断作品的各个部分是否表述清楚的依据是：该段落是否以读者能够读懂的简短语句开头，以及该段是否传达出了下文的意思。

简单句中，简短易懂的语句是主语／话题。比较下面两句话：

1a. <u>Resistance in Nevada against its use as a waste disposal site</u> has been heated.

1b. <u>Nevada</u> HAS heatedly RESISTED its use as a waste disposal site.

在复杂句中，简短易懂的语句是表达了句子的**要点**的**主要从句**。比较下面两句话：

2a. Greater knowledge of pre-Columbian civilizations and the effect of European colonization destroying their societies by inflicting on them devastating diseases has led to a historical reassessment of Columbus' role in world history.

2b. Historians are reassessing Columbus'role in world history, because they know more about pre-Columbian civilizations and how European colonization destroyed their societies by inflicting on them devastating diseases.

段落（2a）的要点在句尾。在段落（2b）中，开篇从句陈述了整个句子的要点，其最重要的主张是：**Historians are reassessing Columbus' role...** 该主张由下文中更长更复杂的从句支撑。

在一个段落中，简短易懂的部分是一两个段首句，它们既表达了段落的要点，又引出了主要概念。比较下列两段话：

3a. Thirty sixth-grade students wrote essays that were analyzed to determine the effectiveness of eight weeks of training to distinguish fact from opinion. That ability is an important aspect of making sound arguments of any kind. In an essay written before instruction began, the writers failed almost completely to distinguish fact from opinion. In an essay written after four weeks of instruction, the students visibly attempted to distinguish fact from opinion, but did so inconsistently. In three more essays, they distinguish fact from opinion more consistently, but never achieved the predicted level. In a final essay written six months after instruction ended, they did no better than they did in their pre-instruction essay. Their training had some effect on their writing during the instruction period, but it was inconsistent, and six months after instruction it had no measurable effect.

3b. <u>In this study, thirty six-grade students were taught to distinguish fact from opinion.</u> They did so **successfully** during the instruction period, but the effect was **inconsistent** and **less than predicted**, and six months after instruction ended, the instruction had **no measurable effect**. （开篇句/观点） In an essay written before instruction began, the writers failed almost completely to distinguish fact from opinion. In an essay written after four weeks of instruction, the students visibly attempted to distinguish fact from opinion, but did so inconsistently. In three more essays, they distinguished fact from opinion more consistently, but never achieved the predicted level. In a final essay written six months after instruction ended, they did no better than they did in their pre-instruction essays. We thus conclude that short-term training to distinguish fact from opinion has no consistent or long term effect.

段落（3a）的开头部分不清晰，且没有陈述该段的关键主题。段落（3b）的开头部分清晰且讲明了观点，并且清楚地陈述了该段的关键主题。

在章、节中，简短易懂的部分可能只是一个段落。在较长的篇章中，这一部分可能也相应地长一些。即使这样，段落的结尾仍要表达该段的要点且引出下文的关键概念。由于篇幅有限，我就不再解释如何在一个几段长的文章中使用这一原则了。但这种情况不难设想。

在一整篇文章中，开头部分可能会长达一段或者几段，也可能长达几页。即使这样，总体来说，这一部分应该比文章主体部分短很多。开头部分的最后一句话应陈述清楚整篇文章的要点并且引出关键概念。

> **快速提示** 合理安排好起草和修改的时间，以便能够把大部分时间用在各个开头部分：整篇文章的导言、主要章节的导言、小章节的导言、长段落的导言以及句子的开头。把开头弄清楚了，剩下的部分自然就容易了。

## 千篇一律写作方式的失与得

有些作者担心，这样千篇一律地写作会抑制他们的创新能力，并且让读者感到厌倦。如果在写一篇文学类的作品时，作者所表达的是自己的思想，而读者正好有时间和耐心沿着你跌宕起伏的思路走，那么这样考虑是有道理的。如果写的是这类作品，读者正好又是这样的人群，那么只管写就行了。不用被我在这里讲的这些条条框框所限制。

然而，大多数情况下，我们大部分人读书的目的是为了了解我们需要知道的东西，而不是为了审美的乐趣。如果遵循了这本书中第二部分和第三部分所探讨的清晰性和连贯性原则，那么就能把读者引导到美学方向上。

对你来说，这样的写作方式似乎显得老套，可能你太拘泥于这个形式了。但是它却很得许多读者的青睐，因为这些读者几乎没有时间阅读、理解以及记忆每一件他们必须要做到的事情，因为在任何情况下，他们更关注的是对作品内容的理解，而不是对作品形式的评论。

## 自我检测

### 练习 8.1

清晰性的一个基本原则是，语篇的任何一个部分——句子、段落、章节、整篇文章——应该以一个简短的部分开头，以引入并构建更长、更复杂的下文。找出你的一篇文章，研究每一章。在简短的部分划线，圈出划线部分表明关键主题的那些词。如果找不到，就修改你的文章，然后用这种方法逐段检查。

### 练习 8.2

为了体会一篇文章（或者一个章节）的连贯性，读者需要知道这篇文章是如何组织的（参考 203—204 页）。但是作者，尤其是在前几次起草的时候，通常以一种最简单的方式组织文章，而不是以一种有利于读者的方式来组织。具体来说，他们经常理所当然地用时间顺序或者叙事的结构来写文章。你会发现他们为什么这么做。当把想法落实到纸上的时候，对作者来说，简单地叙述想法或研究是最容易的。但读者最想要的是理解作者的观点，而不是自己去探索。因此，为了实现整体连贯性，需要把文章的时间顺序或叙事结构转变成并列顺序或逻辑结构。读者可以帮你做到这一点。

仔细研究一篇按照时间顺序所写的文章或文章的一个部分，逐段地标出你的观点，然后把它们抄在检索卡片上。打乱这些卡片的顺序，将其发放给读者。让读者对其进行排序。用读者排列的顺序重新组织你的文章。如此，你需要做哪些修改呢？

# 总结

用这个模板设计段落、章节以及整篇文章：

> Researchers have made strides in the **early and accurate diagnosis** of *Alzheimer's*, [ but those **diagnoses** have raised A NEW HUMAN PROBLEM about **informing** those at risk before they show any *symptoms of it*. ]（要点）

> Not too long ago, when <u>physicians examined an older patient who seemed *out of touch with reality*</u>, they had to **guess** whether that person had *Alzheimer's* or was *only senile*. In the past few years, however, they have been able to use **new and more reliable tests** focusing on genetic clues. But in **the accuracy of these new tests** lies the RISK OF ANOTHER KIND OF HUMAN TRAGEDY: Physicians may be able to **predict** *Alzheimer's* long before its overt appearance, but such an **early diagnosis** could PSYCHOLOGICALLY DEVASTATE AN APPARENTLY HEALTHY PERSON.

每一个部分的开头都是一个相对较短的语句，以引出下文。

该部分的结尾句要陈述清楚这部分的要点。

要点句子的结尾要包含下文的关键主题。

在下文较长的部分，话题需一致（划线部分）。

重复开篇部分的结尾提到的关键词（黑体、斜体、大写）。

每个句子要遵从由熟悉到陌生的原则。

用读者能够理解的方式组织句子、段落和章节。

所有句子要与该部分的要点相关联。

第八课 整体连贯

# 第四部分 优美

> 文采可分为两种。其一实为罕见,它主要由精雕细琢的标点、过分且不自然的人物安排、华丽却毫无内涵的文字组成……另外一种文采则与之大相径庭,据说它具有圣典所具有的一切特点,其文采不是源于矫揉造作且不自然的雄辩术,而是源于朴实与庄严的巧妙结合。
>
> ——劳伦斯·斯特恩
> (Laurencr Sterne)

[ 第九课 ]

# 简 洁

> 我常常想，写作就是去掉繁琐的部分，留下最简洁的部分。
> ——斯科特·菲茨杰拉德
> （Scott Fitzgerald）

> 删繁就简的能力，是指去掉无足轻重的内容，以便让重要的内容表达思想。
> ——汉斯·霍夫曼
> （Hans Hofmann）

> 对不开窍的人，如果我说"最优美的风格就是凝练"的话，想必您已经明白了吧。
> ——玛丽安·摩尔
> （Marianne Moore）

## 简洁的内涵

如果能够做到以下几点，写作就更加清晰了：人物做主语，用动词表达动作；主题中涉及关键人物，重点强调关键词；精心构思导言部分以激励读者；设计段落、章节和文章以帮助读者把握整体连贯性。但是如果像下面这样写，读者会觉得与优美相差甚远：

In my personal opinion, it is necessary that we should not ignore the opportunity to think over each and every suggestion offered.

该作者让人物做主语，用动词表达动作，但是用词累赘：观点通常都是个人的，所以不需要用"personal"；而且既然是观点，也就不需要用"in my opinion"。"Think over"和"not ignore"意思都是"consider"。"Each and every"连用显得累赘。而且顾名思义，"建议"（suggestion）就是"给出"（offered）的，所以"offered"与"suggestion"重复。因此，可改为：

√ We should consider each suggestion.

虽然这样写并不典雅，但至少具备了写作风格中最基本的优美，即凝练，或者称之为我们即将讨论的"简洁"。

## 诊断与修改：简洁的六大原则

我修改上述关于建议的句子时遵循了六大原则：

1. 删除意义不大或没有实际意义的词。
2. 删除意思重复的词。
3. 删除可以通过其他词推测出来的词。
4. 用单词代替短语。
5. 将否定改为肯定。
6. 删除无用的形容词和副词。

这几大原则说起来容易做起来难，因为这需要认真推敲每个句子，删除这里，压缩那里，这是个体力活儿。然而，在此过程中这六大原则会起到指引性作用。

**1. 删除没有实际意义的词。**有些词是人们一开口就无意识说出来的：

kind of   actually   particular   really   certain   various
virtually   individual   basically   generally   given   practically

Productivity **actually** depends on **certain** factors that **basically** involve psychology more than **any particular** technology.

√ Productivity depends on psychology more than on technology.

**2. 删除意思相同的词。**英语这门语言发展初期，作者习惯上将一个拉丁词或法语词与一个本土英语词搭配使用，因为外来词听起来更显得博学。今天使用的这些搭配大部分很累赘。常见的有：

| | | |
|---|---|---|
| full and complete | hope and trust | any and all |
| true and accurate | each and every | basic and fundamental |
| hopes and desires | first and foremost | various and sundry |

**3. 删除读者可以推测出来的词。**这种重复很常见但不易被发现，因为它的形式很多样。

**重复的修饰语**　通常情况下，一些词的意思暗示着另外一些词的意思，尤其是它的修饰语（黑体加粗部分）：

Do not try to *predict* **future** events that will **completely** *revolutionize* society, because **past** *history* shows that it is the **final** *outcome* of minor events that **unexpectedly** *surprises* us more.

√ Do not try to predict revolutionary events, because history shows that the outcome of minor events surprises us more.

一些常见的重复搭配：

| | | |
|---|---|---|
| terrible tragedy | various different | free gift |
| basic fundamentals | future plans | each individual |
| final outcome | true facts | consensus of opinion |

**重复的种类** 每一个词都包含着它更高一级词语的意思，所以可以去掉一个这样的词（黑体加粗部分）：

During that *period* **of time**, the *membrane* **area** became *pink* **in color** and *shiny* **in appearance**.

√ During that *period*, the *membrane* became *pink* and *shiny*.

这样，或许需要将一个形容词转换成副词：

The holes must be aligned in an *accurate* **manner**.

√ The holes must be aligned *accurately*.

有时需要将形容词转换成名词：

The country manages the *educational* **system** and *public recreational* **activities**.

√ The country manages *education* and *public recreation*.

以下是一些经常重复使用的高一级的名词（黑体加粗）：

| large in **size** | round in **shape** | honest in **character** |
| unusual in **nature** | of a strange **type** | **area** of mathematics |
| of a bright **color** | at an early **time** | in a confused **state** |

**普遍的暗指** 这种累赘更难发觉，因为它无处不在：

Imagine someone trying to learn the rules for playing the game of chess.

"Learn"就暗指"trying","rules"暗指"playing the game","chess"本身就是一种"game"。所以更简洁的说法是：

> Imagine learning the rules of chess.

**4. 用单词代替短语。** 这种重复尤其难以发现，它要求具备很大的词汇量并熟悉这些词的使用方法。例如：

> As you carefully read what you have written to improve wording and catch errors of spelling and punctuation, the thing to do before anything else is to see whether you could use sequences of subjects and verbs instead of the same ideas expressed in nouns.

即，

> √ As you edit, first replace nominalizations with clauses.

我将五个短语凝练成了五个单词：

| | | |
|---|---|---|
| carefully read what you have written | → | edit |
| the thing to do before anything else | → | first |
| use X instead of Y | → | replace |
| nouns instead of verbs | → | nominalizations |
| sequences of subjects and verbs | → | clauses |

我并不能提供一个原则，来规定何时需要用单词代替短语，更不要说具体用什么词来代替了。我只能说，很多时候都可以代替。能用单词代替短语时，要尽量使用单词。

以下是一些值得注意的常见短语（黑体加粗部分）。请注意，有一些需要将名词化了的词转换成动词（上下两句中动词均为斜体）：

We must explain **the reason for** the *delay* in the meeting.
√ We must explain **why** the meeting is *delayed*.

**Despite the fact that** the data were checked, errors occurred.
√ **Even though** the data were checked, errors occurred.

**In the event that** you finish early, contract this office.
√ **If** you finish early, contract this office.

**In a situation where** a class closes, you may petition to get in.
√ **When** a class closes, you may petition to get in.

I want to say a few words **concerning the matter of** money.
√ I want to say a few words **about** money.

**There is a need for** more careful *inspection* of all welds.
√ You **must** *inspect* all welds more carefully.

We **are in a position** to make you an offer.
√ We **can** make you an offer.

**It is possible that** nothing will come of this.
√ Nothing **may** come of this.

**Prior to** the *end* of the training, apply for your license.
√ **Before** training *ends*, apply for your license.

We have noted a **decrease/increase in the number of** errors.
√ We have noted **fewer/more** errors.

**5. 将否定式转换成肯定式。**如果用否定式表达一个观点，不仅要加上多余的词，如 same → not different，而且还迫使读者在头脑中进行转换。例如，下面这两个句子意思相同，但是肯定式更直接：

Do not write in the negative. → Write in the affirmative.

大部分否定式都可以改写为肯定式：

| not careful | → | careless | not many | → | few |
| not the same | → | different | not often | → | rarely |
| not allow | → | prevent | not stop | → | continue |
| not notice | → | overlook | not include | → | omit |

如果要强调否定式就不要将否定式转换成肯定式。（这句不就是很好的例子吗？我本可以写成"如果强调否定部分，就保持否定句式"。）

一些动词、介词和连词是间接的否定式：

动词　preclude, prevent, lack, fail, doubt, reject, avoid, deny, refuse, exclude, contradict, prohibit, bar

介词　without, against, lacking, but for, except

连词　unless, except when

如果将 not 与这些否定词连用就会使读者感到困惑。试比较下述句子：

**Except** when you have **failed** to submit applications **without** documentation, benefits will **not** be **denied**.

√ You will receive benefits only if you submit your documents.

√ To receive benefits, submit your documents.

如果将否定词（直接和间接否定词）和被动语态、名词化词语搭配使用，会使读者完全陷入困惑：

There should be **no** submission of payments **without** notification of this office, **unless** the payment does **not** exceed $100.

Do not **submit** payments if you have not **notified** this office, unless you are **paying** less than $100.

现在将否定形式改为肯定形式：

√ If you pay more than $100, notify this office first.

**6. 删除形容词和副词。**许多作者会不自觉地使用一些形容词和副词。试着删掉名词前的形容词和副词，只保留那些帮助读者理解文章的词语。在下面这篇文章中，哪些词语是需要保留的？

At the heart of the argument culture is our habit of seeing issues and ideas as ~~absolute and irreconcilable~~ principles ~~continually~~ at war. To move beyond this ~~static and limiting~~ view, we can remember the ~~Chinese~~ approach to yin and yang. They are two principles, yes, but they are conceived not as ~~irreconcilable polar~~ opposites, but as elements that coexist and should be brought into balance ~~as much as possible~~. As sociolinguist Suzanne Wong Scollon notes, "Yin is always present in and changing into yang and vice versa." How can we translate this ~~abstract~~ idea into ~~daily~~ practice?

——德博拉·泰南,《辩论文化》

---

**要点** 只有当词足以说明要表达的意思时,读者才会认为写得简洁。

1. 删除意义不大或没有实际意义的词。
2. 删除意思重复的词。
3. 删除可以通过其他词推测出来的词。
4. 用单词代替短语。
5. 将否定改为肯定。
6. 删除无用的形容词和副词。

---

## 练习 9.1

删除下列句子中重复的部分

1. Critics cannot avoid employing complex and abstract technical terms if they are to successfully analyze literary texts and discuss them in a meaningful way.

2. Scientific research generally depends on fully accurate data if it is to offer theories that will allow us to predict the future in a plausible way.

3. In regard to desirable employment in teaching jobs, prospects for those engaged in graduate-school-level studies are at best not certain.

4. Notwithstanding the fact that all legal restrictions on the use of firearms are the subject of heated debate and argument, it is necessary that the general public not stop carrying on discussions pro and con in regard to them.

5. Most likely, a majority of all patients who appear at a public medical clinical facility do not expect special medical attention or treatment, because their particular health problems and concerns are often not major and for the most part can usually be adequately treated without much time, effort, and attention.

在合适的地方将否定式改为肯定式，并做其他必要的修改。

6. Except when expenses do not exceed $250, the Insured may not refuse to provide the insurer with receipts, checks, or other evidence of costs.

7. There is no possibility in regard to a reduction in the size of the federal deficit if reductions in federal spending are not introduced.

8. Do not discontinue medication unless symptoms of dizziness and nausea are not present for six hours.

9. No one should be prevented from participating in cost-sharing educational programs without a full hearing into the reasons for his or her not being accepted.

10. No agreement exists on the question of an open or closed universe, a dispute about which no resolution is likely as long as a computation of the total mass of the universe has not been done.

11. So long as taxpayers do not engage in widespread refusal to pay taxes, the

government will have no difficulty in paying its debts.

12. No alternative exists in this country to the eventual development of tar sand, oil shale, and coal as sources of fuel, if we wish to stop being energy dependent on imported oil.

13. Not until a resolution between Catholics and Protestants in regard to the authority of papal supremacy is reached will there be a start to a reconciliation between these two Christian religions.

## 练习 9.2

下面是两个关于赠品的实例。

You will not be charged our first monthly fee unless you don't cancel within the first thirty days.

To avoid being charged your first monthly fee, cancel your membership before your free trial ends.

哪一个清晰性更差？为什么要这样写？对其进行修改。

## 重复的元话语

第四课讨论了作为语言的元话语，它主要指下列几点：

作者的意图：to sum up, candidly, I believe

对读者的指示：note that, consider now, as you see

文本的结构：first, second, finally, therefore, however

写的任何东西都需要元话语，但是过多的元话语会掩埋自己的想法：

> The last point I would like to make is that in regard to men-women relationships, it is important to keep in mind that the greatest changes have occurred in how they work together.

在这 34 个词中只有 9 个说明了男性与女性的关系：

> Men-women relationships... greatest changes... how they work together.

其他的都是元话语。如果将其删除，原文会更加紧凑：

> The greatest changes in men-women relationships have occurred in how they work together.

既然知道了句子的意思，还可以将其说得更直接：

> √ Men and women have changed their relationships most in how they work together.

作者们使用元话语的方式因领域不同而各异，但通常可分为下列两类：

**1. 说明想法出处的元话语** 不要说某事是据观察、据了解、据记载得来的；只需说明事实即可：

High divorce rates **have been observed** to occur in areas that **have been determined to have** low population density.

√ High divorce rates occur in areas with low population density.

**2. 说明自己话题的元话语**　黑体加粗的短语表达了句子的主要内容：

**This section introduces another** problem, that of noise pollution. **The first thing to say about it is** that noise pollution exists not only...

如果减少元话语的数量，读者会更容易抓住主题：

√ **Another** problem is noise pollution. **First**, it exists not only...

另外两种用于引出主题的结构同样需要注意，在文本中通常出现在主题句之前：

**In regard to** a vigorous style, the most important feature is a short, concrete subject followed by a forceful verb.

**So far as** China's industrial development **is concerned**, it has long surpassed that of Japan.

但是，通常可以把这些主题词加进主语里：

√ **The most important feature of a vigorous style** is a short, concrete subject followed by a forceful verb.

√ **China** has long surpassed Japan's industrial development.

## 模糊语与强化语

另外一种元话语反映了作者对自己所陈述话语的确定性。模糊语限制了说话的语气；强化语则加强了说话语气。使用过多，二者都会显得累赘。但是它们也有用，因为通过它们，读者可以看出作者是如何平衡谨慎与自信之间的关系，并由此影响读者对作者所写人物的判断的。

### 模糊语

下列是一些常见的模糊语：

| | |
|---|---|
| 副词 | usually, often, sometimes, almost, virtually, possibly, allegedly, arguably, perhaps, apparently, in some ways, to a certain extent, somewhat, in some/certain respects |
| 形容词 | most, many, some, a certain number of |
| 动词 | may, might, can, could, seem, tend, appear, suggest, indicate |

过多的模糊语听起来会觉得拐弯抹角，就像这样：

There **seems to be some** evidence to **suggest** that **certain** differences between Japanese and Western rhetoric **could** derive from historical influences **possibly** traceable to Japan's cultural isolation and Europe's history of cross-cultural contacts.

另外一方面，只有愚蠢的人或掌握了大量历史证据的人，才会像下面这么肯定地说话：

This evidence **proves** that Japanese and Western rhetorics differ because of Japan's cultural isolation and Europe's history of cross-cultural contacts.

在大部分学术写作中，我们更多地使用类似于这样的说法（注意我使用的模糊语；对比更肯定的说法，"In academic writing, we state claims like this"）：

√ This evidence **suggests** that **aspects** of Japanese and Western rhetoric differ because of Japan's cultural isolation and Europe's history of cross-cultural contacts.

suggest 和 indicate 显示所陈述的主张并不是百分之百确定，但二者也表明你有足够的信心进行陈述：

√ The evidence **indicates** that some of these questions remain unresolved.

√ These data **suggest** that further studies are necessary.

即使是自信的科学家也会使用**模糊语**。下一段介绍了遗传学史上最重大的突破，即发现了 DNA 中的双螺旋。对此最有发言权的就是克里克和沃森，但是他们做了不一样的选择（注意：第一人称使用的是"we"，模糊语已用黑体字加粗）：

We **wish to suggest a** [ not *the* ] structure for the salt of deoxyribose nucleic acid（D. N. A）... A structure for nucleic acid has already been proposed by Pauling and Corey... **In our opinion**, this structure is unsatisfactory for two reasons:（1）**We believe** that the material which gives the X-ray diagrams is the salt, not the free acid...（2）**Some** of the van der Waals distances **appear** to be too small.

——J. D. 沃森和 F. H. 克里克，

《核酸的分子结构》

## 强化语

以下是一些常见的强化语：

| | |
|---|---|
| 副词 | very, pretty, quite, rather, clearly, obviously, undoutedly, certainly, of course, indeed, inevitably, invariably, always, literally |
| 形容词 | key, central, crucial, basic, fundamental, major, principal, essential |
| 动词 | show, prove, establish, as you /we/ everyone knows/ can see, it is clear/obvious that |

不过，最常见的强化语，是指不包含模糊限制成分的词语。

去掉模糊语后，克里克和沃森的话会更简洁，不过也更咄咄逼人。对比下面这句话（我把语气强的词以黑体加粗标出，咄咄逼人的语气主要源于缺乏模糊语的用语）：

We ~~wish to suggest~~ state here ~~a~~ the structure for the salt of deoxyribose nucleic acid（D. N. A.）... A structure for nucleic acid has already been proposed by Pauling and Corey... ~~In our opinion,~~ [ T ] his structure is unsatisfactory for two reasons（1）~~We believe that~~ [ T ] he material which gives the X-ray diagrams is the salt, not the free acid...（2）~~Some of~~ [ T ] he van der Waals distances ~~appear to be~~ **are** too small.

自信的作者使用模糊语的频率高于强化词，因为他们要避免文章听起来像下面这样肯定：

For a century now, **all** liberals have argued against **any** censorship of art, and **every** court has found their arguments so **completely** persuasive that **not** a person **any** longer remembers how they were countered. As a result, today, censorship is **totally** a thing of the past.

一些作者认为，这种咄咄逼人的风格更具说服力。其实恰恰相反。如果平和地进行陈述观点，读者认真思考的可能性更大：

For **about** a century now, **many** liberals have argued against censorship of art, and **most** courts have found their arguments persuasive **enough** that **few** people **may** remember **exactly** how they were countered. As a result, today, censorship is **virtually** a thing of the past.

一些人说使用太多模糊语会使文章显得冗长且缺乏说服力，

或许是这样的。但是这样的文章并不像推土机一样,它同样给读者留有理性的、谨慎的反应空间。

> **快速提示** 当读者看到下列诸如 obviously, undoubtedly, it is clear that, there is no question that 等词语引导的句子时,他们会很自然地想到事情的另一面。

> **要点** 写任何东西都需要某种元话语,尤其是指引读者浏览文章的元话语,如 first, second, therefore, on the other hand 等。还需要使用一些模糊限制性的元话语,以对表达的确定性进行界定,如 perhaps, seems, could 等。若使用过多,则会有风险。

> **快速提示** 在第七课,我们认识到,一些问题的解决方法是阐明观点和主张。但是在陈述解决方法时,一定要谨慎使用元话语,因为它只有助于支持话题,而无助于提出自己的主张。为了避免这种陷阱,请删除元话语(黑体加粗部分),把剩余部分重新改写成句子:
>
> **In this study, I examine** the history of Congressional legislation to protect children in the workplace.
> √ Congress has legislated to protect children in the workplace.

> 如果最后的主张看上去是不言自明的，正如上面的例子，那就需要做更多的叙述，或者继续仔细地思考所要表达的内容。

## 练习 9.3

修改下列句子中不必要的元话语和重复部分：

1. But, on the other hand, we can perhaps point out that there may always be TV programming to appeal to our most prurient and, therefore, lowest interests.

2. In this particular section, I intend to discuss my position about the possible need to dispense with the standard approach to plea bargaining. I believe this for two reasons. The first reason is that there is the possibility of letting hardened criminals avoid receiving their just punishment. The second reason is the following: plea bargaining seems to encourage a growing lack of respect for the judicial system.

3. Turning now to the next question, there is in regard to wilderness area preservation activities one basic principle when attempting to formulate a way of approaching decisions about unspoiled areas to be set aside as not open to development for commercial exploitation.

4. It is my belief that in regard to terrestrial-type snakes, an assumption can be made that there are probably none in unmapped areas of the world surpassing the size of those we already have knowledge of.

5. Depending on the particular position that one takes on this question, the

educational system has taken on a degree of importance that may be equal to or perhaps even exceed the family as a major source of transmission of social values.

## 简洁，而非生硬

至此，我一直强调简练，但是现在必须做出一些让步了。读者不喜欢文章软弱无力，也不喜欢文章精练得只剩下框架。下面一段建议选自阅读最广泛的讨论风格的作品——斯特伦克和怀特合著的《风格的要素》(*The Elements of Style*)：

> Revising is part of writing. Few writers are so expert that they can produce what they are after on the first try. Quite often you will discover, on examining the completed work, that there are serious flaws in the arrangement of the material, calling for transpositions. When this is the case, a word processor can save you time and labor as you rearrange the manuscript. You can select material on the screen and move it to a more appropriate spot, or, if you cannot find the right spot, you can move the material to the end of the manuscript until you decide whether to delete it. Some writers find that working with a printed copy of the manuscript helps them to visualize the process of change; others prefer to revise entirely on screen. Above all, do not be afraid to experiment with what you have written. Save both the original and the revised versions; you can always use the computer

to restore the manuscript to its original condition, should that course seem best. Remember, it is no sign of weakness or defeat that your manuscript ends up in need of major surgery. This is a common occurrence in all writing, and among the best writers. （205 words）

通过删除重复部分可以对上述段落进行简化：

Revising is part of writing. Few writers ~~are so expert that they can~~ produce what they are after on the first try. ~~Quite~~ Often you will discover ~~on examining the completed work, that there are serious~~ flaws in the arrangement of the material. ~~calling for transpositions~~. When this is the case, a word processor can save ~~you~~ time ~~and labor~~ as you rearrange the manuscript. You can ~~select material on the screen and~~ move [ material ] to a more appropriate spot, or, if you cannot find the right spot, you can move the material to the end of the manuscript until you decide whether to delete it. Some writers find that working with a printed ~~copy of the~~ manuscript helps them ~~to~~ visualize ~~the process of~~ change; others prefer to revise ~~entirely~~ on screen. Above all, ~~do not be afraid to~~ experiment ~~with what you have written~~. Save ~~both~~ the original and the revised versions; you can always ~~use the computer to~~ restore the manuscript to its original condition, ~~should that course seem best~~. ~~Remember,~~ it is no sign of weakness ~~or defeat~~ that your manuscript ~~ends up in~~ need[s] ~~of major~~ surgery. This is ~~a~~ common ~~occurrence~~ in all writing, and among the best writers. ( 139 words )

通过进一步改写第二个版本，还可以进一步简化得到第三个版本（改写后的为斜体）：

Revising is part of writing, *because* few writers ~~produce what they are after on the first try~~ *write perfect first drafts. If you use a word processor and find* ~~Often you will discover serious~~ *flaws in your* arrangement, ~~of the material. When this is the case, a word processor can save time as you rearrange the manuscript~~. You can ~~select material on the screen and~~ move material to a more appropriate spot, or, if you cannot find *one*, ~~the right spot,~~ to the end ~~of the manuscript~~ until you decide whether to delete it. Some writers find ~~that working with~~ a printed manuscript helps them visualize change; others revise on screen. Above all, experiment. Save ~~both~~ the original ~~and the revised~~ version; you can always *go back to it* ~~restore the manuscript its original condition.~~ ~~Remember,~~ It is no sign of weakness that your manuscript needs surgery. This is common in all writing, and among the best writers. ( 99 words )

如果将其删得只剩下框架，那么字数还可以缩减一半：

Most writers revise because few write a perfect first draft. If you work on a computer, you can rearrange the parts by moving them around. If you save the original, you can always go back to it. Even great writers revise, so if your manuscript needs surgery, it signals no weakness.（51 words）

但是，文章字数压缩到原文的四分之一，它也丧失了反复叙述的魅力，这是为了简洁而做出的权衡结果，却是大多读者不愿接受的。

我没有办法告诉作者文章何时会显得太过简洁，会使读者觉得生硬，甚至唐突。这也就是为何要听听读者的建议。他们知道一些你永远也不知道的东西——读你的文章有何感受。

## 自我检测

### 练习 9.4

就像我修改斯特伦克和怀特写的《风格的要素》(237—240页)中的段落一样，修改一篇自己的文章。从文章中选取篇幅较长的段落或章节（大约200字）。现在，把它改写成150字左右，然后100字，最后再改成50字。总结一下，在每个改写的版本中你得到了什么，又失去了什么？

## 练习 9.5

———⁂———

每篇文章都需要某种元话语，但是使用过多，会埋没自己的想法。找一个人读自己写的文章的几页，并标出所有的元话语。和读自己文章的人一起解决下列问题：哪些元话语是有用的？哪些是累赘不必要的？有没有需要元话语却没有用的地方？必要时进行改动。

## 总结

仅是简洁还不能保证文章一定优美，然而清理了文中没用的词语，句子会更有条理。

### 1. 无实际意义的词

Some polling sites reported various technical problems, but these did not really affect the election's actual result.

√ Some polling sites reported technical problems, but these did not affect the election's result.

### 2. 重复的搭配

If and when we can define our final aims and goals, each and every member of our group will be ready and willing to offer aid and assistance.

√ If we define our goals, we will all be ready to help.

### 3. 重复的修饰语

In the business world of today, official governmental red tape seriously destroys initiative among individual businesses.

√ Government red tape destroys business initiative.

### 4. 重复的种类

In the area of education, tight financial conditions are forcing school boards to cut nonessential expenses.

√ Tight finances are forcing school boards to cut nonessentials.

### 5. 明显的暗指

Energy used to power industries and homes will in years to come cost more money.

√ Energy will eventually cost more.

### 6. 单词代替短语

A sail-powered craft that has turned on its side or completely over must remain buoyant enough so that it will bear the weight of those individuals who were aboard.

√ A capsized sailboat must support those on it.

7. 间接否定

There is no reason not to believe that engineering malfunctions in nuclear energy systems cannot be anticipated.

√ Malfunctions in nuclear energy systems will surprise us.

8. 过多的元话语

It is almost certainly the case that totalitarian systems cannot allow a society to have what we would define as stable social relationships.

√ Totalitarianism prevents stable social relationships.

9. 模糊语和强化语

这里唯一的原则就是黄金准则：不多不少，刚刚好。这一原则帮助不大，但却是必须培养的能力，只有如此，才能相信自己的判断。

| | |
|---|---|
| 过于确定的说法： | In my research, I **prove** that people with a gun in their home use it to kill themselves or a family member instead of to protect themselves from an intruder. |
| 过于不确定的说法： | **Some** of my recent research **seems** to **imply** that there **may** be a **risk** that certain people with a gun in their homes **could** be **more prone** to use it to kill themselves or a family member than to protect themselves from **possible** intruders. |
| 适度的说法？ | My research indicates that people with a gun in their homes are more likely to use it to kill themselves or a family member than they are to protect themselves from an intruder. |

[ 第十课 ]

# 条理性

> 从逻辑上讲,每个句子的结构都值得研究。
> ——约翰·斯图尔特·米尔
> (John Stuart Mill)

> 长而复杂的句子应该具有感染力,使读者有醍醐灌顶的感觉。
> ——格特鲁德·斯坦因
> (Gertrude stein)

> 只有见识了更好,才知道何为恰到好处。
> ——威廉·布莱克
> (William Blake)

## 句子条理性的内涵

写作如果能做到清晰简洁，那么已经很好了。但是如果作者在一个句子中使用了20多个字，都不能将自己的观点表述清楚，那他就像一个作曲家，沦为只会写广告歌的境地了。一些人反对使用长句子，但是并不是每个复杂的想法都可以用简短的句子表达清楚的，所以必须懂得如何组织长而清晰的句子。

例如，思考下述句子：

> In addition to differences in ethnicity or religion that have for centuries plagued Sunnis and Shiites, explanations of the causes of their distrust must include all of the other social, economic, and cultural conflicts that have plagued them that are rooted in a troubled history that extends 1,300 years into the past.

即使要表达的思想需要用上这52个字（事实上不是），那也本可以将其组织得更有条理。

首先可以将抽象词转换成人物/主语和行为词/动词，然后把句子分解成短句：

> Historians have tried to explain why Sunnis and Shiites

distrust one another today. Many have claimed that the sources of conflict are age-old differences in religion. But they must also consider all the other social, economic, and cultural conflicts that have plagued their 1,300 years of trouble history.

但是上述段落给人的感觉不够连贯。人们更喜欢这样的句子：

√ To explain why Sunnis and Shiites distrust one another today, historians must study not only age-old religious differences, but all the other social, economic, and cultural conflicts that have plagued their 1,300 years of trouble history.

这句话有 36 个字，但并不显得拖沓。所以长句本身并不会使句子冗长累赘。在本课，我重点讲如何写长而复杂、同时又条理清晰的句子。

## 诊断与修改：冗长拖沓

正如写作风格的其他方面一样，与自己的文章相比，总是更能看到别人写作中的拖沓，所以要摒弃个人强烈的主观性，来诊断自己的写作。

首先选出几个长度超过两行的句子，大声朗读。在读其中一句时，要对所有部分进行整合以表达一个整体性的概念结构，如果还没来得及这样做，就觉得快要喘不过气来，那这个句子就是读者希望你修改的句子。如果因为插入语一再地打断而使句子不断地停顿，而且这种现象又很明显，那么读者可能会觉得句子突然失去了条理性，正如本句话一样。

三种情况会使读者觉得长句缺乏条理性：

主要从句中的动词出现太晚

动词后的从句过长且没有条理性

中间的插入语过多使读者不断地停下来

## 修改过长的开场语

一些句子似乎永远也不会进入正题：

1a. Since most undergraduate students change their fields of study at least once during their college careers, many more than once, first-year students who are not certain about their program of studies should not load up their schedules to meet requirements for a particular program.

该句的主要动词是"**should not load up**"，在此之前有 31 个字。关于如何开始一句话，这里有两条经验法则：(1) 快速找到主要从句的主语。(2) 快速找到动词和宾语。

**经验法则一：快速找到主语**。如果一句话开头介绍性短语和从句过长，读起来就会有困难，因为读的过程中要时刻记住主语和动词即将出现，这种记忆上的负担会影响简单的理解。所以要避免使用带有长长的引导性短语和从句的句子开头。

试比较下列几句话。(1b) 中，在主语和动词之前有 17 个词。

（1c）中，在主语和动词之前只有3个词：

> **1b.** **Since most undergraduate students change their major fields of study at least once during their college careers,** *first-year students* who are not certain about the program of studies they want to pursue SHOULD NOT LOAD UP their schedules to meet requirements for a particular program.

> √ **1c. First-year students** SHOULD NOT LOAD UP their schedules with requirements for a particular program if they are not certain about their program of studies they want to pursue, because **most** CHANGE their major fields of study at least once during their college careers.

如果发现过长的介绍性从句，试着将其置于句末。如果放在句末不合适，就使其单独成句。以 if、since、when 和 although 开头的句子一般放在主要从句之前，而非之后，这是英语写作风格的既成事实。所以，如果从句必须放在句首，那么尽量保持简短。

**特例**：在"调尾"和"悬置"写作风格中，作者特意堆砌很多介绍性的从句，以此来扩大和彰显最后的主要从句的影响：

> When a society spends more on its pets than it does on its homeless,
>
> when it rewards those who hit a ball the farthest more highly than those who care most deeply for its neediest,
>
> when it takes more interest in the juvenile behavior of its

richest children than in the deficient education of its poorest,
it has lost its moral center.

这种句子很少见，产生的影响很大，尤其当最后一个从句的最后几个词得到了适当的强调时，效果更明显。我们将在十一课对此进行讨论。

**经验法则二：快速找到动词和宾语。**读者还希望主语后就能看到动词和宾语。因此，

避免使用长而抽象的主语
避免在主语和动词之间加入插入语
避免在动词和宾语之间加入插入语

**避免使用长而抽象的主语** 将长主语改为短主语。首先用下划线标出整个主语。如果发现总主语超过了七八个单词，并包含名词化的词语，试着将其转化成一个动词并为其找到主语：

**Abco Inc.'s *understanding* of the drivers of its profitability in the Asian market for small electronics** helped it pursue opportunities in Africa.

√ **Abco Inc.** was able to pursue opportunities in Africa because it understood what drove profitability in the Asian market for small electronics.

主语也可以很长，如果它包含一个较长的关系从句的话：

A company **that focuses on hiring the best personnel and then trains them not just for the work they are hired to do but for higher-level jobs** is likely to earn the loyalty of its employees.

尽量将关系从句改为由 when 或 if 引导的引导性从句：

√ **When a company focuses on hiring the best personnel and then trains them not just for the work they are hired to do but for higher-level jobs,** it is likely to earn the loyalty of its employees.

但是如果引导性从句与上述句子一样长，就尽量将其置于句末，尤其是在下列情况下：

（1）主句较短且表达句子要点（2）位置可移动的从句表达的是新的复杂信息，且支撑或阐述主句信息。

√ A company is likely to earn the loyalty of its employees **when it focuses on hiring the best personnel and then trains them not just for the work they are hired to do but for higher-level jobs.**

或许将从句改为一个独立句，会更好一点：

√ Some companies focus on hiring the best personnel and then train them not just for the work they are hired to do but for higher-level jobs later. **Such companies are likely to earn the loyalty of their employees.**

**避免在主语和动词之间加入插入语** 如果在主语和动词之间加入插入语，会给读者带来挫败感，就像下面这段话一样：

> Some scientists, **because they write in a style that is impersonal and objective,** do not easily communicate with laypeople.

放在主语后面的 because 从句使读者一眼看到了句子的动词位置，**do not easily communicate**。将该插入语放到句首还是句末，这主要取决于该句与前面还是后面的联系更密切（注意这里应该用 since，而不是 because）。

> √ Since some scientists write in a style that is impersonal and objective, they do **not easily communicate with laypeople. This lack of communication** damages...
>
> √ Some scientists do not easily communicate with laypeople because they write in **a style that is impersonal and objective. It is a kind of style** filled with passives and...

如果插入语较短读者则不会太介意：

> √ Some scientists deliberately write in a style that is impersonal and objective.

**避免在动词和宾语之间加入插入语**　读者还希望在动词后能快速找到宾语。下述句子则没有做到这点：

We must develop, **if we are to become competitive with other companies in our region**, a core of knowledge regarding the state of the art in effective industrial organizations.

将插入语放在句首还是句末取决于下文内容：

√ **If we are to compete with other companies in our region,** we must develop a core of knowledge about the state of the art in **effective industrial organizations. Such organizations provide...**

√ **We** must develop a core of knowledge about the state of the art in effective industrial organizations **if we are to compete with other companies in our region. Increasing competition...**

特例：如果一个位置可移动的介词短语较短，而句子主语又较长，尽量将介词短语置于动词和宾语之间：

In a long sentence, put the newest and most important information that you want your readers to remember **at its end**.

√ In a long sentence, put **at its end** the newest and most important information that you want your reader to remember.

> **要点** 如果读者能很快找到主要从句的主语,并在主语之后很快找到动词和宾语,对读者来说读起来是最容易的。要避免使用过长的引导性短语和从句,避免使用长主语,而且位于主语和动词之间及动词和宾语之间的插入语也不宜过长。

## 另外一条原则:以自己的方式开篇

这里再补充一条原则,它尤其适用于长句。试比较这两个句子:

High-deductible health plans and Health Saving Accounts into which workers and their employers make tax-deductible deposits results in workers taking more responsibility for their health care.

√ Workers take more responsibility for their health care when they adopt high-deductible insurance plans and Health Saving Accounts into which they and their employers deposit tax-deductible contributions.

与结构繁缛的第一个句子不同,第二个句子并没有使用长而抽象的主语,而是简短而具体的词语,且为读者所熟知;主语置于句首,主语后紧跟的是描述具体动作的动词:workers take...

但是二者还有一点不同。第一句中,读者要先读二十多个词才能看到主要立场及最重要的观点:工人们要对自己的医疗卫生负责任。该句给人一种滞后感。只有读到结尾才知道开头部分与主题的联系。

[ High-deductible health plans and Health Saving Accounts into which workers and their employers make tax-deductible deposits ]（说明／支持）[ results in workers taking more responsibility for their health care. ]（要点）

相反地，第二句以八个单词组成的主要从句开头，清晰准确地陈述了最重要的观点：

√[ Workers take more responsibility for their health care ]（要点）[ when they adopt high-deductible insurance plans and Health Saving Accounts into which they and their employers make tax-deductible deposits. ]（说明／支持）

当读者了解了主要观点后，就能对剩余 19 个词与主题间的联系进行预测，**即使还没开始读也能预见**。

下面是一条关于如何阅读的普遍原则：如果能用简短直接的语言框架引出后面更加复杂的信息，句子的复杂性就能得到最为恰当的控制。我们已经见识过，这条原则是怎样运用于单独的主语和动词的。但是它同样适用于长句中**有逻辑联系**的各个要素，适用于句子的要点，适用于对句子的解释性话语及支撑性信息。如果要点被一点一点地透露出来，或没有及时得以表达，就要对其重新构建，在头脑中使其有逻辑性地重新组合。前面清楚陈述的要点为我们提供了一个理解下文复杂性的语境。

要诊断一个长句，首先要找到该句的要点，即希望读者能快速捕捉到的主要信息。如果在句中或句尾才能找到中心句，就要对其进行修改：将其改为一个简短的主句，并置于句首，后面加上更长更复杂的支撑性或解释性信息。（见248—250页与其相矛盾的另一条原则）

事实上，这条简单信息在前、复杂信息在后的原则也适用于更大的语言单位：

开头用一个句子（或两个）来表达段落要点，以使读者能理解下文内容（见205—207页）。

开头用一个段落（或两个）来表达章节要点（见196—198页）。

对于整篇文章也一样：开篇的导言陈述要点，并对下文做出规划（见173—187页）。

句子、段落、章节乃至全文——你如何快速地、简洁地、有效地开篇，直接决定了读者对后面文章难易度的把握。

## 练习 10.1

修改下列句子中的长主语

1. Explaining why Shakespeare decided to have Lady Macbeth die off stage rather than letting the audience see her die has to do with understanding the audience's reaction to Macbeth's death.

2. An agreement by the film industry and by television producers on limiting characters using cigarettes, even if carried out, would do little to discourage young people from smoking.

3. A student's right to have access to his or her own records, including medical records, academic reports, and confidential comments by advisers, will generally take precedence over an institution's desire to keep records private, except when limitations of those rights under specified circumstances are agreed to by students during registration.

下述句子中都有插入语，先将冗长的部分去掉，然后修改插入语部分。

4. The construction of the Interstate Highway System, owing to the fact that Congress, on the occasion when it originally voted funds for it, did not anticipate the rising cost of inflation, ran into serious financial problems.

5. Such prejudicial conduct or behavior, regardless of the reasons offered to justify it, is rarely not least to some degree prejudicial to good order and discipline.

6. TV "reality" shows, because they have an appeal to our fascination with real-life conflict because of our voyeuristic impulses, are about the most popular shows that are regularly scheduled to appear on TV.

7. Insistence that there is no proof by scientific means of a causal link between tobacco consumption and various disease entities such as cardiac heart disease and malignant growth, despite the fact that there is a strong statistical correlation between smoking behavior and such diseases, is no longer the officially stated position of cigarette companies.

8. The continued and unabated emission of carbon dioxide gas into the atmosphere, unless there is a marked reduction, will eventually result in serious

changes in the climate of the world as we know it today.

修改下列句子中长的引导性短语和从句。试着用要点开头引出修改后的句子。

9. While grade inflation has been a subject of debate by teachers and administrators and even in newspapers, employers looking for people with high levels of technical and analytical skills have not had difficulty identifying desirable candidates.

10. Although one way to prevent foreign piracy of DVDs is for criminal justice systems of foreign countries to move cases faster through their systems and for stiffer penalties to be imposed, no improvement in the level of expertise of judges who hear these cases is expected any time in the immediate future.

11. Since school officials responsible for setting policy about school security have said that local principals may require students to pass through metal detectors before entering a school building, the need to educate parents and students about the seriousness of bringing onto school property anything that looks like a weapon must be made a part of the total package of school security.

12. If the music industry ignores the problem of how a rating system applied to offensive lyrics could be applied to music broadcast over FM and AM radio, then even if it were willing to discuss a system that could be used in the sale of music in retail stores, the likelihood of any significant improvement in its image with the public is nil.

# 重构散乱的句子

如果首先抓住了句子要点，就可以勉强理解后文中任何散乱的句子，但读者仍希望避免这种情况。下述句子在开头清楚地陈述了观点，然后用四个散乱的从句进行解释：

No scientific advance is more exciting than genetic engineering, （要点）which is a new way of manipulating the elemental structural units of life itself, which are the genes and chromosomes that tell our cells how to reproduce to become the parts that constitute our bodies.（解释说明）

从结构上看，该句是这样分布的：

No scientific advance is more exciting than genetic engineering
[要点与核心主谓结构]

  **which** is a new way of manipulating the elemental structural units of life itself  [附属从句]

   **which** are the genes and chromosomes  [附属从句]

    **that** tell our cells how to reproduce to become the parts  [附属从句]

     **that** constitute our bodies  [附属从句]

> **快速提示** 阅读时如果因散乱的句子感到困惑，就将注意力放在关系代词 **who**、**which** 和 **that** 上。停顿片刻找出每个代词的所指。然后再读该句，用名词替换代词，这样就可以毫无障碍地理解句子。

第十课 条理性

通过让其他人朗读自己的文章来诊断这个问题。若该读者显得犹犹豫豫，朗读某些词时又磕磕绊绊，或者在读到结尾之前就已上气不接下气，那么其他默读的读者的反应也会一样。对此可从四个方面进行修改：把从句剪切出来，并将其改为独立句，将从句改为修饰性短语或并列句。

## 1. 删除

删除 who/that/which+is/was 等关系代词，从而将关系从句压缩成短语：

√ Of the many areas of science important to our future, few are more promising than genetic engineering, ~~which is~~ a new way of manipulating the elemental structural units of life itself, ~~which are~~ the genes and chromosomes that tell our cells how to reproduce to become the parts that constitute our bodies.

有时要对剪切后的动词进行重写，将其改为动词的 -ing 形式：

The day is coming when we will all have numbers **that will identify** our financial transactions so that the IRS can monitor all activities **that involve** economic activity.

√ The day is coming when we will all have numbers ~~that will~~ **identifying** our financial transactions so that the IRS can monitor all activities that **involving** economic activity.

## 2. 将从句改为独立句

√ Many areas of science are important to our future, but few are more promising than genetic engineering. It is a new way of manipulating the elemental structural units of life itself, the genes and chromosomes that tell our cells how to reproduce to become the parts that constitute our bodies.

## 3. 将从句改为修饰性短语

如果将关系从句改为下列三种修饰性短语的任意一种,就可以写出长而不零乱的句子,即重复性修饰语、总结性修饰语和自由修饰语。你或许从来没有听说过这几个术语,但它们是写作风格上的几种技巧,所以应该知道如何使用。

**重复性修饰语** 下述两个句子是使用关系从句和使用重复修饰语的对比:

Since mature writers often use resumptive modifiers to extend a line of thought, we need a word to name what I have not done in this sentence, **which I could have ended at that comma but extended to show you a relative clause attached to a noun.**

√ Since mature writers often use resumptive modifiers to extend a line of thought, we need a word to name what

I am about to do in this sentence, **a sentence that I could have ended at that comma but extended to show you how resumptive modifier work.**

黑体加粗的重复修饰语重复的是关键词 sentence，其后面的内容保持不变。

要找出重复性修饰语，首先要找到从句修饰的名词，名词后用逗号隔开，重复先行词，然后用 that 引出的限制性关系从句对其进行修饰：

Since mature writers often use resumptive modifiers to extend a line of thought, we need a word to name what I am about to do in **this sentence,**

**a sentence that I could have ended at that comma, but extended to show you how resumptive modifiers work.**

还可以使用形容词或动词重新开始一句话。如果这样就不需要添加关系从句，只需重复形容词或动词，然后继续：

√ It was American writers who found a voice that was both **true** and **lyrical**, **true** to the rhythms of the working man's speech and **lyrical** in its celebration of his labor.

√ All who value independence should **resist** the trivialization of government regulation,

**resist** its obsession with administrative tidiness and compulsion to arrange things not for our convenience but for theirs.

有时可以用 **one that** 作为重复修饰语：

√ I now address a problem we have wholly ignored, **one that** has plagued societies that sell their natural resources to benefit a few today rather than using them to develop new resources that benefit everyone tomorrow.

**总结性修饰语**　下面两句话是关系从句与**总结性修饰语**的对比。注意观察第一句中的 **which** 是如何"附加到"先行词上的：

Economic changes have reduced Russian population growth to less than zero, **which will have serious social implications.**

√ Economic changes have reduced Russian population growth to less than zero, **a demographic event that will have serious social implications.**

为了找出一个总结性修饰语，可在句子中一个语法结构完整的单位后面用逗号隔开，找出一个可对上文内容进行总结的词语，然后用一个 **that** 引出的限制性从句进行修饰：

Economic changes have reduced Russian population growth to less than zero,

<u>a demographic event</u> that will have serious social implications.

总结性修饰语与重复性修饰语会产生相同的效果，即让人产生句子行将结束，却又重新开始之感。

**自由修饰语**　与其他修饰语相同的是，**自由修饰语**也可以出现在从句的结尾，修饰距离动词最近的主语，而不是重复一个关键词或总结前文：

> √ Free modifiers resemble resumptive and summative modifiers, **letting you** [ i.e., the free modifier lets you ] **extend the line of a sentence while avoiding a train of ungainly phrases and clauses.**

自由修饰语通常是以 -ing 形式的现在分词开头，就像前面的例子，不过也可以以过去分词开头，如下：

> √ Leonardo da Vinci was a man of powerful intellect, *driven* by [ i.e., Leonardo was driven by ] **an insatiable curiosity and** *haunted* **by a vision of artistic perfection.**

自由修饰语也可以以形容词开头：

> √ In 1939, we began to assist the British against Germany, *aware* [ i.e., we were aware ] **that we faced another world war.**

[ 264 ] 风格：写作的清晰与优雅

将其称为自由修饰语是因为它们既可以放在句首也可以放在句尾：

√ **Driven by an insatiable curiosity**, Leonardo da Vinci was...

√ **Aware that we faced another world war**, in 1939 we began...

**要点** 写长句子的时候，千万不要只是用毫无条理的一个短语接一个短语或一个从句接一个从句，尤其要避免用一个关系从句紧接另一个关系从句。尽量用重复性修饰语、总结性修饰语和自由修饰语展开句子。

**快速提示** 快速提示：一些长的引导性从句可以很容易转化成独立的从句。最简单的就是 **although** 从句。将下列句子中的 **although** 去掉，用 **but** 或 **however** 引导从句。

**Although** some writers write well on their own, without the help of direct teaching or models of good prose, most benefit from instruction in the basics of writing graceful sentences.

√ Some writers write well on their own, without the help of direct teaching or models of good prose, **but** most benefit from instruction in the basics of writing graceful sentences.

另外一种简单的从句是 **since** 从句。去掉句中的 **since**，用 **so**、**therefore**、**as a result**，或其他类似的连词来引导后面的句子：

> **Since** few writers write well on their own, without the help of direct teaching or models of good prose, most first-year college students would benefit from a course in composition.
>
> √ Few writers write well on their own, without the help of direct teaching or models of good prose, **so** most first-year college students would benefit from a course in composition.

## 4. 并列

并列句是句子有条理因而显得优美的基础。写出好的并列句，比写出好的修饰语更困难，但是一旦完成，句子就会显得更加优美。对比下列两段话，第一段是我写的，第二段是原文：

> The aspiring artist may find that even a minor, unfinished work which was botched may be an instructive model for how things should be done, while for the amateur spectator, such works are the daily fare which may provide good, honest nourishment, which can lead to an appreciation of deeper pleasures that are also more refined.
>
> √ For the aspiring artist, the minor, the unfinished, or even the botched work, may be an instructive model for how things should—and should not—be done. For the amateur spectator, such works are the daily fare which may provide good, honest

nourishment—and which can lead to appreciation of more refined, or deeper pleasures.

——伊娃·霍夫曼,《小众艺术带来的别趣》

我修改后的版本因为使用了一连串的从句，而显得散乱。

The aspiring artist may find that even a minor, unfinished work
 **which** was botched may be an instructive model for
  **how** things should be done,
   **while** for the amateur spectator, such works are the daily fare
  **which** may provide good, honest nourishment,
   **which** can lead to an appreciation of deeper pleasures
    **that** are also more refined.

霍夫曼的原文结构则由众多的并列句组成。从结构上看，类似于这样：

For the aspiring artist, { the minor, the unfinished, or even the botched } work may be

an instructive model for how things { should and should not } be done.

For the amateur spectator, such works are

$$
\text{the daily fare} \begin{cases} \text{which provide} \begin{cases} \text{good,} \\ \text{honest} \end{cases} \text{nourishment---} \\ \text{and} \\ \text{which can lead to appreciation of} \begin{cases} \text{more refined,} \\ \text{or} \\ \text{deeper} \end{cases} \text{pleasures.} \end{cases}
$$

第二个句子尤其表明了并列句带来的优美效果。

## 一个普遍的设计原则：由短到长

应该注意到布局合理的并列句的一大特征。大声朗读下列句子就能听出该特征：

> We should devote a few final words to a matter that reaches beyond the techniques of research to the connections between those subjective values that reflect our deepest ethical choices and objective research.

该句以 **objective research** 结尾似乎有些唐突。从结构上看，其类似于：

... between { Those subjective values that reflect our deepest ethical choices and objective research. }

下面这个版本遵循了由短到长的原则，它将两个并列成分倒置，并增加第二句的长度，使其更好地形成并列结构。大声朗读下列句子：

√ We should devote a few final words to a matter that reaches beyond the techniques of research to the connections between objective research and those subjective values that reflect our deepest ethical choices and strongest intellectual commitments.

从结构上看，其类似于：

√ ... between { objective research and those subjective values that reflect our { deeapest ethical choices and strongest intellectual commitments. } }

尤为典雅的文章的特点是，作者总能巧妙使用这些技巧展开句子，尤其是均衡的并列句。我将在十一课讨论这些技巧，并对其做详细阐述。

**统一的原则**

事实上，由短到长的原则是清晰写作风格统一原则的一条：

适用于单独句子中主谓顺序：介绍长而复杂的信息时，句子越短越好。

适用于"以旧引新"原则：已知信息的字数通常少于新信息，而且人们心理上也觉得已知信息要短于新信息。

适用于长句逻辑要素的排序：把简短的主要信息放在前面，把用于解释和支撑论点的长而复杂的信息放在后面。

适用于平衡的并列句：短信息在前，长信息在后。

> **要点** 与使用从句来展开句子相比，使用并列结构使句子风格更优美。如果句子可以并列，要试着将短信息放在长信息前面，简单信息放在复杂信息前面。

> **快速提示** 可以通过关系连词强调并列结构：both X and Y, not only X but Y, ( n ) either X ( n ) or Y. 试比较：
>
> √ Great Britain is a good trading partner and a reliable ally in the war against terrorism.
>
> √ Great Britain is **both** a good trading partner **and** a reliable ally in the war against terrorism.
>
> 然而，使用这些连词的时候，要确保在与"both""not

> only"" ( n ) either" 这些词引导的句子并列的成分前加上 "and" "but", 或者 " ( n ) or"。在下列第一个句子中, "not only" 放到了句子的动词之前, 而 but 却放到了与之并列的句子的主句之前:
>
> When you punctuate carefully, you not **only** help *readers* understand a complex sentence more easily, **but** *you* enhance your own image as a good writer.
>
> 并列连词应该放在两个并列句的对应位置:
>
> √ When you punctuate carefully, you **not only** *help* readers understand a complex sentence more easily, **but** *enhance* your own image as a good writer.

## 练习 10.2

———❦———

修改下列句子,以解决其中的累赘、冗长、名词化等问题。然后找出合适的重复性修饰语、总结性修饰语及自由修饰语。在前四句中,使用黑体加粗的词开始一个重复性的修饰语。然后使用括号里的词重造一个含有总结性修饰语的句子。例如:

Within ten years, we could meet our energy **needs** with solar power. [ a possibility ]

重复性修饰语：

√ Within ten years, we could meet our energy **needs** with solar power, **needs** that will soar as our population grows.

总结性修饰语：

√ Within ten years, we could meet our energy needs with solar power, **a possibility** that few anticipated ten years ago.

自由修饰语：

√ Within ten years, we could meet our energy needs with solar power, **freeing** ourselves of dependence on foreign oil.

在为这些句子加上修饰语之前，先解决句中累赘、冗长、名词化等问题。

1. Many different school systems are making a return back to traditional education in the **basics**. [ a change ]

2. Within the period of the last few years or so, automobile manufacturers have been trying to meet new and more stringent-type quality control **requirements**. [ a challenge ]

3. The reasons for the cause of aging are a **puzzle** that has perplexed humanity for millennia. [ a mystery ]

4. The majority of young people in the world of today cannot even begin to have an understanding of the **insecurity** that a large number of older people had experienced during the period of the Great Depression. [ a failure ]

5. Many who lived during the period of the Victorian era were appalled when Darwin put forth the suggestion that their ancestry might have included creatures related to apes.

6. In the period known to scholars and historians as the Renaissance, increases in

affluence and stability in the area of political affairs had the consequence of allowing streams of thought of different kinds to merge and flow together.

7. The field of journalism has to an increasing degree placed its focus on the kind of news stories and events that one time in our history were considered to be only gossip of a salacious and sexual nature.

## 解决长句的问题

即使把握好了内部结构，长句仍然会出现问题。

### 语法上的错误并列

一般情况下，只是将相同语法结构的成分进行并列：从句和从句、介词短语和介词短语等。如果将不同的语法结构进行并列，读者会觉得句子明显缺乏并列的条件。认真的作者要避免这样写：

The committee recommends {
**revising the curriculum** to recognize trends in local employment
and
**that the division be reorganized** to reflect the new curriculum.
}

他们会把上句做这样的修改：

√ ... recommends {
  **that the curriculum be revised** to recognize...
  and
  **that the division be reorganized** to reflect...
}

或者这样改：

√ ... recommends {
  **revising the curriculum** to recognize ...
  and
  **reorganizing the division** to reflect...
}

然而，在一些好的作品中也不乏不平行的并列结构。认真的作者会把一个名词短语与一个 how 从句进行并列：

√ We will attempt to delineate {
  **the problems** of education in developing nations
  and
  **how coordinated efforts can address** them in economical ways.
}

他们还会把一个动词与介词短语并列

√ The proposal appears to have been written { **quickly,** **carefully,** **and** **with the help of** many. }

认真的读者不会被这两种情况打断。

## 修辞上的错误并列

并列成分在语法和思想上都平行时,读者最易察觉。一些没有经验的作者只是简单地用 **and** 将两个成分并列起来:

> Grade inflation is a problem at many universities, **and** it leads to a devaluation of good grades earned by hard work **and** will not be solved simply by grading harder.

那些 **ands** 使这些主张间的相互关系模糊了:

> √ Grade inflation is a problem at many universities, **because** it devalues good grades that were earned by hard work, **but** it will not be solved simply by grading harder.

不幸的是,我也无从判断并列成分何时在思想上处于不平行状态,只能提醒你"要注意"。当然,这就像告诉击球手要直接击中球一样。我们知道要这么做,但不知道该怎么做。

**连词不明确**

如果并列成分过长而造成内部关系模糊和指代不清,读者就会不胜其扰:

> Teachers should remember that students are vulnerable and uncertain about those everyday ego-bruising moments that adults ignore and that they do not understand that one day they will become as confident and as secure as the adults that bruise them.

下面这句话中连词所连接的成分不明确:

> ... and that they do not understand that one day they...

如果修改这样的句子,就要缩短并列结构的前半部分,这样可以使后半部分与并列成分的起始点距离更近:

> √ Teachers should remember that students are vulnerable to ego-bruising moments that adults ignore and that they do not understand that one day...

或者重复用于提示并列成分开始的词语(由此创造出一个重复性修饰语):

> √ Teachers should remember that students are vulnerable to ego-bruising moments that adults ignore, **to remember** that they do not understand that...

或者重复名词以避免代词带来的歧义：

√ Teachers should remember that **students** are vulnerable to ego-bruising moments that adults ignore and that **students** do not understand that one day...

## 歧义的修饰语

修饰语带来的另外一个问题是读者有时对其所修饰的成分不确定：

Overtaxing oneself in physical activity too frequently results in injury.

究竟是什么频繁发生，是过度征税还是其带来的伤害？通过移动 **too frequently** 的位置可以降低该句的歧义性：

√ Overtaxing oneself too frequently in physical activity results in injury.

√ Overtaxing oneself in physical activity results too frequently in injury.

位于句尾的修饰语，既可以修饰与其相邻的词又可以修饰距离更远的词，因此会带来歧义：

Scientists have learned that their observations are as subjective as those in any other field **in recent years.**

可以改变修饰语的位置以减少歧义：

√ **In recent years**, scientists have learned that...

√ Scientists have learned that **in recent years** their...

## 悬置的修饰语

长句的另外一个问题就是**悬置修饰语**。如果修饰语所修饰的主语与主句的明确主语不同，这一问题就出现了：

To overcome chronic poverty and lagging economic development in sub-Saharan Africa,（悬置修饰语）a commitment to health and education（完全主语）is necessary for there to be progress in raising standards of living.

动词 overcome 暗示的主语没有明确写出，但是主句的明确主语是 commitment。为了解决悬置的修饰语问题，可以将暗含的主语明确出来：

√ If **developed countries** are to overcome chronic poverty and lagging economic development in sub-Saharan Africa, a commitment to health and education is necessary...

或者更好的方法是将修饰语暗含的主语与主句的明确主语保持一致：

√ To overcome chronic poverty and lagging economic

development in sub-Saharan Africa, **developed countries** must commit themselves to...

## 自我检测

### 练习 10.3

———⁕———

引导句子的两大经验是：(1) 读者能快速找到主语 (2) 能快速找到动词和宾语（见 248—250 页）。浏览一篇自己的文章，用下划线标出每句话的前七八个词。如果每句话的前七个或八个单词中仍没有出现主语和动词，就对其进行修改。

### 练习 10.4

———⁕———

对作者来说，很难发现自己不好的写作习惯，因为他们对自己的写作太熟悉了。所以找个读者来帮你：

是否是花了很长时间才找到主语和动词？

主语是否过长？

主语和动词或动词和宾语间是否有插入语？

是否花了很长时间才找到要点（在句子和段落里）？

是否在从句后叠加了一连串的从句？

找一个读者读几页自己的文章，用横线标出表述不清或理解困难的段落。

尽量让她说出理解困难的原因，如果说不出就和读者一起浏览诊断文章。（若读者觉得文章有问题，要相信他的判断，即使他说不出具体问题在哪）然后对文章进行修改。

## 总结

下列是一些原则，使句子的结构更连贯：

1. 使读者能快速找到主语、动词和宾语：
a. 避免使用过长的引导性短语和从句，将其改为独立的句子：

Since most undergraduate students change their major fields of study at least once during their college careers, many more than once, **first-year students** who are not certain about the program of studies they want to pursue should not load up their schedules to meet requirements for a particular program.

√ **Most undergraduate students** change their major fields of study at least once during their college careers, so **first-year students** should not load up their schedules with requirements for a particular program if they are not certain about the program of studies they want to pursue.

b. 避免使用过长的主语。将长主语改为引导性的从句：

A company that focuses on hiring the best personnel

and then trains them not just for the work they are hired to do but for higher-level jobs is likely to earn the loyalty of its employees.

√ When a company focuses on hiring the best personnel and then trains them not just for the work they are hired to do but for higher-level jobs later, it is likely to earn the loyalty of its employees.

如果改为引导性从句后，从句过长，就要将其置于句末：

√ A company is likely to earn the loyalty of its employees when it focuses on hiring the best personnel...

或者是将其单独成句：

√ Some companies focus on hiring the best personnel and then train them not just for the work they are hired to do but for higher-level jobs later. Such companies are likely to earn the loyalty of their employees.

c. 避免在主语和动词及动词与宾语之间使用插入语，将插入语置于句首或句末，具体主要取决于下文内容：

Some scientists, **because they write in a style that is impersonal and objective**, do not easily communicate with laypeople.

√ **Because some scientists write in a style that is impersonal and objective**, they *do not easily communicate with laypeople. This lack of communication damages...*

√ Some scientists do not easily communicate with laypeople **because they write in a style that is impersonal and objective.** *It is a kind of style filled with passives...*

2. 句首用简短的主句将句子要表达的主要观点陈述出来：

A new sales initiative that has created a close integration between the garden and home products departments has made significant improvements to the customer services that Acme offers.

√ Acme has significantly improved its customer services with a new sales initiative that closely integrates the garden and home products departments.

3. 在主句后避免从句叠加从句的情况：

a. 修剪关系从句，将下列句子改为两句：

Of the many areas of science **that** are important to our future, few are more promising than genetic engineering, **which** is a new way of manipulating the elemental structural units of life itself, **which** are the genes and chromosomes **that** tell our cells how to reproduce to become the parts **that** constitute our bodies.

√ Many areas of science are important to our future, but few are more promising than genetic engineering. It is a new way of manipulating the elemental structural units of life itself, **which** are the genes and chromosomes **that** tell our cells how to reproduce to become the parts that constitute our bodies.

√ Of the many areas of science ~~that are~~ important to our future, few are more promising than genetic engineering, ~~which is~~ a new way of manipulating the elemental structural units of life itself, ~~which are~~ the genes and chromosomes that tell our cells how to reproduce to become the parts ~~that~~ **constituting** our bodies.

b. 使用重复性修饰语、总结性修饰语和自由修饰语来展开句子：

| | |
|---|---|
| √ 重复性修饰语： | When we discovered the earth was not the center of the universe, it changed our understanding of who we are, **an understanding changed again by Darwin, again by Freud, and again by Einstein.** |
| √ 总结性修饰语： | American productivity has risen to new heights, **an achievement that only a decade ago was considered an impossible dream.** |
| √ 自由修饰语： | Global warming will become a central political issue of the twenty-first century, **raising questions whose answers will affect the standard of living in every Western nation.** |

c. 将语法和意义上都平行的成分进行并列：

Besides the fact that no civilization has experienced such rapid alterations in their spiritual and mental lives, the material conditions of their daily existence have changed greatly too.

√ No civilization has experienced such rapid alterations in their spiritual and mental lives and in the material conditions of daily existence.

最后一点注意事项：要写出长而复杂又表述清晰的句子，或许需要借助标点符号帮助读者阅读文章（见附录Ⅰ）。

[第十一课]

# 典 雅

> 写作，最看重的是明白易懂；行文，讲究简洁有力，而非枯燥乏味。这是一个值得尝试的冒险：一头卷曲的假发，往往不如一颗光秃秃的脑袋来得爽利。
>
> ——萨默塞特·毛姆
> （Somerset Maugham）

> 反复阅读你的文章，如果遇到一个自认为极其优美的段落，就将其删掉。
>
> ——塞缪尔·约翰逊
> （Samuel Johnson）

> 在文学圈里，初学者千方百计掌握文学的语言；然而行家却要千方百计摒弃文学的语言。
>
> ——乔治·萧伯纳
> （George Bernard Shaw）

## 典雅的内涵

任何人如能写得清晰、简洁、连贯，都应当为此感到高兴。与臃肿的套路式文章相比，大部分读者更偏爱单调的清晰。但是直白到了极致，文章就会略显枯燥，甚至乏味。正如不加盐的肉和土豆，虽具斯巴达风味，但这样的菜肴却很少令人怀想。然而，惊鸿一瞥的优美不但会将一个思想固定在了我们的脑海里，而且每当回想起来，都会为我们带来丝丝愉悦。不幸的是，我不知道怎样才能写得优美。事实上，我倾向于剥离了直白之后，最优美的典雅才能实现。

不过，总有一些可以用既典雅又清晰的方式将我们思想梳理出来的方法。但是，只明白道理亦无济于事，就像仅仅知道烹调鱼肉汤的材料，并不能保证鱼肉汤做得鲜美一样。写得典雅清晰可能是一种天赋。但是这种天赋必须经过教育和锻炼，才能获得。

## 平衡和对称

最能使句子显得优雅的，是各部分之间保持平衡和对称，在音调、节奏、结构和意义上相互呼应。写作娴熟的作者能够平衡句子的每一部分，而最常见的平衡的基础是协调。

**平衡的协调**

下面是一段分布平衡的段落以及我修订的版本。即使听觉不灵敏的人也能够区分开来：

> The national unity of a free people depends upon a sufficiently even balance of political power to make it impracticable for the administration to be arbitrary and for the opposition to be revolutionary and irreconcilable. Where that balance no longer exists, democracy perishes. For unless all the citizens of a state are forced by circumstances to compromise, unless they feel that they can affect policy but that no one can wholly dominate it, unless by habit and necessity they have to give and take, freedom cannot be maintained.
>
> ——瓦尔特·李普曼

The national unity of a free people depends upon a sufficiently even balance of political power to make it impracticable for an administration to be arbitrary against a revolutionary opposition that is irreconcilably opposed to it. Where that balance no longer exists, democracy perishes, because unless all the citizens of a state are habitually forced by necessary circumstances to compromise in a way that lets them affect policy with no one dominating it, freedom cannot be maintained.

我的句子前后失去了平衡。然而在李普曼的版本里，在词序、音调和意义上从句和短语之间总能够相互呼应，从而使整个段落形成一种复杂的建筑学上的对称。

话题和重读原则不仅适用于句子，也适用于文章的每个部分。如果我们运用此原则来分析这个段落，就可以看出李普曼是如何平衡这些异常简短的片段的了。注意短语中每个有实际意义的词和相应短语中的词呼应的方式（话题短语用黑体，重读词用斜体）：

The national unity of a free people depends upon a sufficiently even balance of political power to make it impracticable.

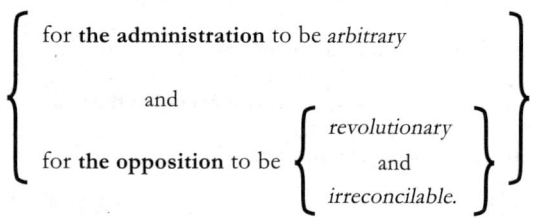

李普曼让以短语形式出现的话题"administration"和"opposition"保持了平衡，结尾时让"arbitrary""revolutionary"和"irreconcilable"在重读和意义上保持了平衡。后面跟着一个简短的概括句，它的重读词虽不协调但仍保持了平衡（我用方括号来表示非协调的平衡部分）：

Where [ **that balance** *no longer exists,* **democracy** *perishes.* ]

然后，他构建了一个十分复杂的结构，结果使许多音调和意义保持了平衡：

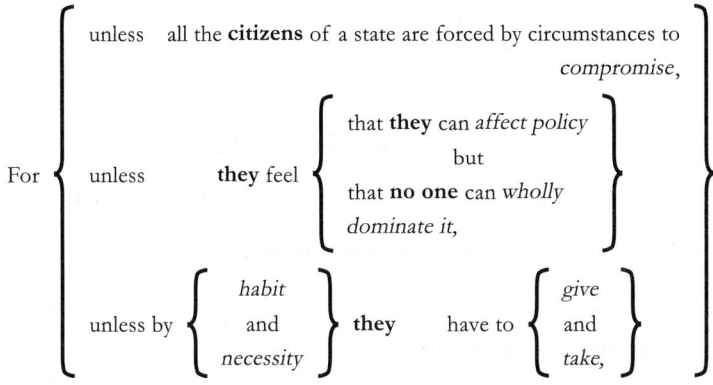

他重复使用"citizens"，将之当作每个从句的主语/话题：all the citizens, they, they（注意第一句中的被动句：citizens are forced; 主动句就会使协调性失衡）。

他使 force 的读音和意义与 feel 的保持平衡，并且 affect policy 与 dominated it 在意义上保持平衡。

在"unless"从句中，他使"habit"与"necessity"在意义上保持平衡，被重读的"give"和"take"在意义上保持平衡。

他使"compromise""affect""dominate"与"give and take"在意义上保持平衡。

然后，为了使前面简短的从句 balance no longer exists 与 democracy perishes 保持平衡，他写了一个同样简短的从

第十一课 典雅 [289]

句 freedom cannot be maintained，该句的意义和结构都与前句中相应的部分呼应：

| | |
|---|---|
| balance | no longer exists |
| democracy | perishes |
| freedom | cannot be maintained |

对于有心人来说，这样的结构让他们记忆深刻。

**不平行结构的平衡**　我们也可以使语法上不平行的结构保持平衡。在下面的例子中，主语和宾语就保持了平衡：

$$\left[\begin{array}{l}\textbf{Scientists}\text{ whose research }\textit{creates revolutionary views of the universe}\\ \qquad\qquad\qquad\qquad\text{invariably confuse}\\ \textbf{those of us}\text{ who }\textit{construe reality from our common-sense experience of it.}\end{array}\right]$$

下面的句子中，修饰主语的关系从句中的**谓语**与整个句子的**谓语**保持了平衡。

$$\text{A government}\left[\begin{array}{l}\textit{that is unwilling to }\text{listen}\textit{ to the }\text{moderate hopes}\textit{ of }\text{its citizenry}\\ \textit{must eventually }\text{answer}\textit{ to the }\text{harsh justice}\textit{ of }\text{its revolutionaries.}\end{array}\right]$$

下面句子中，直接宾语和介词的宾语保持了平衡：

Those of us concerned with our school systems will not sacrifice

$$\left[\begin{array}{ll} \text{the } \textit{intellectual growth} \text{ of} & \text{our } \textit{innocent children} \\ & \text{to} \\ \text{the } \textit{social engineering} \text{ of} & \textit{incompetent bureaucrats.} \end{array}\right]$$

下面是一个更复杂的平衡结构:

$$\text{Were I trading}^{1a} \left[\begin{array}{c} \text{scholarly principles}^{2a} \\ \text{for} \\ \text{financial security,}^{2b} \end{array}\right]$$

$$\text{I would not be writing}^{1b} \left[\begin{array}{c} \text{short books}^{3a} \\ \text{On} \\ \text{minor subjects}^{3b} \\ \text{for} \\ \text{small audiences.}^{3c} \end{array}\right]$$

在上面的句子结构中,

从句(1a),"Were I trading"和主句(1b)"I would not be writing"保持了平衡;

从句(2a)的宾语"scholarly principles"和介词短语(2b)里的宾语"financial security"保持了平衡;

主句(3a)中的宾语"short books"和两个介词短语的宾语,(3b)中"minor subjects"以及(3c)中的"small audiences"(用 short、minor 和 small 实现这种平衡)保持了平衡。

切记：如果每个连续的平衡元素比前一个稍长，那通常就实现了最有节奏的平衡。（参见 268—269 页）

这些模式激励我们以一种意想不到的方式去思考。从这种意义上讲，它们不只是塑造了思维，也创造了思维。试想句子以这样开头：

> In his earliest years, Picasso was a master draftsman of the traditional human form.

现在尝试这样写：

> In his earliest years, Picasso was **not only** a master draftsman of the traditional human form, **but also**...

为了了解完整的信息，你不得不想弄明白，毕加索可能有，也可能没有，或者早已有其他的身份了。

---

**要点** 典雅文章的最显著特征是句式结构保持平衡。很容易通过使用连接词 and、or、nor、but 和 yet 使句子的各个部分保持平衡，不过，也可以使不协调的短语和从句保持平衡。过度使用这些套路，只会显示写作技巧的娴熟；然而谨慎地使用，则可以强调重点，或者用令人难忘的方式结束推论的过程，这足以使细心的读者注意到。

## 最大程度的强调

句子是否清晰是由开头决定的；而句子是否有节奏、是否优美则是由结尾决定的。下面是五种句子结尾的方法，都运用了特殊的强调：

### 1. 举足轻重的词

当读到句子结尾时，我们期望看到应得到强调的词（见150—152页）。因此，如果一个句子的结束词在语法上或者语义上无足轻重，那么就会使文章虎头蛇尾。在句子的结尾处使用介词，就不会引起读者的注意，这是有时避免使用介词结尾的一个原因。句子的节奏应当带给读者力量。对比下面两句：

> Studies into intellectual differences among races are projects that only the most politically naive psychologist would be willing to give support to.

> √ Studies into intellectual differences among races are projects that only the most politically naive psychologist would be willing to support.

与介词相比，形容词和副词更能引起读者的注意，但它们都不如名词，而名词中最引人注意的是名词化的词。如果它们出现在主语里，读者就会感到疑惑，但是当它们位于句尾时，尤其是两个词协调平衡的时候，读者则会感到满意，而且印象深刻。思考下面一节选自丘吉尔《最光辉的时刻》("Finest Hour")的选段。他用平行结构来结束句子，该结构通过一对平衡的名词引起读者的注意：

> ... until in God's good time.
>
> the New World, with all its { power and might } steps forth to
>
> { the **rescue** and the **liberation** } of the old.

他本可以写得更加直白和平衡：

> ... until the New World rescues us.

## 2. Of + 有分量的词

这种搭配似乎不大可能，但却是事实。看一下丘吉尔是如何结束他的句子的：仅在这个重点强调的单音节词 old 之前，轻音 of（后面跟着一个更轻的 a 或者 the）加快了句子的节奏感：

> ... the rescue and the liberation of the **old**.

我们有意识地将这种句型和典雅联系起来，正如在爱德华·吉本（Edward Gibbon）的《罗马帝国衰亡史》(*History the Roman Empire's Decline and Fall*) 中开篇的一些句子一样（请与下面书名做对比：*History of the Roman Empire's Decline and Fall*）：

√ In the second century of the Christian era, the Empire of Rome comprehended **the fairest part** *of* **the earth,** AND **the most civilized portion** *of* **mankind.** The frontiers of that extensive monarchy were guarded **by ancient renown** AND **disciplined valour.** The gentle but powerful influence of laws and manners had gradually cemented **the union** *of* **the provinces.** Their peaceful inhabitants **enjoyed** AND **abused the advantages of wealth** AND **luxury.** The image of a free constitution was preserved with decent **reverence:** the Roman senate appeared to possess the sovereign authority, and devolved on the emperors all **the executive powers** *of* **government.**

相比之下,下面这段就显得平淡无奇了:

In the second century AD, the Roman Empire comprehended **the earth's fairest, most civilized part.** Ancient renown and disciplined valour guarded **its extensive frontiers.** The gentle but powerful influence of laws and manners had gradually **unified the provinces.** Their peaceful inhabitants enjoyed and abused luxurious wealth while decently preserving what seemed to be **a free constitution.** Appearing to possess the sovereign authority, the Roman senate devolved on the emperors all **executive governmental powers.**

## 3. 强调前后呼应

在句子的结尾,如果一个重读单词/短语在发音和意义上与

前面某个词 / 短语保持平衡，那么读者会听出来特殊的强调意味。下面的例子均选自皮特·盖伊（Peter Gay）的著作《历史的风格》(*Style in History*)

> √ I have written these essays to anatomize this familiar yet really strange being, **style the centaur**; the book may be read as an extended critical commentary on Buffon's famous saying that **the style is the man.**

如果一个重读词和前面的某个词相呼应，这种平衡就更具强调性的意味：

> √ Apart from a few mechanical tricks of rhetoric, **manner** is indissolubly linked to **matter**; **style shapes**, and in turn is **shaped** by, **substance.**

> √ It seems frivolous, almost inappropriate, to be **stylish** about **style.**

盖伊用 matter, shape by, style 分别呼应了 manner, style, shapes 和 stylish 的读音和意义。

### 4. 交错法

或许，只有那些醉心于艰涩写作风格的人对交错法（Chiasmus [kɪˈæzmes]）感兴趣。"Chiasmus"一词来自希腊语，意思是"交叉"。它的功能是使句子中两部分的元素保持平衡，但是，第二部分中相呼应的元素的顺序颠倒了。例如，下面的句子不但协调，而且平行，但是它没有使用交错法结尾，因为这两部分的元素顺序相同（1A1B : 2A2B）：

$$\checkmark \text{ A concise style can improve both} \begin{Bmatrix} \text{our own}^{1A} \ thinking^{1B} \\ \text{and} \\ \text{our readers'}^{2A} \ understanding.^{2B} \end{Bmatrix}$$

要是寻求特殊的效果的话，我们本可以颠倒第二部分的顺序来呼应第一部分的对应元素。现在的句型不是 1A1B 对应 2A2B，而是 1A1B 对应 2B2A：

$$\checkmark \text{ A concise style can improve not only} \begin{Bmatrix} \text{our own}^{1A} \ thinking^{1B} \\ \text{but} \\ \text{the } understanding^{2B} \text{ of our readers.}^{2A} \end{Bmatrix}$$

下面的例子更加复杂。两句的前两个元素是对称的，但是最后三部分是相互呼应的，其格式为 AB CDE，AB EDC：

$$\begin{bmatrix} \text{You}^A \ reveal^B \ \textbf{your own}^C \ \ \ highest \ rhetorical^D \ \text{SKILL}^E \\ \text{by the way} \\ \text{you}^A \ respect^B \ \text{THE BELIEFS}^E \ most \ deeply \ held^D \ \textbf{by your reader.}^C \end{bmatrix}$$

## 5. 悬置

最后，不采纳我此前讨论过的方法，直接运用戏剧性高潮结束句子。在第十课，我建议过使用要点词引出句子。但是，自觉优雅的作者通常将一系列平行、并列的短语和从句放在句子的开头，这样他们可以推迟高潮到来的时间，从而增强高潮感。

> If [journalists] held themselves as responsible for the rise of public cynicism as they hold "venal" politicians and the "selfish" public; if they considered that the license they have to criticize and defame comes with an implied responsibility to serve the public—if they did all or any of these things, they would make journalism more useful, public life stronger, and themselves far more worthy of esteem.
>
> ——詹姆斯·法洛斯，《传播新闻》

这句（法娄斯书的最后一句）用三个 if 从句开头，三个并列结构结尾。该句最后一个并列部分是最长的，该部分用一个 of+名词化的词（worthy of esteem）结束。然而，像如此长的悬置句这类的手法，其效果与它使用的频率正好成反比：使用的越少，效果越好。

> **要点** 典雅句子的结尾应该响亮有力。可以用下面五种方法达到这种效果：
>
> 1. 用一个有分量的词，或最好用一对这样的词结尾。
> 2. 用 of 引导的介词短语结尾。
> 3. 用前后呼应的强调结尾。
> 4. 用交错句结尾。
> 5. 高潮开头，高潮结尾。

## 过度典雅

如果作者把所有的元素都放到一个句子里,其目的是要强调某些成分,正如下面这个段落一样:

> Far from being locked inside our own skins, inside the "dungeons" of ourselves, we are now able to recognize that our minds belong, quite naturally, to a collective "mind", a mind in which we share everything that is mental, most obviously language itself, and that the old boundary of the skin is not boundary at all but a membrane connecting the inner and outer experience of existence. Our intelligence, our wit, our cleverness, our unique personalities—all are simultaneously "our own" possessions and the world's.
>
> ——乔伊斯·卡洛尔·欧茨,《新天地》

下面是关于这段话的一个解析:

Far from being locked **inside** our own skins,
     **inside** the "dungeons" of ourselves.

我们能够辨别 {
    that our minds belong, quite naturally, to a collective **"mind"**,
        **a mind** in which we share { everything that is *mental*, most obviously *language itself*, }
    and
    that the old boundary of the skin is { not *boundary* at all but *a membrane* connecting the inner and outer **experience of existence.** }
}

{ Our intelligence, our wit, our cleverness, our unique personalities } —all are simultaneously { "our own" possessions and the world's. }

除了所有的并列外，注意下面两个简明的修饰语：

> Far from being locked **inside** our own skins,
>         **inside** the "dungeons" of ourselves…
> Our minds belong… to a collective **"mind"**,
>         **a mind** in which we share…

还要注意首句句尾两个被强调的名词化的词，以及第二句句尾并列的名词化的词：

> … the inner and outer experience of existence.
> … "our own" possessions and the world's.

但是，这样的句型还可以得到更详尽的阐述。下面这段选自弗雷德里克·杰克逊·特纳（Frederick Jackson Turner）的《美国历史前沿》(*The Frontier in American History*) 中的最后一句：

This then is the heritage of the pioneer experience—a passionate belief that a democracy was possible which should leave the individual a part to play in a free society and not make him a cog in a machine operated from above; which trusted in the common man, in his tolerance, his ability to adjust differences with good humor, and to work out an American type from the contributions of all nations—a type for which he would fight against those who challenged it in arms, and for which in time of war he would make sacrifices, even the temporary sacrifice of his individual freedom and his life, lest that freedom be lost forever.

注意下面的内容：

开篇部分中的总结性修饰语：a passionate belief that...

每个并列成分（甚至包括并列中的并列部分）中加长加重的第二元素。

用 type 和 sacrifice 开始的两个重复性修饰词。

接近句尾处，尤其是最后十六个词中的四重交错搭配：

the temporary[1] sacrifice[2] of his individual FREEDOM[3] and his life[4], lest[4] that FREEDOM[3] be lost[2] forever[1].

temporary 和 forever 的意义保持平衡；sacrifice 和 lost 保持平衡；freedom 和 freedom 相呼应；life 的读音和 lest（更不用说 lest 在 lost 的韵律相近了）保持平衡。像这样优美的句子恐怕再也写不出来了。

下面是关于该段落的解析：

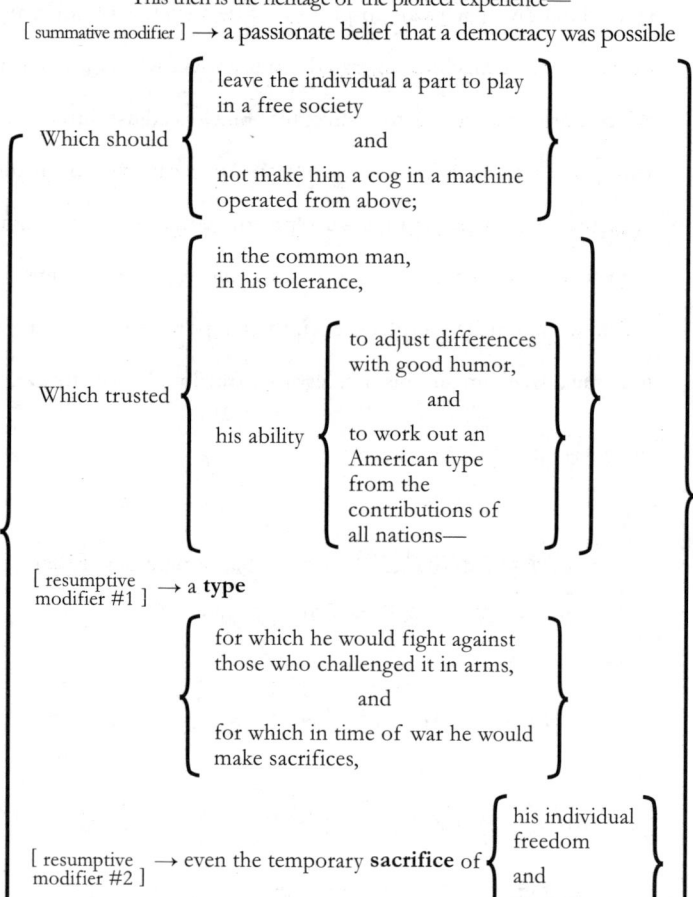

## 练习 11.1

下文给出了句子的前半部分,根据例句,采用前后平衡的方法完成句子的后半部分。

Those who keep silent over the loss of small freedoms... finish with something like this:

... will be silenced when they protest the loss of large ones.

1. Those who argue stridently over small matters...

2. While the strong are often afraid to admit weakness, the weak...

3. We should pay more attention to those politicians who tell us how to make what we have better than to those...

4. When parents raise children who scorn hard work, the adults those children become will...

5. Some teachers mistake neat papers that rehash old ideas for...

## 练习 11.2

下面的句子结尾虚弱无力。首先将它们修改得清晰、简洁,然后用强重读的词结尾,尤其要使用 of 引导的介词短语。例如:

Our interest in paranormal phenomena testifies to the fact that we have **empty spirits and shallow minds.**

√ Our interest in paranormal phenomena testifies to **the emptiness of our**

**spirits and the shallowness of our minds.**

在前三句中,我将可以被名词化的词用黑体字标出。

1. If we invest our sweat in these projects, we must avoid appearing to work only because we are **interested** in ourselves.

2. The plan for the political campaign was concocted by those who were not sensitive to what we **needed** most critically.

3. Throughout history, science has made progress because dedicated scientists have ignored a **hostile** public that is uninformed.

4. Not one tendency in our governmental system has brought about more changes in American daily life than federal governmental agencies that are very powerful.

5. The day is gone when school systems' boards of education have the expectation that local taxpayers will automatically go along with whatever extravagant things incompetent bureaucrats decide to do.

## 长度和节奏的细微差别

大部分作者不规划句子的长度,在他们看来,除非每个句子不超过十五个词,或者除非它特别长,否则这将不是问题。然而,老练的作者确实会通过规划句子的长度来达到某种目的。一些作者使用短句来突出内容的紧迫性:

> Towards noon Petrograd again became the field of military action; rifles and machine guns rang out everywhere. It was not

easy to tell who was shooting or where. One thing was clear; the past and the future were exchanging shots. There was much casual firing; young boys were shooting off revolvers unexpectedly acquired. The arsenal was wrecked... Shots rang out on both sides. But the board fence stood in the way, dividing the soldiers from the revolution. The attackers decided to break down the fence. They broke down part of it and set fire to the rest. About twenty barracks came into view. The bicyclists were concentrated in two or three of them. The empty barracks were set fire to at once.

——利昂·托洛茨基,《俄国革命》, 马克思·东曼译

或者精悍短小, 显示其必然性:

The teacher or lecturer is a danger. He very seldom recognizes his nature or his position. The lecturer is a man who must talk for an hour.

France may possibly have acquired the intellectual leadership of Europe when their academic period was cut down to forty minutes.

I also have lectured. The lecturer's first problem is to have enough words to fill forty or sixty minutes. The professor is paid for his time, his results are almost impossible to estimate...

No teacher has ever failed from ignorance.

That is empiric professional knowledge.

Teachers fail because they cannot "handle the class".

Real education must ultimately be limited to men who INSIST on knowing, the rest is mere sheep-herding.

——埃兹拉·庞德,《阅读ABC》

或者显示直接性。下面的文章中,马克·吐温使用简短的语法句模仿成人对小孩子的说教,用长而加标点的句子——不只是长的单词——给心照不宣的读者以暗示(关于语法句和加标点句的差异,见十一课,346—347页):

These chapters are for children, and I shall try to make the words large enough to command respect. In the hope that you are listening, and that you have confidence in me, I will proceed. Dates are difficult things to acquire; and after they are acquired it is difficult to keep them in the head. But they are very valuable. They are like the cattle-pens of a ranch—they shut in the several brands of historical cattle, each within its own fence, and keep them from getting mixed together. Dates are hard to remember because they consist of figures; figures are monotonously unstriking in appearance, and they don't take hold, they form no picture, and so they give the eye no chance to help. Pictures are the thing. Pictures can make dates stick. They can make nearly anything stick—particularly *if you make the pictures yourself*. Indeed, that is the great point—make the pictures *yourself*. I know about this from experience.

——马克·吐温,《巧记历史日期》

敏感的文体家也写超长的句子。下面就是其中一例,那曲折蜿蜒的长句似乎反映出抗议队伍的艰难历程:

> In any event, up at the front of this March, in the first line, back of that hollow square of monitors, Mailer and Lowell walked in this barrage of cameras, helicopters, TV cars, monitors, loudspeakers, and wavering buckling twisting line of notables, arms linked ( line twisting so much that at times the movement was in file, one arm locked ahead, one behind, then the line would undulate about and the other arm would be ahead ) speeding up a few steps, slowing down while a great happiness came back into the day as if finally one stood under some mythical arch in the great vault of history, helicopters buzzing about, chop-chop, and the sense of America divided on this day now liberated some undiscovered patriotism in Mailer so that he felt a sharp searing love for his country in this moment and on on this day, crossing some divide in his own mind wider than the Potomac, a love so lacerated he felt as if a marriage were being torn and children lost—never does one love so much as then, obviously, then—and an odor of wood smoke, from where you knew not, was also in the air, a smoke of dignity and some calm heroism, not unlike the

sense of freedom which also comes when a marriage is burst—Mailer knew for the first time why men in the front line of battle are almost always ready to die; there is a promise of some swift transit... [ it goes on ]

——诺曼·梅勒,《夜幕下的大军》

我们几乎认为,我们是在窃听梅勒(Mailer)的思想。但是,这种句子当然不是情感自然流露的产物,而是精心策划的艺术品。

梅勒用简短且断音的短语引出句子,从而表明困惑,但是他用并列结构来组织它们。

他用并列的自由修饰定语展开句子。

几个更自由的修饰语之后,他中间使用了重复性的修饰语(a love so lacerated...)。

在一个语法句之后,他增加了另一个重复性修饰语(a smoke of dignity and some calm heroism...)

> **要点** 除非文章的句子超过了三十个词,或者少于十五个词,否则就要考虑句子的长度。如果用这章学到的方法写作,句子会变换得很自然。不过,情况允许的话,可以自由地尝试。

# 自我检测

## 练习 11.3

———⁂———

通过模仿例子——不是词对词，只是大体的句型，你可以掌握平衡的技巧。可以从布道词、政治演讲词，或者词典的引用词中挑一些喜欢的精致的平衡段落，选择自己文章的一个主题，遵循模型的框架去写，就像下面这位作者引用弗雷德里克·杰克逊·特纳一个段落做的练习一样。

Survival in the wilderness requires the energy and wit to overcome the brute facts of an uncooperative. Nature but rewards the person who acquires that power with the satisfaction of having done it once and with the confidence of being able to do it again.

Life as a college student offers a few years of intellectual excitement but imposes a sense of anxiety on those who look ahead and know that its end is in sight.

你也可以模仿这一课中的例子。

## 练习 11.4

———⁂———

祝贺你，已经通过十一课学习到了清晰和优美的原则。这个练习是一个检验你学习成果的机会。把两篇自己写的五百字的文章交给一位读者，一篇是开始读这本书之前写的，另一篇是最近完成的。读者可以辨认出它们吗？在写作风格中，你做了哪些特别的改变？用本课中的规则去描述新作和旧作中的差别。

# 总结

总的来说,优美的特点不胜枚举,也特别微妙,从而难以把握。不过,典雅的文章具有三个特征,这些特征看似相互矛盾,其实不然:

人物做主语和动词表达动作时的简洁性。
平衡句式、意义、读音和节奏的复杂性。
巧妙重读结尾所实现的强调效果。

仅通过读本书,并不能掌握典雅的文风。必须读文风优美的作者的文章,直到他们的风格渗透到你的骨髓之中。只有那时,才可以查看你自己的文章,才知道何处优美,何处矫揉造作。为使文章与众不同,我认为唯一的规则就是"少即是好"。在许多风格优美的作品中,我认为,压缩篇幅仍然是首位的。

# 总结:第四部分

在第二部分中已经列出的规则上,我们添加以下四条:
1. 删除冗余。

删除意义不大或者没有意义的词。
删除重复其他词意的词。
删除其他词中隐含的词。

用词替代短语。

被动语态转换为主动语态。

2. 从简练的主句中得到句子的主要观点。

3. 从主句中迅速找到动词。

保持引导性从句和短语的简短。

保持主语简短。

不要在主语—动词结构中插入其他成分。

4. 不要在句子结尾的从句后添加多于一个的同类从句。而是：

使短语和从句并列，如果想达到特殊的效果，就要使之保持平衡。

使用重复性的、总结性的自由修饰语。

5. 努力使句子的每一部分保持平衡，尤其是它们中的最后几个词。

# 第五部分 伦理

> 从根本上讲，伦理是一种为了寻求合作而建议别人做出必要牺牲的艺术。
>
> ——伯特兰·罗素
> （Bertrand Russell）

[第十二课]

# 伦 理

任何事情都应该尽可能简单,但不能过于简单。

——阿尔伯特·爱因斯坦

(Albert Einstein)

朴实绝不是不劳而获的。它是一种成就、一项人类的发明、一个发现、一种人们钟爱的信仰。

——威廉·加斯

(William Gass)

风格是心灵的终极道德。

——阿尔弗雷德·诺斯·怀特海

(Alfred North Whitehead)

## 超越润色

我们很容易把风格理解为使句子流畅的润色,然而在下列两句中主语和动词的选择会比润色的魅力更加重要:

1a. **Shiites and Sunnis** DISTRUST one another because **they** HAVE ENGAGED in generations of cultural conflict.

1b. **Generations of cultural conflict** HAVE CAUSED distrust among Shiites and Sunnis.

这两个句子哪一个更能准确地反映出他们彼此不信任的原因——是(1a)中有意的行为,还是(1b)中的历史环境?主语和动词的选择甚至会暗示人类行为的哲学:我们能自由地选择行动吗?还是当时的环境使然?后面,我们会在探讨《独立宣言》时看到这一问题是如何展开的。

我们究竟选择哪一类主人公(人或者人们的环境)讲述故事,这不仅超越了阅读的难易度的范畴,也超越了一种行动的哲学,因为每一个此类选择都包含着一个伦理的维度。

## 作者和读者的道德责任

前十一课中，我已经强调了为了做到写作清晰，作者应该为读者承担的责任。但是，读者也有责任，去下功夫理解比 Dick-and-Jane 这类简单句难得多的句子。例如，让一位工程师把下面这段表述得更清晰，简直不太可能：

The drag force on a particle of diameter $d$ moving with speed $u$ relative to a fluid of density $p$ and viscosity $\mu$ is usually modeled by $F=0.5C_D u^2 A$, where A is the cross-sectional area of the particle at right angles to the motion.

大多数人的确会为此下功夫——至少在意识到作者的问题之前是如此，作者没有花费同样的精力帮助我们有效地理解文章内容；或者更糟糕的是，作者故意使阅读变得更艰难。一旦我们认定作者粗心、懒惰，或者任性，好吧，既然他们漠视我们的需求，我们又怎能舍得把宝贵的时间浪费在他们身上呢！

但是应对这种不必要的复杂性，唯一的方法是再度强调作者应对读者承担起责任，因为如果不想让别人把"粗心、晦涩"的标签贴在自己身上，就不应该把"粗心、晦涩"的作品推给读者，这一点似乎是不言自明的。如果作者有社会责任心，他就不应该将自己的思想表达得过于直白，也不应该过于艰涩。

有责任心的作者往往遵循着一个规则，其更普遍的含义是：

己不愿读，勿写予人。

很少有人故意违背写作伦理的第一规则。问题是，我们总是会认为自己的写作是清晰的：即便读者很难理解，我们也会认为一定不是自己作品的问题，而是读者的阅读水平太过肤浅。

然而，这种想法是错误的，因为你若低估读者的实际需求，那么你失去的很可能不仅仅是读者的关注，而且也很可能失去被自亚里士多德以来作家们信奉的可信赖的准则——读者从作品中推断出你的品性：你是可接近的，还是不可接近的？是可信赖的，还是虚伪的？是和蔼率直的，还是冷酷无情的？

随着时间的推移，个人的写作理念会凝注在自己的声名之中。因此，额外努力去帮助读者理解，并不只是一种无私的慷慨。实际上，它也是一种智慧，因为我们更愿意信任一位拥有"思想深刻、值得信赖、关注读者需要"的名声的作者。

然而，重要的是这不仅关乎声望，而且也是文化界的道德基础。作为写作原则，如果我们愿意站在目标读者的角度，体验读者阅读后的感受，我们就遵循了写作伦理。不幸的是，这并没有那么简单。例如，我们如何评判那些写作晦涩却毫无察觉的人，或那些明知写作晦涩还为自己辩解的人？

### 无心的晦涩

一些人写得晦涩难懂，但很少有意为之。例如，我并不认为下面这段话的作者是**故意**写得如此不清晰：

> A major condition affecting adult reliance on early communicative patterns is the extent to which the communication

has been planned prior to its delivery. Adult speech behaviour takes on many of the characteristics of child language, where the communication is spontaneous and relatively unpredictable.

——伊利诺尔·欧克斯、班比·B.谢夫林，

《非即兴和即兴语篇》

大意是（我认为）：

When we speak spontaneously, we rely on patterns of child language.

他们可能会反对我将其观点过分地简化，但是这 11 个词表达了我从 44 个词中所记住的信息，毕竟，文章的真正价值并不在于理解所读的内容，而在于第二天还能记起多少。

这个伦理问题并不属于作者有意疏忽的范畴，而是由于他们无意地忽视而造成的。这种情况下，如果作者不太了解，那么读者就有义务去履行读者与作者之间契约的另一条款：不但要仔细地阅读，而且一旦有机会，还要给出坦率、有益的回馈。

**有意的误导**

如果作者故意使用语言伪装自己，而不是为了增强读者的兴趣，此时写作伦理问题就显得尤为突出了。

例一：谁的错？西尔斯公司（Sears）曾被控告汽车修理费索价过高。西尔斯公司用广告语言来回应：

Which over two million automotive customers serviced last year in California alone, mistakes may have occurred. However, Sears wants you to know that we would never intentionally violate the trust customers have shown in our company for 105 year.

在第一句，作者避免提到西尔斯公司作为承担错误责任的一方。他本可以使用一个被动句：

... mistakes **may have been made**.（错误本来可以犯。）

但是，这样会促使我们去考虑 By whom（由谁犯）？相反，作者发现了一个使西尔斯公司避免承担责任的动词 occurred，他通过表述错误只是"发生了"（occurred）来表达好像责任在于消费者自己。

在第二句，尽管作者把重点放在西尔斯公司这个责任主体上，但是作者想强调的是公司的善意：

**Sears**... would never intentionally violate...

（西尔斯公司绝无意违反……）

如果我们将第一句聚焦在西尔斯公司，在第二句中隐藏西尔斯公司，我们会得到不一样的效果：

When we serviced over two million automotive customers last year in California, we made mistakes. However, you should know that no intentional violation of 105 years of trust occurred.

这是风格处理中的一个小要点，纯属自我娱乐，毫无不良动机。下面的会更有意义。

**例二：谁付钱？** 思考一下这封天然气公用事业公司发出的信，它通知我和其他成千上万的用户：税率就要提高了。（在每个小句、主句或从句中，主语／话题标注为黑体。）

> **The Illinois Commerce Commission** has authorized a restructuring of our rates together with an increase in Service Charge revenues effective with service rendered on and after November 12, 1990. **This** is the first increase in rates for Peoples Gas in over six years. **The restructuring of rates** is consistent with the policy of the Public Utilities Act that **rates for service to various classes of utility customers** be based upon the cost of providing that service. **The new rates** move revenues from every class of customer closer to the cost actually incurred to provide gas service.

该通知是一个误导的典范：写完第一句以后，作者再也不用人物来开始一个句子，至少不用利益紧密相关者，如作者或者读者。作者只用第三人称提到自己两次，却不用来做主语／话题／行为主体：

> ... for service to various classes of utility **customers**
>
> ... move revenues from every class of **customer**

作者只提到了公司一次，而且它仅仅是用第三人称出现的，并且也不是作为承担责任的主语／话题／行为主体：

> ... increase in rates for **People Gas**

如果公司真想澄清谁是真正的"执行者",谁是被执行者,那么通知就应该更像是这样的：

> According to the Illinois Commerce Commission, **we** can now make **you** pay more for your gas service after November 12, 1990. **We** have not made **you** pay more in over six years, but under the Public Utilities Act, now **we** can.

如果作者想替公司推卸责任,那么我们就可以合理地控诉他违反了写作伦理的第一原则。肯定的是,他当然不愿意写像上面这类突出自己的文章,结果就在与自己利益密切相关的事情上,系统地隐藏了"执行者"及其"所作所为"。

**例三：谁死了？** 最后,这里有一个段落引起了一个更大的写作伦理争论,它涉及生和死。此前,政府会计处调查了半数以上的车主收到召回信却没有修车的原因。调查发现,车主之所以没有把车返回到经销商那里维修,是因为车主不理解召回信的内容,或者是因为召回信没有起到足够的警示作用。

我收到了下面这封信。(当被问到汽车品牌时,我避开了这个问题。)它显示了作者是如何履行法律义务,如何规避道德义务的(我给这些句子编了号码)：

> 1A defect which involves the possible failure of a frame

support plate may exist on your vehicle. 2This plate ( front suspension pivot bar support plate ) connects a portion of the front suspension to the vehicle frame, and 3its failure could affect vehicle directional control, particularly during heavy brake application. 4In addition, your vehicle may require adjustment service to the hood secondary catch system. 5The secondary catch may be misaligned so that the hood may not be adequately restrained to prevent hood fly-up in the event the primary latch is inadvertently left unengaged. 6Sudden hood fly-up beyond the secondary catch while driving could impair driver visibility. 7In certain circumstances, occurrence of either of the above conditions could result in vehicle crash without prior warning.

首先，看句子的主语 / 话题：

1a defect          2this plate                    3its failure
4your vehicle      5the secondary catch
6sudden hood fly-up  7occurrence of either condition

故事的主要人物 / 话题不是"我"，也不是司机，而是我的车和车的部件。事实上，作者几乎完全把"我"忽略了（"我"作为 your vehicle 出现两次，作为 driver 出现一次），并且省略了所有和他们相关的事物。总之，它的意思是：

There is a car that might have defective parts. Its plate could fail and its hood fly up. If they do, it could crash without warning.

作者们——可能是律师委员会——把能警示我们的动词,一部分转化成了名词,另一部分转化成了被动式。(n= 名词 [nominalization], p= 被动式 [passive]):

| Failure (n) | vehicle directional control (n) | heavy brake application (n) |
| be misaligned (p) | not be restrained (p) | hood fly-up (n) |
| is left unengaged (p) | driver visibility (n) | warning (n) |

如果作者打算转移我的恐惧或者愤怒,他们就没有尽到道德义务:给我写的信就应该像他们希望我写给他们的那样。他们肯定不会和我这样的读者——我们之所以忽视了威胁自己生命的状况,是因为受到了故意诱导——交换位置。

当然,做一个公正的作者要付出代价。如果希望每个人都可以依其所愿而自由地写作,那就太天真了。尤其是该作者的工作涉及要保护雇主的个人利益时,这种想法就更不切实际了。或许,作者们在写信时觉得是被迫这样写的,尽管事实的确如此。但是这对造成的后果于事无补。如果故意使用大家都难以接受的方式写作,就会损害维系文明社会的信任。

当然,我们不应该混淆恶意的含蓄和善意的欺瞒之间的界限。例如,如果一个管理者说,**我担心我们没有新的资金来源了**,我们都清楚这就意味着**我们就要失业了**。但是这种含蓄就是一种善意的表达,而非故意欺骗。

总之，主语的选择很关键，这不仅关系到我们表达得是否清晰，也关系到我们是否诚实。

## 练习 12.1

———⁂———

请修改天然气税率的通知，用 you 作为一个主语 / 话题 / 行为主体。之后用 we 再做一次修改。例如：

As the Illinois Commerce Commission has authorized, *you* will have to pay us higher service charges after November 12, 1990/*we* can charge you more after November 12...

该公司会拒绝发布哪一个版本？为什么？原版写的"好"吗？"好"意味着什么？

## 练习 12.2

———⁂———

修改召回书，尽可能多地使用 you 做动词的主语，并且使用动词表示动作。其中一个句子可以这样写：

If **you** BRAKE hard and the plate FAILS, **you** could...

公司会不情愿发布修改过的召回书吗？原版的召回书写的"好"吗？下面的句子，哪一个更接近"真相"？修改的问题是症结所在吗？

If the plate fails, you could crash.

If the plate fails, your car could crash.

# 晦涩的合理性

## 必要的复杂

一个棘手的伦理问题是我们如何回应那些明知道写得艰涩却又声称必须这样（是因为他们正在开拓一个新的知识领域）的人。他们是正确的吗，或者说他们在为自己的艰涩找借口？这是一个令人头疼的问题，不仅因为问题要一个一个地解决，而且也因为一些问题根本得不到彻底地解决，至少不能令所有的人满意。

下面的例子选自当代文学理论领军人物的作品：

> If, for a while, the ruse of desire is calculable for the uses of discipline soon the repetition of guilt, justification, pseudo-scientific theories, superstition, spurious authorities and classifications can be seen as the desperate effort to "normalize" *formally* the disturbance of a discourse of splitting that violates the rational, enlightened claims of its enunciatory modality.
>
> ——霍米·巴巴

该句表达的思想如此微妙而且复杂，是只能这样写？还是说它只是学术上的胡言乱语？考虑到大多数人弄懂这种细微差别所需的时间，至少对于水平一般的读者来说，如何去判断事实是属于上述哪种情况呢？

作者应给读者奉献简洁而精妙的文章，却不该认为读者必须花费大量的时间去理解。如果作者非要坚持用一种令读者痛苦的方式写作，那我就无话可说了，毕竟写作是一个自由的领域。在思想的市场里,真理居于价值之本,但不是唯一的。另一个则是寻找真理的代价。

在最后的分析中,我只能说,如果作者因为其观点新颖就声称他们的文章必须写得晦涩,那么就实际情况而言,他们多数情况下是错的。语言哲学家路德维希·维特根斯坦曾说:

"只要是能思考的,都可以思考得很清楚;只要是能写的,都可以写得很清晰。"

(Whatever can be thought can be thought clearly; whatever can be written can be written clearly.)

我再补充一小点:

付出的努力稍多一点,就会更清晰一点。

(... and with just a bit more effort, more clearly still.)

**有用的复杂性/无益的清晰性**

这里还有两条为复杂性辩护的规则:一条是复杂性对我们有益;另一条则是写作清晰对我们有害。

就第一条而言,有人认为越是努力地去理解所写的东西,就会思考得越深刻,理解得越好。每个人都应该庆幸自己明白,没有明显的例证支持这种愚蠢的说法,而且大量的例证都与此相悖。

就第二条而言,有些人认为,表述清晰是掌握在当权者手中的武器,以用来混淆谁才是真正主宰我们生命的人。他们认为,这些掌控事实真相的人以迷惑性的手段言说,简化真相,导致我们不能完全理解复杂的政治和社会环境：

> The call to write curriculum in a language that is touted as clear and accessible is evidence of a moral and political vision that increasingly collapses under the weight of its own anti-intellectualism... [T]hose who make a call for clear writing synonymous with an attack on critical educators have missed the role that the "language of clarity" plays in a dominant culture that cleverly and powerfully uses "clear" and "simplistic" language to systematically undermine and prevent the conditions from arising for a public culture to engage in rudimentary forms of complex and critical thinking.
>
> ——史丹利·阿洛诺维茨，《后现代教育》

该作者阐明了一点：语言与政治、意识形态和控制有联系。在最早期的历史中，受过教育的精英利用写作去排斥文盲，后来会拉丁文和法文的人排斥只会英文的人。近代，权威人士依据名词化拉丁词汇和标准英语，要求那些希望加入"圈内"的"圈外人"接受长达数十年的教育，在这期间他们不仅被要求掌握"圈内人"的语言，而且也要掌握他们的价值观。

此外，清晰的写作不是天生就有的美德，一些堕落的学者、官僚和那些小肚鸡肠的人为了维护他们的权威，而将此美德搞得污浊不堪。清晰的写作是一种社会创造出来的价值观，社会必须努力地维护它。因为写得清晰十分困难，事实上，它需要人们后天的努力。人们必须学习，甚至有时候很痛苦（正如书中所展示的那样）。

那么，清晰的写作是一种意识形态上的价值观吗？当然了，否则，它是什么呢？

但是，为了过分简化复杂的社会问题，一些人将清晰写作诋毁为阴谋，他们和那些攻击科学的人一样是错误的，因为有些人是想达到中伤的目的——实际上，无论科学还是写作清晰都不是一种威胁；而威胁来自那些使用清晰原则（或科学）进行欺骗的人。写作清晰并没有带来破坏，而是被不道德地利用了。原则上，我们必须坚持，从事写作的人，承担着尽可能清楚地告诉我们真相的责任。他们可能不会，但是我们有义务提醒他们去承担这样的责任。

我们要写的每一句话都必须经过慎重的选择，而我们选择的伦理取决于背后的动机。只有了解了这些动机，我们才能知道写作清晰或复杂的作者是否情愿被外界认为是这种风格的人，是否受到同种写作风格的影响。

这看起来似乎很简单。但实际上并非如此。

## 外延分析

出于个人私利，一些作者似乎在通过语言操控读者，这些人容易备受诟病。然而，当那些貌似诚实可靠的人操控读者时，读者就不太容易考虑这些事情了。不过，正是这些情况，才迫使读者思考风格与伦理这类最困难的事情。

美国历史上最有名的文章当属《独立宣言》《宪法》、亚伯拉罕·林肯的《葛底斯堡演讲》和《第二次就职演讲》。在之前的版本中，我讨论过在《葛底斯堡演讲》和《第二次就职演讲》中，林肯如何巧妙地操控他的语言。这里，我们仔细分析《独立宣言》中托马斯·杰斐逊如何调整其行文风格来影响读者对其论证逻辑的接受。

《独立宣言》因其逻辑性而著名。在讨论了人权及其起源之后，杰斐逊列出了一个简单的三段论：

| | |
|---|---|
| **Major premise:** | When a long train of abuses by a government evinces a design to reduce a people under despotism, they must throw off such government. |
| **Minor premise:** | These colonies have been abused by a tyrant who evinces such a design. |
| **Conclusion:** | When therefore declare that these colonies are free and independent states. |

他的论证就像其表达技巧一样直截了当。

他采用导言开篇，解释了殖民地居民决定为独立辩护的原因，这种辩护以革命者必有的和推崇的大胆想法为依据，理由十分充足：

> When, in the course of human events, it becomes necessary for one people to dissolve the political bonds which have connected them with another, and to assume among the powers of the earth, the separate and equal station to which the laws of nature and of nature's God entitle them, a decent respect to the opinions of mankind requires that they should declare the causes

which impel them to the separation.

之后，他将宣言分成三部分。第一部分，他提出了大前提，即摆脱暴政而代之以人民政府的哲学依据：

> We hold these truths to be self-evident, that all men are created equal, that they are endowed by their Creator with certain unalienable rights, that among these are life, liberty and the pursuit of happiness. That to secure these rights, governments are instituted among men, deriving their just powers from the consent of the governed. That whenever any form of government becomes destructive to these ends, it is the right of the people to alter or to abolish it, and to institute new government, laying its foundation on such principles and organizing its powers in such form, as to them shall seem most likely to effect their safety and happiness. Prudence, indeed, will dictate that governments long established should not be changed for light and transient causes; and accordingly all experience hath shown that mankind are more disposed to suffer, while evils are sufferable, than to right themselves by abolishing the forms to which they are accustomed. But when a long train of abuses and usurpations, pursuing invariably the same object evinces a design to reduce them under absolute despotism, it is their right, it is their duty, to throw off such government, and to provide new guards for their future

security.

第二部分，杰斐逊将此原则运用到殖民地居民的实际状况上：

Such has been the patient sufferance of these colonies; and such is now the necessity which constrains them to alter their former systems of government. The history of the present King of Great Britain is a history of repeated injuries and usurpations, all having in direct object the establishment of an absolute tyranny over these states. To prove this, let facts be submitted to a candid world.

这些例证是乔治国王攻击殖民地的理由，却提供了支撑杰斐逊小前提的证据：国王打算建立一个"统治美国的绝对暴政"：

He has refused his assent to laws, the most wholesome and necessary for the public good.

He has forbidden his governors to pass laws of immediate and pressing importance, ...

He has refused to pass other laws for the accommodation of large districts of people, ...

He has called together legislative bodies at places unusual, uncomfortable, and distant...

第三部分，以回顾殖民地居民反对分裂的抗争史开篇：

In every stage of these oppressions we have petitioned for redress in the most humble terms: Our repeated petition have been answered only by repeated injury. A prince, whose character is thus marked by every act which may define a tyrant, is unfit to be the ruler of a free people.

Nor have we been wanting in attention to our British brethren. We have warned them from time to time of attempts by their legislature to extend an unwarrantable jurisdiction over us. We have reminded them of the circumstances of our emigration and settlement here. We have appealed to their native justice and magnanimity, and we have conjured them by the ties of our common kindred to disavow these usurpations, which, would inevitably interrupt our connections and correspondence. We must, therefore, acquiesce in the necessity, which denounces our separation, and hold them, as we hold the rest of mankind, enemies in war, in peace friends.

第三部分以真正的独立宣言结尾：

We, therefore, the representatives of the United States of America, in General Congress, assembled, appealing to the Supreme Judge of the world for the rectitude of our intentions, do, in the name, and by the authority of the good people of these colonies, solemnly publish and declare, that these united colonies are, and of right ought to be free and independent states; that they are absolved from all allegiance to the British Crown, and that all political connection between them and the state of the Great Britain, is and ought to be totally dissolved; and that as free and independent states, they have full power to levy war, conclude peace, contract alliances, establish commerce, and to do all other acts and things which independent states may of right do. And for the support of this declaration, with a firm reliance on the protection of divine providence, we mutually pledge to each other our lives, our fortunes and our sacred honor.

杰斐逊的辩论是逻辑严密的范例,他巧妙地组织语言,以使读者接受他的逻辑。

第二部分和第三部分反映了在第三课至第六课中讨论过的清晰性原则。在第二部分中,杰斐逊使用 He(乔治国王)这个简短、具体的词作为所有动作的主语 / 话题 / 行为主体:

**He** has refused...

**He** has forbidden...

**He** has refused...

**He** has called together...

他本可以这样写:

**His assent to laws,** the most wholesome and necessary for the public good, *has not been forthcoming...*

**Laws of immediate and pressing importance** *have been forbidden...*

**Places unusual, uncomfortable, and distant from the depository of public records** *have been required* as meeting places of legislative bodies...

或者,他本可以一直把殖民地居民放在中心的位置:

**We** *have been deprived* of Laws, the most wholesome and necessary...

**We** *lack* Laws of immediate and pressing importance...

**We** *have* had to meet at places usual, uncomfortable...

换句话说,杰斐逊没有为事情的本质所动,而是让乔治国王成为所有压迫行为的执行者。但是这一选择正好支撑了他的论证,即国王是一个任意妄为的暴君。这样的选择显得如此自然,以至于我们没有注意到它是一个**选择**。

第三部分,杰斐逊仍然以一种体现清晰原则的风格在写作:他再次将其故事中的人物和句子的主语/话题进行搭配。但是这里他把人物转换成了殖民地居民,并用第一人称复数"we"来指称:

Nor *have* **we** *been wanting* in attentions to our British brethren...

> **We** *have warned* them from time to time...
>
> **We** *have reminded* them of the circumstances of our emigration...
>
> **We** *have appealed* to their native justice and magnanimity...
>
> ... **we** *have conjured* them by the ties of our common kindred...
>
> **They** too *have been deaf* to the voice of justice and of consanguinity.
>
> **We** *must*, therefore, *acquiesce* in the necessity...
>
> **We**... *do*... solemnly *publish and declare*...
>
> ... **we** mutually *pledge* to each other our Lives...

上述句子中，除了 They too have been deaf 之外，所有的主语／话题都是我们（we）。

杰斐逊又一次没有为事情的本质所动。他本应该把他的英国同胞们（**British brethren**）作为主语／话题：

> **Our British brethren** *have heard* our request...
>
> **They** *have received* our warnings...
>
> **They** *know* the circumstances of our emigration...
>
> **They** *have ignored* our pleas...

但是他选择让殖民地居民做主语，是为了首先强调他们尝试谈判不成功，其次才强调了宣布独立的行动。

再次，他的选择并不是不可避免的，但是这一切看上去很自然，甚至没有引起注意：King George did all those bad things, so we must declare our independence. 但是这些选择确实是可以避免的。在第二部分和第三部分中，除了杰斐逊明显的正确选择之外，还有哪些风格方面的特点？

杰斐逊在第一部分中的遣词尤为精彩，这些词汇已经成为了民族记忆的一部分。在这一部分中，他选用了一种截然不同的风格，事实上，只有两句话是用"人"作了动词的主语：

... **they** [ the colonists ] *should declare* the causes...

**We** *hold* these truths to be self-evident...

另外，还有四个主—谓词句，它们都有简短、具体的主语，但是这些主语都用在被动式中：

... **all men** *are created* equal...

... **they** *are endowed* by their Creator with certain unalienable Rights...

... **governments** *are instituted* among **Men**...

... **governments long established** *should* not *be changed* for light and transient causes...

在前两句中，主语明显是上帝；但是在后两句中，被动语态将普通意义上的人和具体的殖民地居民模糊化了。

在第一部分的剩余部分中，杰斐逊选用了一种更加客观的风格，从而使抽象词成为每一个重要动词的主语／话题／行为主体。事实上，大部分句子都属于第三课至第六课讨论过的修改范畴：

When in the course of human events, **it** *becomes necessary* for one people to dissolve the political bands which have connected them with another...

√ When in the course of human events, **we** *decide* **we** *must dissolve* the political bands which have...

... **a decent respect to the opinions of mankind** *requires* that they should declare **the causes** which *impel* them to the separation.

√ If **we** decently *respect* the opinions of mankind, **we** *should declare* why **we** *have decided to separate.*

... **it** *is the right* of the people to alter or to abolish it, and to institute new Government...

√ **We** *may alter or abolish* it, and *institute* new government...

**Prudence,** indeed, *will dictate* that governments long established should not be changed for light and transient causes.

√ If **we** *are prudent,* **we** *will not change* governments long established for light and transient causes...

... **all experience** *hath shewn,* that **mankind** *are more disposed* to suffer, while evils are sufferable...

√ **We** *know* from experience that **we** *choose* to suffer, while **we** *can suffer* evils...

... **a long train of abuses and usurpations**... *evinces* a design to reduce them under absolute Despotism.

√ **We** *can see* a design in a long train of abuses and usurpations pursuing invariably the same Object—to reduce us under absolute Despotism.

**Necessity**... *constrains* them to alter their former Systems of government.

√ **We** now *must alter* our former Systems of government.

为什么在第一部分杰斐逊选择用这种间接而且客观的风格，而不采用像第二和第三部分那样清晰、直接的风格呢？一个现成的答案是，他希望为普遍意义上的革命奠定一个理论基础，而不是为了具体的美国革命，前者是指西方政治思想中具有深刻颠覆意义的观念，并且比殖民地居民仅仅希望推翻他们厌恶的政府理由更充分。

第一部分风格中最显著的不仅仅是客观的普遍性，而且是杰斐逊如何使用这种风格无情地剥夺属于殖民地居民的自由意志，并且赋予主语更大的力量去迫使他们采取行动：

**respect** for opinion *requires* that [ the colonists ] explain their action

**causes** *impel* [ the colonists ] to separate

**prudence** *dictates* that [ the colonists ] not change government lightly

**experience** has *shown* [ the colonists ]

**necessity** *constrains* [ the colonists ]

即使抽象词汇不能对殖民地居民起到明显的强制作用，杰斐逊也暗示了他们不是自由的行为主体：

It [ is ] *necessary* to sever bonds.

Mankind *are disposed* to suffer.

It is their *duty* to throw off a tyrant.

从这个角度来看，即使这句 We hold these truths to be self-evident 只是一个声明，也暗示了殖民地居民没有发现那些真相，更确切地说，是这些真相自己显露给他们的。

总之，杰斐逊曾三次润色这篇演讲的语言，其中前两次使用的方法似乎一目了然、毫无特点，那么老套，以至于我们根本没有注意到他遣词方面的特色，即在第二部分，通过让乔治国王做每一句的主语/话题，杰斐逊使他成为动作的自由主体；在第三部分，杰斐逊让殖民地居民作为动作的行为主体。

但是，杰斐逊为了使第一部分发挥力量，他就必须让殖民地居民成为受至高无上的权力支配的客体。因为在《独立宣言》中，唯一至高无上的权力被称为创造者——自然的上帝，该创造者暗示着"阻止人们去改变他们原有政府体系"的强制性力量。杰斐逊并没有明确地表达出这个观点，更不用说去为其做辩护了。相反，他让句子的语法成为他论点的一部分。

《独立宣言》是一篇庄严的文章，起作用的除了语法和风格之外，还有很多。同样是这些词汇促使我们的民族得以诞生，确立了我们的基本价值观——民族自治在任何地方都是合理的。

但是，我们不应该忽视杰斐逊运用修辞手法的能力，尤其是他使用写作风格的才能。他创造的客观性的逻辑论证方法为我们的独立提供了辩护的理由，同时他也操控、管理、润色语言，从而用一种难以察觉的方式来支持他的逻辑。

如果他的出发点与使用的方法不相符的话，我们可能会认为杰斐逊具有欺骗性，因为他是使用语言而不是用逻辑去建立论证的前提，即殖民地居民没有自由做其他事情，除了反叛别无选择。最终，这就属于写作伦理的范畴了。对于那些不仅直接通过逻辑论证，而且间接通过文章风格试图控制我们反应的作者，我们能否给予信任呢？对于汽车召回书的作者，我们会说 No（不），因为它几乎确实是有意要欺骗我们。然而，对于杰斐逊，我们只能说 Yes（是），但前提是他的意图和使用方法相一致，不过这个原则通常在道德层面上是不被采纳的。

## 自我检测

### 练习 12.3

―――⁂―――

写作伦理的第一条原则是，用你希望别人写给你的方式去写作。回忆一个你违背了或者是被诱导违背该原则的一个场景。该场景是什么？你当时做了什么？你现在会做一些不同的事情吗？

## 练习12.4

―――∽∾―――

在写作中，我们每天都会遇到伦理问题。在一个星期之内，持续关注日常生活中遇到的文字：产品上的标签、票据上的附属细则、大宗邮件广告、邮箱里的垃圾邮件等。从那些能够引起伦理问题的文本中，选出三个，和一个同事或者班级分享。你提出的伦理问题是什么？作者之所以这么写，猜想一下是为什么？怎样修改才会使它们更符合写作伦理？

## 总结

最终，如何判断"好"文章？即使它没有达到目的，但是否清晰、优美、坦诚？或者说不考虑完整性和方法，它是否起到了一定的作用？如果"好"意味着道德层面上是可信赖的，或者实用层面上是成功的，那么我们的疑问就出现了。

我们用写作伦理第一条原则来解决这个困境：

> 如果我们把自己放在读者的位置，并且经历读者在阅读我们文章时所经历的，那么我们就是有道德的作者。

这样就把球踢到作者这边了，它要求作者需要将读者和他们的感受考虑进来。

如果你在学术或是职业生涯中处于较为领先的位置，那么你一定碰到过写作不清晰的情况，尤其在自己的作品中。如果现在正处于大学生涯的初期，那么你可能想知道关于清晰、道德、理念的讨论是否只是无端的指责。发现自己能够用足够多的词写满三页纸的那一刻，你一定会很高兴，根本就不会担心它的风格问题了。你可能正在读那些已被大力修改过的课本，它们之所以被修改，是为了使那些对内容知之甚少或者一无所知的大一学生读起来更为清晰。因此，你可能还没有遇到过太过粗糙、晦涩的文章。但是你迟早会遇到的，这只是时间问题而已。

还有些人想知道，在拙劣的文章如此普遍而作者似乎又不用付出多少代价之时，他们为什么还要费力地学习清晰写作呢？有经验的作者知道，而且最终你也会知道，文风清晰且优美的作者凤毛麟角，以至于一旦发现这样的作者，我们就会由衷地感激他们。他们不是得不到回报的！

我也知道，对于许多作者来说，雕琢出一个好句子或者好的段落，足以给他们带来极大的快乐。我们有些人发现这种道德上的满足感不仅出现在写作中，也出现在我们做的每件事情中：工作进展顺利，我们就会乐在其中，不管工作是什么，也不管有没有人注意到我们的工作。用清晰和优美来形容一种观点是哲学家阿尔弗雷德·诺斯·怀特海提出的，他认为任何艺术或相关努力中的风格意识都是一种审美，并且最终也是为最大效果地实现既定目标而培养的道德审美。

> 具有风格意识的管理者讨厌浪费；具有风格意识的工程师节约原材料；具有风格意识的艺术家偏爱上乘的作品。风格就是心灵的终极道德。
>
> ——阿尔弗雷德·诺斯·怀特海，《教育的目标》

[ 附录一 ]

# 标点

在音乐上,标点符号的使用非常严格,音节和休止符同样受到绝对的限定。但是散文却没有如此严格,因为我们必须把它和读者联系在一起。换句话说,作家总是不断地修改着自己的乐谱。

——拉尔夫·理查森
（Ralph Richardson）

有些标点很有趣,有些则不然。

——格特鲁德·斯坦因
（Gertrude Stein）

## 标点的内涵

大部分作者认为,标点必须遵循同一种语法规则,所以使用逗号和分号就如主谓一致一样有趣。事实上,对标点符号所提供的选择方式远比想象的要多。如果认真选择,不仅可以让读者更简单地理解复杂的句子,还可以帮助读者察觉强调带来的细微差别。要将单一音调变为多音调需要很多逗号,但是这一过程中只需稍加用心就可以产生一个令人满意的结果。

我将把标点当作功能问题来解决:首先是如何在句末加标点,然后是句首,最后是句中。但是,首先要对不同种类的句子进行区分。

### 简单句、复合句和复杂句

传统上讲,句子可分为**简单句**、**复合句**和**复杂句**。如果一个句子只有一个独立句,那么该句就称为**简单句**:

The greatest English dictionary is the *Oxford English Dictionary*.

如果一个句子有两个或两个以上的独立句,那么该句称为**复合句**:

[ There are many good dictionaries, ] ¹

[ but the greatest is the *Oxford English Dictionary*. ] ²

如果一个句子有一个独立的主句和一个及一个以上的从句，那么该句就称为**复杂句**：

[ While there are many good dictionaries ] 从句

[ the greatest is the *Oxford English Dictionary*. ] 独立主句

（至于什么是**复合—复杂句**，则不言自明）

这几类句子的名称可能会给人一种错觉，误认为语法结构简单的句子，**理解**起来也会比那些语法结构复杂的句子容易，这种观点并不总是正确的。例如，大多数人读完下面两句话后，觉得语法结构简单的句子比语法结构复杂的句子**理解**起来更困难：

| | |
|---|---|
| 语法简单的句子： | Our review of the test led to our modification of it as a result of complaints by teachers. |
| 语法复杂的句子： | After we reviewed the test, we modified it because teachers complained. |

我们还需要另外一组术语，它们更可靠地显示了读者对这些句子的反应。

## 标点句和语法句

我们可以在**加标点的句子**和**合乎语法的句子**之间找到更多有用的区别：

标点句以大写字母开头,以一个句号、问号或感叹号结束。可能由一个单词也可能由一百个单词组成。

语法句由主句中的主语和动词及依附于主句的其他成分组成。

对这两种句子进行区分,是因为读者对这两种句子的反应是大相径庭的。例如,现在读的这个句子是一个较长的标点句,但是,读起来并不比那些由许多从句构成的较短的句子理解起来困难;我将那些本可以分成一系列短句的成分合成了一个长句。例如:冒号、分号和"**but**"前面的逗号本可以写成句号,破折号也可以写成句号。

We distinguish these two kinds of sentences because readers can respond to them very differently: the one you are now reading, for example, is one long punctuated sentence, but it is not as hard to read as many shorter sentences that consist of many subordinate clauses; I have chosen to punctuate as one long sentence what I might have punctuated as a series of shorter ones: that colon, those semicolons, and the comma before that **but** could have been periods, for example—and that dash could have been a period too.

下面就是刚才提到的长句,停顿并没有带来语法上的变化,但却分成了七个标点句:

We must distinguish these two kinds of punctuated sentences because readers respond to them very differently. The one you are now reading, for example, is a short punctuated sentence, consisting of just one subject and one verb plus what depends on them. But this paragraph is not as hard to read as many shorter sentences that consist of many subordinate clauses. I have chosen to punctuate as separate sentences what I could have punctuated as one long one. The period before that **but**, for example, could have been a comma. The last two periods could have been semicolons. And that period could have been a dash.

虽然改动不大,但是七个语法句变成了七个标点句,语法结构保持不变,但是读起来的感觉却与单一的标点句不同。简言之,不同的停顿方式可以带来不同的文体效果——标点取决于作者的选择,而不是规则。

## 句尾的标点

除上述标点的规则之外,最重要的是作者必须明白如何给语法句句尾加上标点。在加哪种标点方面,作者有很多种选择,但是千万要标记清楚,因为读者需要知道一个语法句何时结束,另一个语法句何时开始。下面这句话的停顿就没有达到这样的效果:

In 1967, Congress passed civil rights laws that remedied problems of registration and voting this had political consequences throughout the South.

此类句子会造成**句式杂糅**或**句式无停顿**,这种后果是不可挽回的,因为它表明作者连基本的写作知识都不明白。

你可以**选择**把成组的语法句分开,有十种方法,常见的主要有三种。

### 三种常见的句尾标点形式

**1. 只有句号(或问号/感叹号)** 语法句结尾最简单最不引人注意的方法就是用句号:

√ In 1967, Congress passed civil rights laws that remedied problems of registration and **voting. This** had political consequences throughout the South.

但是如果简短的标点句太多,读者会觉得文章过于简单且不够连贯。有经验的作者会将一系列短的语法句改为从句或短语,将两个或更多的语法句改为一个语法句:

√ **When Congress passed civil rights laws to remedy problems of registration and voting in 1967, they** had political consequences throughout the South.

√ The civil rights laws **that Congress passed in 1967**

**to remedy problems of registration and voting** had political consequences throughout the South.

不过，需要注意的是：将过多简短的语法句合并成一个长句，会使该句显得零乱（见第十课）。

**2. 只有分号**　一定程度上，分号相当于缓和的句号；不管分号两边的成分是什么，它们都应该是语法完整的句子（375 页讨论的内容除外）。只有当第一个语法句由十五个左右单词组成，而第二个语法句的内容又与前一个紧密相关时才使用分号代替句号：

In 1967, Congress passed civil rights laws that remedied problems of registration and **voting; those** laws had political consequences throughout the South.

**使用分号和"however"时的特殊问题**　在一种语境中，即使是受过良好教育的作者也会错误地用逗号为一个语法句结尾，用 however 来引出下一个句子。

Taxpayers have supported public education, **however,** they now object because taxes have risen so steeply.

必须用一个分号将这些句子分开（但是要将逗号置于"however"之后）：

√ Taxpayers have supported public education; **however,** they now object because taxes have risen so steeply.

许多作者不用分号，因为他们觉得分号会使人有点害怕，所以，如果想做一个有经验的作者，就有必要花时间学学分号的用法。一旦每隔几页需要分号，要知道如何正确使用。

**3．逗号+并列连词**　当读者看到逗号后有下列两个标记时，就会意识到是语法句的结尾了：

并列连词：**and, but, yet, for, so, or, nor**
另外一组主语和动词

√ In the 1950s religion was viewed as a bulwark against **communism, so it was** not long after that that atheism was felt to threaten national security.

√ American intellectuals have often followed **Europeans, but our culture has proven** inhospitable to their brand of socialism.

如果两个语法句过长，而且每个句子都有各自内部的标点，选择使用句号。

当读者读到三个及三个以上语法句并列时，他们只接受在句与句间使用逗号，而且是只有当这些句子较短且没有内部的标点时：

√ Baseball satisfies our admiration for **precision, basketball** speaks to our love of speed and **grace, and** football appeals to our lust for violence.

如果任何的语法句有内部的标点，用分号将其隔开：

√ Baseball, the oldest indigenous American sport and essentially a rural one, satisfies our admiration for **precision; basketball**, our newest sport and now more urban than rural, speaks to our love of speed and **grace; and** football, a sport both rural and urban, appeals to our lust for violence.

**特例**：如果引入两个并列且较短的语法句时，使用了二者共同适用的修饰语，那么可将二者间的逗号省略：

√ Once the upheaval after the collapse of the Soviet Union had settled down, the economies of its former satellites had begun to **rebound but Russia's** had yet to hit bottom.

使用"and"和"so"来连接过多的语法句会使人觉得文章过于简单，所以一页使用不要超过一两个。

## 四种不太常见的句尾标点形式

关于下列标识语法句结尾的四种形式，一些读者持保留态度，而认真的作者却频繁使用。

**4. 句号 + 并列连词** 一些读者认为使用诸如 and 和 or 这样的并列连词引导标点句是不正确的，但他们错了，这是完全正确的：

√ Education cannot guarantee a **democracy. And** when it is available to only a few, it becomes a tool of social repression.

使用这种形式时,尤其是用"**and**"引导标点句时,一页不要超过一两次。

**5. 分号 + 并列连词**　作者有时会使用分号结束一个语法句,用并列连词来引导下一句话:

√ In the 1950s religion was viewed as a bulwark against **communism; so** soon thereafter atheism was felt to threaten national security.

如果两个语法句较短,要使用逗号而不用分号。但是如果两个语法句较长,且各自内部又有逗号时,使用分号会使读者更容易理解:

√ Problem solving, one of the most active areas of psychology, has made great strides in the last decade, particularly in understanding the problem-solving strategies of experts; **so** it is no surprise that educators have followed that research with interest.

但是,这种情况下读者更希望看到的是句号。

**6. 只有连词**　一些作者在较短的语法句之间只使用并列连词进行连接,省略了逗号:

√ Oscar Wilde violated a fundamental law of British **society and** we all know what happened to him.

但有个警告:尽管一些优秀文章的作者这样做,但一些教师认为这样用是错误的。

**7. 只有逗号** 读者并不期望只用逗号将语法句分开,但是如果句子较短,意思又紧密相关,读者也能理解,例如 cause-effect、first-second、if-then 等。

Act in haste, repent at leisure.

然而要确保两个语法句中都没有逗号;不要这样写:

Women, who have always been underpaid, no longer accept that discriminatory treatment, they are now doing something about it.

这时使用分号会更清晰:

√ Women, who have always been underpaid, no longer accept that discriminatory treatment; they are now doing something about it.

**同样的警告**:虽然一些优秀文章的作者只用逗号来分隔较短的语法句,但是,许多教师却持反对态度,因为传统上讲,仅仅使用逗号会导致犯"逗号粘连"的错误,在他们看来这是极其严重的错误。所以使用之前,一定要熟悉文章的读者。

> **快速提示** 如果使用 **but** 来引导语法句，可以在第一个句子后面加上逗号，还可以使用句号结束第一个句子，开始一个新的标点句，这时要把 **but** 大写。如果下文很重要，而且还想继续加以讨论，就使用句号 +**But** 这一结构：
>
> √ The immediate consequence of higher gas prices was some curtailment of driving. But the long-term effect changed the car buying habits of Americans, perhaps permanently, a change that the Big Three car manufacturers could not ignore. They...
>
> 如果下文只是对前文进行说明，就使用逗号 +but 的结构。
>
> √ The immediate consequence of higher gas prices was some curtailment of driving, but that did not last long. The long-term effect was changes in the car buying habits of Americans, a change that the Big Three car manufacturers could not ignore. They...

### 三种特殊情况：冒号、破折号、括号

最后三种标识语法句结尾的方式是需要作者有意为之的，但是对那些想把自己与其他作者加以区别的人来讲，这一做法或许很有趣。

**8. 冒号**　如果能在句尾恰当地使用冒号，眼光敏锐的读者会觉得该作者很有经验：他们认为这种方法是对 **to illustrate**、**for example**、**that is**、**therefore** 这些词的简写：

√ Dance is not widely **supported: no** company operates at a profit, and there are few outside major cities.

在平衡两个句子的结构、发音和意义方面，使用冒号也比使用逗号或分号的效果明显：

√ Civil disobedience is the public conscience of a democracy: mass enthusiasm is the public consensus of a tyranny.

如果冒号后面是一个语法句，那么该句首字母是否需要大写，取决于对后面信息的强调程度（注意：一些手册认为冒号后面句子首字母不需要大写）。

---

**快速提示**　如果使用的冒号将一个句子分成了两部分，每部分在语法上都不是完整的句子，那么要避免这样使用：

**Genetic counseling requires: a knowledge** of statistical genetics, an awareness of choices open to parents, and the psychological competence to deal with emotional trauma.

相反地，要将冒号置于完整的主谓宾结构之后：

> ✓ **Genetic counseling requires the following:** a knowledge of statistical genetics, an awareness of choices open to parents, and the psychological competence to deal with emotional trauma.

**9. 破折号** 破折号表明句子间的平衡更随意些,它说明这是一个随意的补充说明:

> ✓ Stonehenge is a **wonder—only** a genius could have conceived it.

将其与更加正式的冒号相比,破折号产生的效果是不同的。

**10. 括号** 如果一个简短的语法句属于补充说明的部分,那么用括号将其括起来插入另一个语法句中。不要在括号内的句子结尾加句号;在括号外加一个句号即可:

> ✓ Stonehenge is a **wonder**(**only** a genius could have conceived it).

---

**要点** 语法句结尾有十种方法,
其中三种是传统常见的:

| | |
|---|---|
| 句号 | I win. You lose. |
| 分号 | I win; you lose. |
| 逗号 + 并列连词 | I win, and you lose. |

> 下述四种方法有些争议，但是一些写作水平高的作者也使用，尤其是第一种：
>
> | | |
> |---|---|
> | 句号 + 并列连词 | I win. And you lose. |
> | 分号 + 并列连词 | I win; and you lose. |
> | 只用并列连词 | I win and you lose. |
> | 只用逗号 | I win, you lose |
>
> 下面三种方法是针对那些在使用标点上标新立异的作者而言的：
>
> | | |
> |---|---|
> | 冒号 | I win: you lose. |
> | 破折号 | I win—you lose. |
> | 括号 | I win (you lose). |

虽然一些句尾的标点使用是完全错误的，但你可以选择正确的使用方法，而且每种方法都会产生不同的效果。回过头再看 305 至 307 页的短句和 307 至 308 页梅勒的长句，就会发现不同的选择产生的对比效果。这些作者本可以选择另外一种方法，从而产生不同的风格效果。

## 有意而为的不完整句子

如果误将语法句的一部分作为完整句加上了标点，大多数读者会觉得这是一个非常严重的错误。从主句中分离出来的从属子句是一种最常见的不完整句，尤其是用 **because** 引导的句子：

You cannot break a complex sentence into two shorter ones merely by replacing commas with periods. **Because if you do, you will be considered at best careless, at worst uneducated.**

另外一种常见的不完整句是用 which 来引导的：

Most fragments occur when you write a sentence that goes on so long and becomes so complicated that you start to feel that you are losing control over it and so need to drop in a period to start another sentence. **Which is why you must understand how to write a long but clearly constructed sentence that readers can follow easily.**

传统上来讲，没有独立主句的标点句是不正确的，至少理论上是这样的。

事实上，一些经验丰富的作者常常故意写片段句，就像我所做的一样。有意而为的那些片段句有两个典型的特点：

句子比较短，不超过十个词。

这些句子要反映出一种工作中的思想，好像是作者在同读者讲话，每当说完一个句子，随后就将其展开，并做出进一步说明。它们几乎是作为一种补充说明出现的，通常很具讽刺意味。

在下面这篇文章中，马克·吐温使用了一些片段句（以及用连词引导的句子），以此来捕捉故事发生环境中的细节，也正是这点使他成了一名作家（不完整句已用黑体加粗）：

For amusement I scribbled things for the Virginia City *Enterprise*... One of my efforts attracted attention, and the *Enterprise* sent for me and put me on its stall.

And so I became a journalist—**another link**. By and by Circumstance and the Sacramento *Union* sent me to the Sandwich Islands for five or six months, to write up sugar. I did it; **and threw in a good deal of extraneous matter that hadn't anything to do with sugar.** But it was this extraneous matter that helped me to another link.

It made me notorious, and San Francisco invited me to lecture.**Which I did. And profitably.** I had long had a desire to travel and see the world, and now Circumstance had most kindly and unexpectedly hurled me upon the platform and furnished me the means. So I joined the "Quaker City Excursion".

——马克·吐温，《我一生中的转折点》

要知道在学术文章中作者很少使用片段句，人们觉得片段句过于随意。如果一定要尝试，就要确保读者能真正理解你的思想。

## 句首标点

如果句首直接用主语来引导，就不会遇到为句首加标点的问题。当一个句子有不同的引导性单词、短语和从句时，尤其是当这些成分内部还有各自的标点时，读者就会彻底感到迷惑不解，从而忘了试着为其加上正确的标点，对其进行修改。

下面是一些读者希望作者遵循的规则，但更多的时候还需要自己判断。

**五条可靠原则**

1. 如果读者有可能对句子结构产生误解，就将引导性成分从句子主语中分离出来并加上逗号，如下句：

> When a lawyer concludes her argument has to be easily remembered by a jury.

要这样写：

> √ When a lawyer **concludes, her** argument has to be easily remembered by a jury.

2. 不要在引导性从句或短语后使用分号，无论它有多长。读者认为分号是语法句结尾的标志（但请看第374页）。千万不要这样写：

> Although the Administration knew that Iraq's invasion of Kuwait threatened American interests in Saudi **Arabia; it** did not immediately prepare a military response.

这种情况下要多使用逗号：

√ Although the Administration knew that Iraq's invasion of Kuwait threatened American interests in Saudi **Arabia**, it did not immediately prepare a military response.

3. 如果从句后面的成分是句子主语，切忌在从属连词后使用逗号。不要这样写：

**Although, the art** of punctuation is simple, it is rarely mastered.

4. 如果并列连词"and""but""yet""for""so""or"和"nor"后是句子主语，要避免在这些连词后面使用逗号。不要这样写：

**But, we** cannot know whether life on other planets exists.

如果并列或从属连词后面是引导性单词或短语，一些喜欢使用标点的作者会在这些连词后加上逗号：

**Yet, during this period, prices** continued to rise.
**Although, during this period, prices** continued to rise, interest rates did not.

频繁使用标点符号会妨碍读者阅读，但这是作者的选择。下面两个句子对读者来说也正确，或许有些更显轻快：

√ Yet during this **period, prices** continued to rise.
√ Yet during this **period prices** continued to rise.

5. 如果一个引导性单词或短语是对后面整个句子的评论，或是连接两个句子,要在这个单词或短语后加上逗号。这类词和短语包括"fortunately""allegedly"等,而连接副词包括"however""nevertheless""otherwise"等。说完这些词之后会有片刻停顿。

√ **Fortunately, we** proved our point.

但是要避免使用一个引导性成分和一个逗号来引导过多的句子。如果包含太多此类句子,整篇文章就会缺乏说服力。

三个特例:在"now""thus"和"hence"之后尤其会省略逗号:

√ **Now it** is clear that many will not support this position.

√ **Thus the** only alternative is to choose some other action.

## 两个可行性原则

**1. 简短的引导性短语和主语之间通常不需要标点:**

√ **Once again we** find similar responses to such stimuli.

√ **In 1945 few** realized how the war had transformed us.

在这些句子中使用逗号并没有不妥之处,但是如果希望读者加快阅读速度的话,就不要用,因为逗号会减缓其速度。

**2. 在一个长的引导性短语(或者从句)和主语之间,通常需要一个逗号:**

√ When a lawyer begins her opening statement with a dry recital of the law and how it must be applied to the case before the **court, the jury** is likely to nod off.

---

**要点**　下面是关于标点符号使用的一些硬性规则，请遵循它们。

1. 如果读者可能会误解句子的结构，那么就要把引导性的成分从主语中分离出来。
2. 绝对不能在引导性从句中或者短语的结尾使用分号。
3. 如果从句的下一部分做该句的主语，就不能将逗号放在一个从属连词之后。
4. 如果从句的下一部分做该句的主语，就不能把逗号放在一个并列连词之后。
5. 如果一个简短的引导词或者短语统领后面所有的句子，或者连接两个句子，那么要在它后面加逗号。

下面是一些可行性原则：

1. 简短的引导性短语或其他引导成分后面是否加逗号，由你决定。
2. 较长的引导性短语或从句之后要加逗号。

---

## 句中标点

关于句中加标点，越解释越糟糕，因为在句子里加标点，更加确切地说，是在一个从句内加标点，不仅要考虑从句的语法，还要考虑句子在读者脑海中产生的韵律、意义和强调的细微差别。然而，这里有一些可靠原则。

## 主语—动词,动词—宾语

无论主语有多长(不在动词和宾语间),不要在主语和动词间加逗号。不要像下面这样:

> A sentence that consists of many complex subordinate clauses and long phrases that all precede a **verb, may** seem to some students to demand a comma somewhere.

如果主语很简短,就不需要逗号。

有时,作者不得不使用长主语,尤其是在它由一串夹杂着标点的头衔组成的时候。

例如:

> **The president, the vice president, the secretaries of the departments, senators, members of the House of Representatives, and Supreme Court justices take** an oath that pledges them to uphold the Constitution.

可以使用总结性的主语帮助读者梳理一下句子:

在长主语的尾部加冒号或者破折号;
添加一个能总结长主语的词:

> √ The president, the vice president, the secretaries of the departments, senators, members of the House of Representatives, and Supreme Court justices: **all** take an oath that pledges them to

uphold the Constitution.

文章的正式程度决定了破折号或者冒号的选择。

## 插入

如果打断主语—动词或者是动词—宾语的结构，那么读者在理解句子的语法联系时会更困难。因此，一般来说，除非为了强调或者表现差别，否则要避免这样的打断。

如果必须要在主语和动词或者是动词和主语之间加入几个词，那么要在插入部分前后加上一组逗号。

√ A sentence, **if it includes subordinates clauses,** may seem to need commas.

一般而言，在一个独立句之后添加一个从属句时，如果从句对于主句的理解非常必要的话（相当于限定性关系从句），那么不用加逗号：

√ No one should violate the law just because it seems unjust.

如果该从句对于句子意思的理解不是必要的，那么要将其与主要从句用逗号隔开。

√ No one should violate the law, because in the long run, it will do more harm than good.

有时候，一些差异是很微妙的。

根据想要强调的程度，可以把**副词短语**放在从句的前面、后面或者是其里面。如果是在从句中间，就在短语前后加逗号。对比下面句子中不同的强调：

√ **In recent years** modern poetry has become more relevant to the average reader.

√ Modern poetry **has, in recent years, become** more relevant to the average reader.

√ Modern poetry has **become, in recent years, more** relevant to the average reader.

√ Modern poetry has become more relevant to the average reader **in recent years.**

## 随意注释

"随意注释"不同于一个插入结构，因为通常可以移动插入结构到句子的任何部位。但是，随意注释修饰的是后面紧跟的部分，所以通常不能被移动。除非是在句子的末尾，否则它仍然需要成对的逗号、括号或者破折号将其括起来；在这种情况下，可以用句号替代第二个逗号或者破折号。

很难准确地解释随意注释到底是什么，因为它取决于语法和意义。限定性从句和非限定性从句（见第40至43页），也包括**同位语**，都有点似是而非的意味。

当限定性修饰语只修饰唯一的名词时，不加逗号：

√ The house **that I live in** is 100 years old.

但是通常用一对逗号将非限定性修饰语分开（除非修饰语在句子结尾）：

√ We had to reconstruct the **larynx, which is the source of voice**, with cartilage from the shoulder.

同位语只是缩短的非限定性从句：

We had to rebuild the **larynx,** ~~which is~~ **the source of voice,** with cartilage from the shoulder.

可以用破折号或者括号来实现随意的效果：

√ We had to rebuild the **larynx—the source of voice—with** cartilage from the shoulder.

√ We had to rebuild the **larynx（the source of voice）with** cartilage from the shoulder.

如果随意注释中间有逗号，那就需要使用破折号。下文中长长的主语使读者不明所以：

The nations of Central Europe, Poland, Hungary, Romania, Bulgaria, the Czech Republic, Slovakia, Bosnia, Serbia have for centuries been in the middle of an East-West tug-of-war.

如果看到用破折号或是括号断开的随意修饰语，读者会更容易理解这类结构：

√ The nations of Central **Europe—Poland, Hungary, Romania, Bulgaria, the Czech Republic, Slovakia, Bosnia, Serbia—have** for centuries been in the middle of an East-West tug-of-war.

如果想让读者在不知不觉中听到注释，那就加上括号。

√ The brain (**at least that part that controls nonprimitive functions**) may comprise several little brains operating simultaneously.

或者在句子中用括号做一个解释性的注脚：

√ Lamarck (**1744—1829**) was a pre-Darwinian evolutionist.

√ The poetry of the *fin de siècle* (**end of the century**) was characterized by a world-weariness and fashionable despair.

如果较为松散的解释性成分出现在句尾，就用一个逗号将其和句子的第一部分隔开。然而要确定的是，该成分的意义对整个句子的意义并非至关重要。否则，不要使用逗号。对比下面这些句子：

√ I wandered through **Europe, seeking a place** where I could write undisturbed.

√ I spent my **time seeking a place** where I could write undisturbed.

√ Offices will be closed July **2–6, as announced in the daily bulletin.**

√ When closing offices, secure all safes **as prescribed in the manual.**

√ Historians have studied social changes, **at least in this country.**

√ These records must be kept **at least until the IRS reviews them.**

---

**要点**  下面是几条关于句子内部加标点的可靠原则，请遵循：

1. 除非是为了达到清晰这一绝对性的要求，否则不要把任何标点插入主语和动词或者动词和宾语之间。

2. 在从句中，通常用成对的标点，如括号或者逗号、破折号去分离较长的插入语。但绝对不能用分号。

3. 如果一个附加的从句对于整个句子的意义不是至关重要的，那么就在该从句前的独立从句末尾加逗号。

---

## 并列成分之间的标点

### 两个并列成分之间的标点

一般来说，不要在两个并列成分间加逗号。对比下面的句子：

As computers have become **sophisticated, and** powerful they have taken over more **clerical, and** bookkeeping tasks.

√ As computers have become **sophisticated and** powerful they have taken over more **clerical and** bookkeeping tasks.

**四种特例**

1. 为了达到显著的对比效果，要在前一个并列成分之后加逗号，以强调第二个成分（要保证第二个成分的简短）：

√ The ocean is nature's most glorious **creation, and** its most destructive.

为了强调对比，在"**but**"之前加逗号（保证第二部分的简短）：

√ Organ transplants are becoming more **common, but** not less expensive.

2. 如果想要读者感到并列成分的语气在逐渐增强，就删掉"**and**"，只留一个逗号。对比下面句子：

√ Lincoln never had a formal **education and** never owned a large library.

√ Lincoln never had a formal **education, never** owned a large library.

√ The lesson of the pioneers was to ignore conditions that seemed difficult or even **overwhelming and** to get on with the business of subduing a hostile environment.

√ The lesson of the pioneers was to ignore conditions that seemed difficult or even **overwhelming, to** get on with the business of subduing a hostile environment.

3. 如果觉得读者需要喘口气，或对语法进行分类，就在一对较长的并列成分之间加逗号。对比下面的句子：

It is in the graveyard that Hamlet finally realizes that the inevitable end of life is the **grave and clay and that the** end of all pretentiousness and all plotting and counter-plotting, regardless of one's station in life, must be dust.

**clay** 之后的逗号表示一个自然停顿：

√ It is in the graveyard that Hamlet finally realizes that the inevitable end of all life is the **grave and clay, and that the** end of all pretentiousness and all plotting and counter-plotting, regardless of one's station in life, must be dust.

更重要的是，clay 后的逗号将潜在的困惑结构 grave and clay and that regardless 进行了分类。

在下面的句子中，并列的前半部分较长，因此将其与后半部分连接时，读者可能会遇到问题：

> Conrad's *Heart of Darkness* brilliantly dramatizes those primitive impulses that lie deep in each of us and stir only in our darkest **dreams but asserts** the need for the values that control those impulses.

下句中 dreams 后面的逗号会清楚地表示出前一并列成分的结束和后一部分的开始：

> √ Conrad's *Heart of Darkness* brilliantly dramatizes those primitive impulses that lie deep in each of us and stir only in our darkest **dreams, but asserts** the need for the values that control those impulses.

另一方面，如果只用一个标点就可以弄明白一个复杂句子的意思，那就需要对该句进行修改。

4. 如果用一个短语，或一个修饰两个独立并列句的从句来引导一个句子，那么请在引导性短语或者从句后加逗号，但是不能在两个独立的并列句之间加逗号：

> √ After the Soviet Union collapsed, Russia's economy declined for several years [ **no comma here** ] but the economies of former satellites to the west began to expand.

## 在三个或三个以上的并列成分之间加标点

最后，要在三个或者三个以上的并列成分间加标点。作者们在该问题上有争议。一些人会省略逗号，但是大多数坚持认为逗号要加在最后一个成分之前：

√ His wit, his **charm and his loyalty** made him our friend.

√ His wit, his **charm, and his loyalty** made him our friend.

这两种都是正确的，但要保证前后一致。

如果并列成分中任何一项有内逗号，就要用分号将这些并列分类：

√ In mystery novels, the principal action ought to be economical, organic, and **logical; fascinating,** yet not **exotic; clear,** but complicated enough to hold the reader's interest.

> 要点　如果这些并列成分之间没有标点，就用逗号去分开它们。若有标点，就用分号分开。

## 撇号

使用撇号有一些注意原则，并且它们是可靠原则（见第 35–37 页）。违背这些原则的人往往会滥用撇号，并且这些人常常是那些监督这些原则的人。

### 缩写形式

在所有缩写词中用撇号：

don't    we'll    she'd    I'm    it's

学术界中，作者在专业著作中经常避免使用缩写形式，因为他们怕文章显得不正式。我在本书中使用缩写形式，因为我想去避免一种正式的语气。在尝试使用前，让指导者和你一起检查你的文章。

### 复数

除了下述两种情况外，**不能用撇号表示复数**。不能这样写：bus's, fence's, horse's. 这种错误是带有讽刺意味儿的滥用。

只有在两种情境中才能用撇号表示复数：（1）在所有小写的单个字母中；（2）在单个的大写字母中，如 A、I 和 U（如果只加 s 就会拼写出单词 As、Is 和 Us）：

Dot your i's and cross your t's        many A's and I's

然而，如果一个词全都由数字或者多个大写字母组成，那就只加 s，不加撇号：

The ABCs    the 1950s    767s
CDs         URLs         45s

### 所有格

除了几个特例，所有格的形式都是在一个普通的单数名词或者专有名词末尾加撇号，之后再加 s。

FDR's third term    the U.S.'s history    a 747's wingspan

有几个特例，它们指单数名词，但总是以 s 结尾或者发 s 音。对于这些词，只需要在词尾加撇就表示它们的所有格：

politics' importance                the United States' role
Descartes' *Discourse on Method*    Sophocles' plays
the audience' attention             for appearance' sake

（关于这个问题，一些指导书给出了不同的建议，它们推荐在所有的情况中都用"'+s"的形式。无论选择哪一种，要保持一致。）

对于普通名词和专有名词的复数，其所有格形式只需在"s"后加一个撇号。

workers' votes      the Smiths' house

单数合成词的所有格形式要在最后一个词尾加撇号和"s"。

the attorney general's decision    his sister-in-law's business

## 练习 A.1

———❦———

下面的段落缺少标点符号。斜线表示语法上的断句。要给文章加三次标点，第一次使用尽可能少的标点，第二次使用尽可能多的标点，第三次使用你认为最合适的标点。你可以从典雅的特征入手分析句子，尤其分析句子是如何开始和结束的，并且可以完善部分句子。

1. Scientists and philosophers of science tend to speak as if "scientific language" were intrinsically precise as if those who use it must understand one another's meaning even if they disagree/but in fact scientific language is not as different from ordinary language as is commonly believed/it too is subject to imprecision and ambiguity and hence to imperfect understanding/moreover new theories or arguments are rarely if ever constructed by way of clear-cut steps of induction deduction and verification or falsification/nether are they defended rejected or accepted in so straightforward a manner/in practice scientists combine the rules of scientific methodology with a generous admixture of intuition aesthetics and philosophical commitment/the importance of what are sometimes called extra-rational or extra-logical components of thought in the *discovery* of a new principle or law is generally acknowledge/... but the role of these extra-logical components in persuasion and acceptance in making an argument convincing is less frequently discussed partly because they are less visible/ the ways in which the credibility or effectiveness of an argument depends on the realm of common experiences or extensive practice in communicating those experiences in a common language are hard to see precisely because such commonalities are taken for granted/only when we step out of such a "consensual domain" when we can stand out on the periphery of a community with a common language do we begin to become aware of the unarticulated premises mutual understandings and assumed practices of the group/even in those subjects that lend themselves most readily to quantification discourse depends heavily on conventions and interpretation conventions that are acquired over years of practice and participation in a community.

—Evelyn Fox Keller, *A Feeling for the Organism:*
*The Life and Work of Barbara McClintock*

## 练习 A.2

用自己文章中的一个段落来重做练习 A.1。把段落中所有的标点去掉,然后用斜线断出语法上的句子。接着,在段落中添加尽可能少的标点,之后再添加尽可能多的标点。(我假设你最初的标点是你认为最合适的。)和你的读者分享这三段——一段有最少的标点,一段有最多的标点,还有一段是原稿。读者更喜欢哪一个?为什么?

## 总结

不是对该部分做详细的总结,我只是提供四个小小的建议:

通常要标记出语法句的句尾。
一直要遵循第 362 至 364 页上的五条可靠原则。
一直要用逗号隔开较长的插入成分。
在一个主语和它的动词或者一个动词和它的宾语之间绝对不能加单个的逗号。

此外,还需判断在文章的何处应该加上标点,以帮助读者找到意义连接和分离的点,他们只有发现了这些连接和分离的点,才能明白句子的意思。这一过程意味着作者必须把自己放在读者的位置上思考问题,这其实并不容易,但是作者必须学习。另一方面,要写出一个结构清晰的句子,然后再用标点对其进行加工。

[ 附录二 ]

# 资源的使用

> 每一件重要的事情都被并未发现这些事情的人说过了。
> ——阿尔弗雷德·诺斯·怀特海
> （Alfred North Whitehead）

> 正确地运用在书中发现的思想所体现的智慧,并不比思想的原创者少多少,其创造性也不差多少。
> ——皮埃尔·贝勒
> （Pierre Bayle）

## 恰当地使用资源

几乎没有哪个作家仅靠自己的想法包打天下,研究人员就更不可能了。如果我们运用从其他人那里学到的知识来丰富自己的思想,那么我们就会写得好一些。但使用别人的语言和思想也有规则要遵循:一些规则是读者用来判断作者的品性,即此人是否值得信赖;还有一些规则是绝不能忽视的,否则后果堪忧。在这一点上所犯的错误会损坏他们的信誉、降低他们的等级,甚至损害他们的名誉。作者有一些选择,但并不多。他们面临的挑战是学习并按照计划行事,这能帮他们恰当地使用资源,不会犯巨大的错误,但也不会一遍又一遍地做无用功。

虽然在资源的引用和其他用途方面有一些原则可循,但是我还是要强调作家心中要有读者,也要记住自己的选择:这并不意味着为了遵循这些原则作者必须做什么,而是意味着作者如何使自己在利用资源上是准确的、公正的。

**避免剽窃**

我从最严重的错误入手。在作家所有可能违背道德的事情中,说谎和其他的欺骗固然很糟糕,但最糟糕的是盗取其他人的话语和想法。

剽窃者窃取的不只是别人的语言。他（她）同时也窃取了别人对该作品的尊敬和认可。作为学生，剽窃者不仅仅剽窃了他人的语言和思想，还把同学的作品比下去了，从而来获得认可。如果该类窃取变得司空见惯，该社会就会让人生疑，然后导致互不信任，最后便是愤世嫉俗——那么，这是谁造成的？每个人都逃不了干系。结果，老师不得不花少量的心思关注教学，而花大量的精力去发现不诚实的行为。这些剽窃者不仅背叛了使用资源时应承担的责任，而且破坏了整个社会的道德结构。

从未打算剽窃的诚实学生可能认为他们没必要为此而担心受到审查。但是我们读的是其语言而不是其思想。如果他们不知道避免抄袭的原则，或者更糟的是，他们不注意避免使用让老师产生怀疑的资源的话，那么就是主动让不诚实的行为发生了。

### 三个原则

为了避免这一风险，你必须理解并遵从每个老师期望每一位作者都遵从的那些原则。最重要的原则是：**避免让学识渊博的读者怀疑，你将别人的语言或者思想占为己有**。这一原则适用于任何形式的资源：打印的、在线的、记载的或者口头的。有些学生认为如果有些资源在网上是随意流通的，那么他们就可以认为这些东西是自己的。他们这么想就错了：你需要标明引用的任何资源。

尤其要遵循下面的原则：

1. 如果你想引用某一资源中的原文，先标明出处（包括页码），并把这些话语放在括号里或者字体加粗（见 387—390 页）。

2. 如果你改述了某一资源，先标明出处（包括页码）。你不需要使用引号，但是你必须用自己的话以新的结构来重新改写这一资源。

3. 你使用某一资源中的观点或者方法，先标明出处。如果整个资源都在论述这一观点或者方法，就不用标出页码。

如果遵循了这三个原则，你就不会有试图将别人的语言和思想据为己有的嫌疑了。

**做好笔记**

为了正确地使用和引用资料，必须从做好笔记开始。由于这个过程会很无聊，首先需要建立一个框架以把事情安排妥当，这样你就不用一遍又一遍地检查了。

**1.** 拿到一份资料，首先记录书目的基本信息。尽早这样做，不要等到最后。

读书时需要记录以下内容：
- ☐ 作者
- ☐ 标题（和副标题）
- ☐ 各级标题（若有的话）
- ☐ 版本或者册数（若有的话）
- ☐ 城市和出版商
- ☐ 出版年代
- ☐ 章节页码（若有的话）

读文章时需要记录以下内容：
- ☐ 作者
- ☐ 标题（和副标题）
- ☐ 日报、杂志等
- ☐ 册数和版本号
- ☐ 在线数据库（若有的话）
- ☐ 出版日期
- ☐ 文章页码

网络资源不好掌控。除了以上信息外，至少还要记录网址和访问日期，以及其他任何有助于向读者证明资料来源的信息。

**2. 准确记录引语。** 使用引语时要和原文保持完全一致，连逗号和分号也不能有误。如果引语很长，把它影印或者下载下来。

**3. 明确地标出引语和改述出自他人。** 这一点很重要：做好笔记，这样的话，即使几个星期或者几个月过去了，你也不可能认为某一资料上的语言和思想是你自己的。不管你是手写还是用电脑做笔记，用不同颜色的标记、横线或者不同的字体来区分直接引语。然后用另外一种方式区分改述和总结。有些优秀的学者曾被指责剽窃，因为他们声称他们没有清楚地标记引用和改述的话语，所以就"忘了"这些东西不是自己的了。

**4. 改述不要与原文太接近。** 如果你在笔记中改述了某一资料，你要做的不仅仅是把资料中的内容用同义词代替。如果这样的话，即使你注明了来源也被视为剽窃。例如，下文第一个改述就是剽窃，因为句子结构没变，只是词对词地做了调整。第二个改述是一种公正的使用方式。

| | |
|---|---|
| 原作： | The drama is the most social of literary forms, since it stands in so direct a relationship to its audience. |
| 剽窃： | The theater is a very social genre because it relates so directly with its viewers. |
| 公正的使用： | Levin claims that we experience the theater as the most social form of literature because we see it taking place before us. |

## 引语的使用

如果把引语和自己的文字融为一体,那么你就把引语使用到了最佳程度。如果读者发现你的文章中的基本引语和你的观点没有关系,那么他们就会产生怀疑:是你,还是你的资料有这些想法?**使用引语之前**,先站在读者的角度阐释清楚每条引文和论点之间究竟有何契合之处。然后尽可能使引语和你的文字衔接得天衣无缝。

### 四行或者少于四行

**顺便引入引语** 有一种方式可以把引语插入文章中,虽可接受但毫无艺术性,那就是将引语简单地顺便引入,用的是下面这些词:

Smith says, states, claims, etc.    As Smith says, asserts, suggests, etc.
According to Smith, In Smith's view, etc.

动词暗示了你对引语的态度,所以要认真地挑选:

says vs. asserts vs. claims vs. suggests vs. thinks vs. wants to believe

当引语中首字母在原文中大写的情况下,请在引导性短语的后面加逗号,并大写引语的首字母:

> Williams said, "An acceptable but artless way to insert a quotation into your text is simply to drop it in."

如果你用 stated that、claimed that、said that 等词引入引语的时候，不要使用逗号且第一个单词不用大写：

> He went on to say that "if you introduce the quotation with **stated that**, **claimed that**, **said that**, etc., do not use a comma."

**编织引语**　使用引语的一个更好的方式是，把它和你的句子结构交织在一起（这样做能够帮助你把引语融入你自己的想法里）：

> In *The Argument Culture*, Deborah Tannen treats the male-female polarity "more like ends of a continuum than a discrete dualism," because the men and women we know display "a vast range of behaviors, personalities, and habits."

为了让引语和句子搭配，可以修改引语的语法，甚至可以增加一两个词，只要遵循下面原则：

> 不要改变引文的意义。
> 用中括号标出增加的或者做了改变的词语。
> 用省略号标出删除的部分，我们称之为省略。

下面这个句子原封不动地引用了原文：

> Although it is clear that we have long thought of argument as verbal combat, Deborah Tannen suggests that there is something

new in the way we argue: "The increasingly adversarial spirit of our contemporary lives is fundamentally related to a phenomenon that has been much remarked upon in recent years: the breakdown of a sense of community".

下面这一版本既缩短又修改了引语，使得它能够与作者的句子语法相匹配：

Although it is clear that we have long thought of argument as verbal combat, Deborah Tannen suggests that our "increasingly adversarial spirit... is fundamentally related" to new social developments in "the breakdown of a sense of community".

如果删除了整个句子或者更多，那么你就需要使用省略号。

你可以用斜体、加粗或者下划线标出引语中的词来表示强调，但是如果你用这种方法的话，要在中括号里加上 my emphasis 或者 emphasis mine：

Lipson recommends that when you paraphrase you "write it down in your own words [ my emphasis ] ... and then compare your sentence with the author's original".

## 五行或者多于五行

如果使用的引语是五行或者更多，就需要把引语放到引语段中（周围没有引语标志）。引语段的缩进字符和普通段落缩进的

字符相同。如果引语的开头缩进了,那么第一行再缩进:

Lipson offers this advice about paraphrase:
> So, what's the best technique for rephrasing a quote? Set aside the other author's text and try to think of the point **you** want to get across. Write it down in your own words (with a citation) and then compare your sentence to the author's original. If they contain several identical words or merely substitute a couple of synonyms, rewrite yours.

正如上述例子一样,用暗示性的词语引出大部分的引语段,后面用句号或者冒号。但是也可以让引语和导入性的句子共同组成一个完成的语法句。这样一来,给句子的结尾加标点,就像把引语段放在文章中一样自然:

A good way to avoid paraphrasing too closely is to
> think of the point **you** want to get across. Write it down in your own words (with a citation) and then compare your sentence to the author's original. If they contain several...

不要在连续文本中使用引语,引语需要在引语段中完成。如下:

> A good way to avoid paraphrasing too closely is to "think of the point" **you** want to get across. Write it down in your own words (with a citation) and then compare your sentence to the author's original. If they...

### 五个词或者少于五个词

即使仅仅借用了某一资源中的几个词语，或许也不得不把它们当作引语对待。如果这些词是任何人都可能会使用的，那么可以把它们当作自己写的。如果这些词很明显是原创的或者特别重要的，就必须把它们放在引号中，并标明出处。例如：读下面一段来自贾雷德·戴蒙德（Jared Diamond）的《枪炮、病菌和钢铁》（Guns, Germs, and Steels）的一段：

> Because technology begets more technology, the importance of an invention's diffusion potentially exceeds the importance of the original invention. Technology's history exemplifies what is termed an autocatalytic process: that is, one that speeds up at a rate that increases with time, because the process catalyzes itself.

the importance of the original invention 等词太普通了，既不需要引证，也不需要引号。但是有两个词组却需要，因为他们太明显了：technology begets more technology 和 autocatalytic process：

> The power of technology goes beyond individual inventions because technology "begets more technology". It is, as Diamond puts it, an "autocatalytic process".

一旦你引用了这些词，再次使用的时候你就可以不加引证或者引号了：

As one invention begets another one and that one still another, the process becomes a self-sustaining catalysis that spreads exponentially across all national boundaries.

### 给引语加标点

用引号做标点时有三个原则需要注意：

**1. 如果引语是以句号、逗号、分号或者冒号结尾的，那么就用自己句子中的标点来代替这些符号。**

如果标点是句号，或者逗号，把它放在引号里：

President Nixon said, "I am not a crook".
Falwell claimed, "This is the end", but he was wrong.

如果标点是问号、冒号或者分号，把它放在引号外：

My first bit of advice is "Quit complaining"; my second is "Get moving."
The Old West served up plenty of "rough justice": lynchings and other forms of casual punishment were not uncommon.
How many law professors believe in "natural law"?
Was it Freud who famously asked, "What do women want"?

**2. 如果引语以问号或者感叹号结束，而你使用的标点是句号**

或者逗号，那么你要把自己的标点去掉，把问号或者感叹号放在引号里：

> Freud famously asked, "What do women want?"

**3.** 如果引语内存在引号，要把句号或者逗号放在这两个引号前面：

> She said, "I have no idea how to interpret 'Ode to a Nightingale'".

## 恰当地引用资源

最后一项任务是完整、准确并且恰当地引用资源。没有人会因为你放错一个逗号而指控你剽窃，但是有人会就此得出结论，认为你连小事情都搞不定，在大事情上就更不值得相信了。有很多种格式的引证，你要找出读者期望使用的那一种。以下三种最常见：

> Chicago 格式，源自《芝加哥大学风格指导手册》(*University of Chicago Manual of Style*)，在人文及一些社会科学中比较常见。
> MLA 格式，全称 Modern Language Association（现代语言协会），在文学作品中比较常见。
> APA 格式，全称 American Psychological Association（美国心理协会），在社会科学中比较常见。

你几乎可以在任何书店的参考书目中或者网上找到一本引证指南。

## 总结

为了准确、公正、有效地使用资源，需要遵循以下三个原则：

1. 不论何时使用资料中的语言或者思想，都要对之加以信任。

  不论何时使用某一资料的语言，都要标明资料出处和页码，把引语放在引号或者引用段中。
  不论何时改述某一资源，都要标明资料出处和页码。
  不论何时参考某一资料的思想或者方法，都要标明资料出处。

2. 使引语和你的文字衔接得天衣无缝。

  使用引语之前，都要提示二者的关联方式。
  任何时候都不要随便插入引语，而是要把它和整个文章整合在一起。
  插入四行或者少于四行的引语。
  五行或者多于五行的引语要分开作为引语段。
  第一次使用特殊的词或者词组时要注明。

3. 使用标准的引证格式。以下三类最常见：

Chicago 格式，在人文及一些社会科学中比较常见
MLA 格式，在文学作品中比较常见
APA 格式，在社会科学中比较常见

当使用某一文献中的材料时，作者就在自己和自己的文章、引文和引文所在的文献之间创造了一个思考链。这一思考链必须是一个信任链。作者可以信任自己的文献（以及文献中的资料），因为文献告诉作者，它们不仅已经处理好了自己的资料，而且已经处理好了它们从别处借用的资料。相反，如果你想让读者相信你的话，你不得不向他们展示你也处理好了这些环节。这些原则能够帮助你取得读者的信任。

# 参考答案

可能你的答案和参考答案不一样,或者要比参考答案写得好。不要担心你的答案和参考答案是否做到一字不差;重点在于遵循每课和每个练习的总体性原则即可。

### 练习 3.2

主语下面加了下划线,动词使用了大写,人物用斜体表示,动作用了黑体加粗。

**1a.** There IS **opposition** among many *voters* to nuclear power plants BASED on a **belief** in their **threat** to human health.

**1b.** Many *voters* **OPPOSE** nuclear power plants because *they* **BELIEVE** that such *plants* **THREATEN** human health.

**3a.** There IS a **belief** among some *researchers* that *consumers'* **choices** in fast food restaurants WOULD BE healthier if there WERE **postings** of nutrition information in their menus.

**3b.** Some *researchers* **BELIEVE** that *consumers* **WOULD CHOOSE** healthier foods if fast food *companies* **POSTED** nutrition information in their menus.

**5a.** Because the *student's* **preparation** for the exam WAS thorough, none of the questions on it WERE a **surprise**.

**5b.** Because the *student* **PREPARED** thoroughly for the exam, *she* WAS not **SURPRISED** by any of the questions on it.

练习 3.4

1a. 动词：argue, elevate.

没有名词化的词。

1b. 动词：has been.

名词化的词：speculation, improving, achievement.

3a. 动词：identified, failed, develop, immunize.

名词化的词：risk.

3b. 动词：met.

名词化的词：attempts, defining, employment, failure.

5a. 动词：resulted.

名词化的词：loss, share, disappearance.

5b. 动词：discover, embrace, teach.

没有名词化的词。

7a. 动词：fail, realize, are unprepared, protect, face.

名词化的词：life.

7b. 动词：have, are.

名词化的词：understanding, increases, resistance, costs, education.

练习 3.5

1b. Some educators have speculated about whether families can improve educational achievement ( help students achieve more ) .

3b. Economists have attempted but failed to define full employment.

5a. When domestic automakers lost market share to the Japanese, hundreds of thousands of jobs disappeared.

7b. Colleges now understand that they can no longer increase tuition yearly because parents are strongly resisting the soaring cost of higher education.

练习 3.6

1. Lincoln hoped to preserve the Union without war, but when the South attacked Fort Sumter, war became inevitable.

3. Business executives predicted that the economy would quickly revive.

5. Because the health care industry cannot control costs, the public may decide that Congress must act.

7. Several candidates attempted to explain why more voters voted in this year's elections.

9. The business sector did not independently study why the trade surplus suddenly increased.

### 练习 3.7

下面是依据虚拟的人物写的几个合理的答案。

1. Although we use models to teach prose style, students do not write more clearly or directly.

3. If members depart from established procedures, the Board may terminate their membership.

5. To implement a new curriculum successfully, faculty must cooperate with students to set goals that they can achieve within a reasonable time.

### 练习 4.1

1. We were required to explain the contradictions among the data.

3. In recent years, historians have interpreted the discovery of America in new ways, leading them to reassess the place of Columbus in Western history.

5. Medical professionals usually decide on-scene whether to forcibly medicate patients who are unable to legally consent.

7. Although critics panned the latest installment of the series, loyal fans still loved it.

9. We were disappointed but not surprised when they rejected the proposal, because we expected that they had made a political decision.

### 练习 4.2

1. Those on welfare become independent when they learn skills valued by the marketplace.［我喜欢此处为了强调"marketplace"而用的被动语态。］

3. In this article, I argue that the United States fought the Vietnam War to extend its influence in Southeast Asia and did not end it until North Vietnam made it clear

that it could be defeated only if the United States used atomic weapons.

练习 4.3

1. We believe that students binge because they do not understand the risks of alcohol.

3. We suggest that Russia's economy has improved because it has exported more crude oil for hard currency.

5. In Section Ⅳ, I argue that the indigenous culture overcultivated the land and thereby exhausted it as a food-producing area.

7. To evaluate how the flow rate changed, the current flow rate was compared to the original rate on the basis of figures collected by Jordan in his study of diversion patterns of slow-growth swamps.［该句很巧妙地使用了悬置修饰语，由于很常见，所以科技文章的读者都能理解句末的名词化用法，因为这是一个术语。］

练习 4.4

1. When the author treats the conspiracy theories, he abandons his impassioned narrative style and adopts a cautious one, but when he picks up the narrative line again, he invests his prose with the same vigor and force.

3. We have undervalued how the brain solves problems because we have not studied it in scientifically reliable ways.

练习 4.6

1. Diabetic patients may reduce their blood pressure by applying renal depressors.

3. On the basis of these principles, we may now attempt to formulate rules for extracting narrative information.

5. The Federal Trade Commission must be responsible for enforcing the guidelines for the durability of new automobile tires.

练习 5.1

1. When the president assumed office, he had two aims—the recovery of... He succeeded in the first as testified to by the drop in... But he had less success with the

second, as indicated by our increased involvement... Nevertheless, the American voter was pleased by vast increases in the military...

### 练习 5.2

1. Except for those areas covered with ice or scorched by continual heat, the earth is covered by vegetation. Plants grow most richly in fertilized plains and river valleys, but they also grow at the edge of perpetual snow in high mountains. Dense vegetation grows in the ocean and around its edges as well as in and around lakes and swamps. Plants grow in the crakes of busy city sidewalks as well as on seemingly barren cliffs. Vegetation will cover the earth long after we have been swallowed up by evolutionary history.

3. In his paper on children s thinking, Jones ( 1985 ) stressed the importance of language skills in the ability of children to solve problems. He reported that when children improved their language skills, they improved their ability to solve nonverbal problems. Jones thinks that they performed better because they used previously acquired language habits to articulate the problems and activate knowledge learned through language. We might therefore explore whether children could learn to solve problems better if they practiced how to formulate them.

### 练习 6.1

One can imagine different rationales for different stresses.

1. In my opinion, at least, the Republic is most threatened by the President s tendency to rewrite the Constitution.

3. In large American universities the opportunities for faculty to work with individual students are limited.

5. College students commonly complain about teachers who assign a long term paper and then give them a grade but no comments.

### 练习 6.2

1. During the reign of Queen Elizabeth, the story of King Lear and his daughters was so popular that by the time she died, readers could find it at least a dozen books.

Most of these stories, however, did not develop their characters and were simple narratives with an obvious moral. Several versions of this story must have been available to Shakespeare when he began work on *Lear*, perhaps his greatest tragedy. But while he based his characters on these stock figures of legend, he turned them into credible human beings with complex motives.

3. Because the most important event in Thucydides' *History* is Athens' catastrophic Sicilian Invasion, Thucydides devotes three-quarters of his book to setting it up. We can see this anticipation especially in how he describes the step-by-step decline in Athenian society so that he could create the inevitability that we associate with the tragic drama.

练习 9.1

1. Critics must use complex and abstract terms to analyze literary texts meaningfully.

3. Graduate students face an uncertain future at best in finding good teaching jobs.

5. Most patients who go to a public clinic do not expect special treatment, because their health problems are minor and can be easily treated.

7. We can reduce the federal deficit only if we reduce federal spending.

9. A person may be rejected from a cost-sharing educational program only if that person receives a full hearing into why she was rejected. 或者 An agency may reject a person from... only when that agency provides a full hearing into why it rejected her.

11. If we pay taxes, the government can pay its debts.

13. Catholics and Protestants will reconcile only when they agree on the Pope's authority.

练习 9.3

1. On the other hand, some TV programming will always appeal to our most prurient interests

3. One principle governs how to preserve the wilderness from exploitation.

5. Schools transmit more social values than do families.

## 练习 10.1

1. To explain why Shakespeare had Lady Macbeth die off-stage, we must understand how the audience reacted to Macbeth s death.

3. A student s right to access his records generally takes precedence over an institution s desire to keep those records private, unless the student agree to limits on his rights during registration.

5. Regardless of its justification, such conduct is prejudicial to good order.

7. Cigarette companies no longer claim that smoking does not cause heart disease and cancer.

9. Employers have had no difficulty identifying skilled employees, even though teachers, administrators, and even newspapers continue to debate grade inflation.

11. Parents and students need to understand how serious it is to bring to school anything that looks like a weapon, since, as school officials have said, principals may require students to pass through metal detectors before entering a school building.

## 练习 10.2

1. Many school systems are returning to the basics, basics that have been the foundation of education for centuries. /... a change that is long overdue.../trying to stem an ever rising drop-out rate.

3. For millennia, why we age has been a puzzle, a puzzle that only now can be answered with any certainty. /... a mystery that we can answer either biologically or spiritually./... hoping that one day we might stop our inevitable decline into infirmity and death.

5. Many Victorians were appalled when Darwin suggested that their ancestry might include apes, a suggestion that seemed to be at odds with Christian teaching/... a reaction deeply rooted in Victorian religious beliefs/... objecting to a perceived challenged to their religious convictions.

7. Journalism has increasingly focused on stories that were once considered salacious gossip, stories that would not have been seen as news even a decade age/... a trend that signal the decline of journalism as a profession/... catering to a seemingly

incessant demand for titillating news.

### 练习 11.1

1. Those who argue stridently over small matters are unlikely to think clearly about large ones.

3. We should pay more attention to those politicians who tell us how to make what we have better than to those who tell us how to get what we don t have.

5. Some teachers mistake neat papers that rehash old ideas for great thoughts wrapped in impressive packaging.

### 练习 11.2

1. If we invest our sweat in these projects, we must avoid appearing to be working only for our own self-interest.

3. Throughout history, science has progressed because dedicated scientists have ignored the hostility of an uninformed public.

5. Boards of education can no longer expect that taxpayers will support the extravagancies of incompetent bureaucrats.

### 练习 12.1

As the Illinois Commerce Commission has authorized, **you** will have to pay... **You** have not had to pay... but **you** will now pay rates that have been restructured consistent with the policy of The Public Utilities Act that lets us base what **you** pay on what it costs to provide you with service.

As the Illinois Commerce Commission has authorized, **we** are charging you... **We** have not have not raised rates... but **we** will are restructuring the rates now... so that we can charge you for what **we** pay to provide you with service.

### 练习 12.2

Your car may have a defective part that connects the suspension to the frame. If you brake and the plate fails, you won t be able to steer. We may also have to adjust the secondary latch on your hood because we may have misaligned it. If you don t latch the primary latch, the secondary latch, might not hold the hood down. If the hood flies up while you are driving, you won t be able to see. If either of these things occurs, you could crash.

**练习 A.1**

下面的两个段落，首先我加了最少的标点，之后又加上了更多的标点。

1. Scientists and philosophers... precise, as if those... disagree. But in fact scientific language... believed. It too is subject to... understanding. Moreover, new theories or arguments are rarely if ever constructed by way of clear-cut steps of induction,... falsification. Neither are they defended, rejected or accepted in so straightforward a manner. In practice scientists combine... of intuition, aesthetics commitment. The importance... generally acknowledged.... But the role of... less visible. The ways in... common experiences, on extensive practice... taken for granted. Only when we step out of such a "consensual domain", when we can stand out... the unarticulated premises, mutual understanding and assumed practices of the group. Even in those subjects... to quantification, discourse depends heavily on conventions and interpretation, conventions that are acquired over years of practice and participation in a community.

2. Scientists and philosophers of science... were intrinsically precise, as if those who use it... meaning, even if they disagree. But, in fact, scientific language... commonly believed: it, too, is subject to imprecision and ambiguity, and hence to imperfect understanding. Moreover, new theories, or arguments, are rarely, if ever, constructed by way of clear-cur steps of induction, deduction, and verification or falsification; neither are they defended, rejected, or accepted in so straightforward a manner. In practice, scientists combine the rules of scientific methodology with a generous admixture of intuition, aesthetics, and philosophical commitment. The importance of what are, sometimes, called extra-rational, or extra-logical components of... law is generally acknowledged... But the role of these extra-logical... frequently discussed, partly because they are less visible. The ways in which the credibility, or effectiveness, of an argument depends on the realm of common experiences, on extensive practice... a common language, are hard to see precisely, because such

commonalities are taken for granted. Only when we step out of such a "consensual domain," when we can stand... language, do we begin to become aware of the unarticulated premises, mutual understandings, and assumed practices of the group. Even in those subjects... quantification, discourse depends heavily on conventions and interpretation, conventions that... participation in a community.

# 术语表

语法是一切的基础。

——威廉·朗格兰
（William Langland）

世界上大部分问题都源于语法。

——蒙田
（Montaigne）

纯粹的词汇出现于世人面前之前，需要一种令人满意的语法结构。为了语法而研究语法，如果不与其功能联系在一起，那完全是疯狂的行为。

——安东尼·伯吉斯
（Anthony Burgess）

你存心不良，设立什么文法学校来腐蚀国内青年。……我要径直向你指出，你任用了许多人，让他们大谈什么名词呀，什么动词呀，以及这一类的可恶的字眼，这都是任何基督徒的耳朵所不能忍受的。

——威廉·莎士比亚，《亨利四世》第四幕第七场
（William Shakespeare, 2 Henry VI, 4.7）

下文不是与语法紧密相连的理论，而是本书相关词条的定义。文中详细讨论到的词条，我都指明了参考出处。如果想快速回顾一下前文以便着手阅读，试读 SUBJET、SIMPLE SUBJECT、WHOLE SUBJECT 和 VERB 这些词条。

**Action**（动作）：从原型上讲，可以用动词表达其意思：move, hate, think, discover。但是"动作"也常常出现在名词化中：movement, hatred, thought, discovery。"动作"有时也暗含在形容词中：advisable, resultant, explanatory 等。

**Active**（主动语态）：参见 102 页。

**Adjectival Clause**（形容词性从句）：形容词从句修饰名词，也称之为关系从句。这类句子通常以关系代词开头：which, that, whom, whose, who。可分为两类：限制性关系从句和非限制性关系从句。参见 40–43 页。

  限制性关系从句  The book that *I read* was good.

  非限制性关系从句  My car, which *you saw*, is gone.

**Adjective**（形容词）：之前可以放置 very 的一类词：very old, very interesting。也有例外：major, additional 等。因此，以上这一条也是对副词（ADVERBS）的检验。通过把形容词和副词放在 the 和名词之间，可以把形容词从副词中区分出来：The **occupational** hazard, the **major** reason 等。有些名词也可以放在 the 和名词之间——the **chemical** hazard。

**Adjective Phrase**（形容词性短语）：指 ADJECTIVE（形容词）和与之连在一起的部分：so **full** that it burst。

**Adverb**（副词）：副词修饰话语中除了 NOUN（名词）的所有部分：

  Adjectives  **extremely** large, **rather** old

  Verbs  **frequently** spoke, **often** slept

  Adverbs  **very** carefully, **somewhat** rudely

  Articles  **precisely** the man I meant, **just** the thing I need

  Sentences  **Fortunately**, we were on time.

**Adverb Phrase**（副词性短语）：指副词和与之连在一起的部分：as **soon** as I could。

**Adverbial Clause**（状语从句）：指一种 SUBORDINATE CLAUSE（从句）。修饰 VERB（动词）或 ADJECTIVE（形容词），包括时间、原因、条件等。句子通常以 SUBORDINATING CONJUNCTION（从属连词）开头，例如 because, when, if, since, while, unless：

  **If you leave**, I will stop.  **Because he left**, I did so.

**Agent**（施事者/动作执行者）：从原型上讲，代理是 ACTION（动作）活生生动作的发出者。但是我们的目的是，代理是任意动作表面上的根源，是一个实体，动作离开这个实体就不能发生：**She** criticized the program in this report。我们通常用一个表面意义来诠释真正意义：**This report** criticizes the program。不要把 SUBJECTS（主语）和代理混淆。代理原型上是主语，但是代理也可以是语法上的 OBJECT（宾语）：I underwent an interrogation by **the police**。

**Appositive**（同位语）：指位于被删除的 which 和 be 之后的名词词组：My dog, ~~which is~~ a dalmatian, ran away。

**Article**（冠词）：相比定义而言，我们更容易罗列出这些冠词：a, an, the, this, these, that, those。

**Character**（人物）：参见 62—65 页。

**Clause**（从句）：从句有两个定义特征：

1. 至少包含一个 SUBJECT + VERB（主语 + 动词）结构。
2. 动词必须与主语性数一致，并且可以转换成过去式和现在式。

就这个定义而言，下列这些属于从句：

She left　　　that they leave　　　if she left　　　why he is leaving

而下列这些不属于从句，因为动词既不能转换成过去式，并且与假定的主语性数不一致：

for them to go　　　her having gone

**Comma Splice**（逗号粘连）：如果只能用一个逗号连接两个独立从句，那么就需要逗号粘连：

Oil-producing countries depend too much on oil revenues, they should develop their educational and industrial resources, as well.

参见 355 页

**Complement**（补语）：指补充 VERB（动词）的任何成分：

I am **home**.　　　You seem **tired**.　　　She helped **me**.

**Compound Noun**（复合名词）：参见 115—116 页。

**Conjunction**（连词）：指连接词语、词组或者句子的词。相比定义而言，我们更容易对其作出阐释（前两个也归属于 SUBORDINATING［从属］连词）：

adverbial conjunctions　　because, although, when, since

relative conjunctions　　　who, whom, whose, which, that

sentence conjunctions　　　thus, however, therefore, nevertheless

coordinating conjunctions　and, but, yet, for, so, or, nor

correlative conjunctions　　both X and Y, not only X but Y, (n) either X (n) or

Y, X as well as Y

**Coordination**（并列）：指用 and, or, nor, but, yet 把两个相同顺序的语法单位连在一起：

| same part of speech | you and I, red and black, run or jump |
| phrases | in the house but not in the basement |
| clauses | when I leave or when you arrive |

**Dangling Modifier**（悬置修饰语）：参见 278 页

**Dependent Clause**（附属从句）：该 CLAUSE（从句）加上标点后不能作为 MAIN CLAUSE（主从句），以大写字母开头，以句号或者问号结尾。附属从句常以从属连词 because, if, when, which, that 等开头：

why he left    because he left    which he left

**Direct Object**（直接宾语）：指位于 TRANSITIVE VERB（及物动词）之后的 NOUN（名词），还可以作 PASSIVE（被动）动词的主语：

I found the money. → The money was found by me.

**Finite Verb**（限制性动词）：指既有过去时又有现在时的 VERB（动词），因为我们可以将其过去式变成被动式，或者将被动式变成过去式：

She wants to leave. → She wanted to leave.

下列不属于限制动词，因为我们不能把 INFINITIVE（不定式）转换成过去式：

She wants to leave. → She wanted to left.

**Fragment**（片段）：指以大写字母开头，以句号、问号或者感叹号结尾的 PHRASE（词组）或者 DEPENDENT CLAUSE（附属从句）：

| Because I left. | Though I am here! | What you did? |

下列是完整句子：

| He left because I did. | Though I am here, She is not! | I know what We did. |

**Free Modifier**（自由修饰语）：参见 264—265 页。

**Gerund**（动名词）：指动词加上 ing 后变成的名词化的词：

When she left we were happy. → Her leaving made us happy.

**Goal**（目标）：指动词的动作所指的内容。大部分情况下，目标是 DIRECT OBJECTS（直接宾语）：

I see you.    I broke the dish.    I built a house.

但是在有些情况下，动作的直接目标可能是 ACTIVE VERB（主动动词）的 SUBJECT（主语）：

I underwent an interrogation.　　She received a warm welcome.

**Grammatical Sentence**（语法句子）：参见 346 页。

**Hedge**（模糊语）：参见 231—233 页。

**Independent Clause**（独立从句）：该从句加上标点后可作为语法句。

**Infinitive**（不定式）：指不可以转化成过去时或者现在时的动词。常常由 to 引导：

He decided to stay。但有时并非如此：We helped him repair the door。

**Intensifier**（强化语）：参见 233—235 页。

**Intransitive Verb**（不及物动词）：指后面不接宾语且没有被动式的动词。下列这些不是 TRANSITIVE VERB（及物动词）：

He **exists**.　　They **left** town.　　She **became** a doctor.

**Linking Verb**（系动词）：带有 COMPLEMENT（补语）指称 SUBJECT（主语）的 VERB（动词）：

He **is** my brother.　　They **became** teachers.　　She **seems** reliable.

**Main Clause**（主要从句）：主要从句或独立从句至少有一套 SUBJECT（主语）和 VERB（动词）（祈使语气除外），加标点后可以作为独立句子出现：

I left.　　Why did you leave?　　We are leaving.

A SUBORDINATE（从属）或 DEPENDENT CLAUSE（附属从句）加标点后不能作为独立句子出现。下列句子是不正确的：

Because she left.　　That they left.　　Whom you spoke to.

**Main Subject**（主要主语）：SUBJECT of the MAIN CLAUSE（主要从句的主语）。

**Metadiscourse**（元话语）：参见 109—112 页。

**Nominalization**（名词化）：参见 68—70 页。

**Nonrestrictive Clause**（非限制性从句）：参见 40—43 页。

**Noun**（名词）：满足下列结构的词：The [ ] is good。有些词是具体的：dog, rock, car；有些词是抽象的：ambition, space, speed。

跟我们关系最大的名词是 NOMINALIZATION（名词化的词），那些从 VERB（动词）或 ADJECTIVES（形容词）派生出来的名词：act → action，wide → width。

**Noun Clause**（名词从句）：名词从句的功能等同于名词，例如，作为 VERB（动词）的 SUBJECT（主语）或者 OBJECT（宾语）：**That you are here** proves that you love me。

**Object**（宾语）：有三类宾语：

1. DIRECT（直接）宾语：指跟在 TRANSITIVE VERB（及物动词）后的 NOUN（名词）：

I read the book.　　We followed the car.

2. PREPOSITIONAL（介词）宾语：跟在介词后的宾语：

in the house　　by the walk　　across the street　　with fervor

3. INDIRECT（间接）宾语：位于 VERB 及其直接宾语中间的名词：

I gave him a tip.

**Parallel**（平行）：如果 COORDINATED（并列）词、PHRASES（短语）或者 CLAUSES（从句）的语法结构一致，那么其顺序就是平行的。下列句子是平行的：

I decided to work hard and do a good job.

不能像下面这样写：

I decided to work hard and that I should do a good job.

**Passive**（被动式）：参见 102—104。

**Past Participle**（过去分词）：通常情况下和过去式形式相同 -ed：jumped, worked。不规则动词的过去分词形式不规则：seen, broken, swum 等。过去分词紧接 be 或 have：I have gone. It was found。过去分词有时候充当修饰词：found money。

**Personal Pronoun**（人称代词）：相比给出一个明确的定义而言，我们更容易列举一些人称代词：I, me, we, us, my, mine; our, ours; you, your, yours; he, him, his; she, her, hers; they, them, their, theirs.

**Phrase**（短语）：一组词构成不包含 SUBJECT（主语）和 FINITE VERB（限定动词）的单位：the dog, too old, was leaving, in the house, ready to work。

**Possessive**（所有格）：my, your, his, her, its, their, 或者名词以 - s 或 -s' 结尾：the dog's tail。

**Predicate**（谓语）：跟在总 SUBJECT（主语）后面，以动词短语开头，包括 COMPLEMENT（补语）及其附属部分：

He [left yesterday to buy a hat]. (谓语)

**Preposition**（介词）：列举出来比给出定义要简单得多：in, on, up, over, of, at, by 等。

**Prepositional Phrase**（介词短语）：即介词 + OBJECT（宾语）：in+ the house。

**Present Participle**（现在分词）：VERB（动词）的 -ing 形式：running, thinking。

**Progressive**（进行时）：VERB（动词）的 PRESENT PARTICIPLE（现在分词）：Running streams are beautiful。

**Punctuated Sentence**（标点句）：参见 347 页

**Relative Clause**（关系从句）：参见 250—252 页。

**Relative Pronoun**（关系代词）：who, whom, which, whose，还有关系从句中的 that。

**Restrictive Clause**（限制性从句）：参见 40—43 页。

**Resumptive Modifier**（重复性修饰语）：参见 261—263 页。

**Run-on Sentence**（连写句）：包含两个或两个以上未被 COORDINATING CONJUNCTION（并列连词）或标点符号分开的语法句子，这一整体叫作连写句。

**Simple Subject**（简单主语）：简单主语是总主语中的最小单位，决定着动词的单复数：

[The [books] (简单主语) that are required reading] (总主语) are listed.

简单主语应尽可能地靠近它的动词。

If a **book** is required reading, **it** is listed.

**Stress**（重读）：参见 150—152 页。

**Subject**（主语）：主语是 VERB（动词）在数上与之保持一致的词：

Two **men** are at the door.　　One **man** is at the door.

区别 WHLOE SUBJECT（总主语）和 SIMPLE SUBJECT（简单主语）。

**Subjunctive**（虚拟语气）：动词的一种形式，用来表达与事实相反的事情：

If he were President...

**Subordinate Clause**（从句）：通常以 if, when, unless 或者 which, that, who 等 SUBORDINATING CONJUNCTION（从属连词）开头的从句。有三类从句：NOUN（名词），ADVERBIAL（状语）和 ADJECTIVE（形容词）。

**Subordinating Conjunction**（从属连词）：because, if, when, since, unless, which, who, that, whose 等。

**Summative Modifier**（总结性修饰语）：参见 263 页。

**Thematic Thread**（主题线）：贯穿整个段落的一系列 THEMES（主题）。

**Theme**（主题）：参见 159—162 页。

**Topic**（话题）：参见 133—134 页。

**Topic String**（话题链）：贯穿句子的一系列 TOPICS（话题）。

**Transitive Verb**（及物动词）：指带有 DIRECT OBJECT（直接宾语）的 VERB（动词）。原型上讲，直接宾语"接受"一个 ACTION（动作）。原型的直接宾语可以作为 PASSIVE（被动）动词的 SUBJECT（主语）：

We **read** the book. → The book **was read** by us.

从这一意义上讲，resemble、become 和 stand（例如：He stands six feet tall）不属于及物动词。

**Verb**（动词）：指与主语在数上保持一致的词，并且有过去式和现在式之间的屈折变化：

This book **is** ready.　　The books **were** returned.

**Whole Subject**（总主语）：定义了总主语的 VERB（动词）之后就可以定义总主语了：把 who 或者 what 放在动词前，然后调换句子顺序，使之成为问句。这一问句的完整答案就是总主语：

The ability of the city to manage education is an accepted fact.

Question: **What** is an accepted fact?

Answer (and the whole subject)：the ability of the city to manage education

区分清楚总主语和 SIMPLE SUBJECT（简单主语）：

The **ability** of the city to manage education **is** an accepted fact.